IN TRANSITION

Children's Literature Association Series

IN TRANS ITION

Young Adult Literature and Transgender Representation

Emily Corbett

University Press of Mississippi / Jackson

The University Press of Mississippi is the scholarly publishing agency of
the Mississippi Institutions of Higher Learning: Alcorn State University,
Delta State University, Jackson State University, Mississippi State University,
Mississippi University for Women, Mississippi Valley State University,
University of Mississippi, and University of Southern Mississippi.

www.upress.state.ms.us

The University Press of Mississippi is a member
of the Association of University Presses.

A version of chapter two was previously published by the
International Journal of Young Adult Literature: Corbett, Emily.
"Transgender Books in Transgender Packages: The peritextual materials
of young adult fiction." *The International Journal of Young Adult Literature*,
vol. 1, no. 1, 2020, pp. 1–25. http://doi.org/10.24877/ijyal.32.

Copyright © 2024 by University Press of Mississippi
All rights reserved

∞

Library of Congress Cataloging-in-Publication Data

Names: Corbett, Emily, author.
Title: In transition : young adult literature and transgender representation / Emily Corbett.
Other titles: Children's Literature Association series.
Description: Jackson : University Press of Mississippi, 2024. | Series: Children's literature association series | Includes bibliographical references and index.
Identifiers: LCCN 2024002727 (print) | LCCN 2024002728 (ebook) | ISBN 9781496852601 (hardback) | ISBN 9781496852618 (trade paperback) | ISBN 9781496852625 (epub) | ISBN 9781496852632 (epub) | ISBN 9781496852649 (pdf) | ISBN 9781496852656 (pdf)
Subjects: LCSH: Young adult literature—History and criticism. | Young adult fiction—History and criticism. | Sexual minorities in literature. | Transgender people in literature. | Gender identity—Juvenile literature.
Classification: LCC PN1009.5.S483 C67 2024 (print) | LCC PN1009.5.S483 (ebook) | DDC 809.93353—dc23/eng/20240226
LC record available at https://lccn.loc.gov/2024002727
LC ebook record available at https://lccn.loc.gov/2024002728

British Library Cataloging-in-Publication Data available

TABLE OF CONTENTS

vii	Acknowledgments
3	Introduction
31	Chapter 1. The Transgender Problem: A New Subcategory of Young Adult Fiction
59	Chapter 2. The Peritextual Materials of Transgender Young Adult Fiction
83	Chapter 3. Can Transgender Representation Get More Fantastic? Speculative Young Adult Fiction
113	Chapter 4. There's No Place Like Home: Parent-Adolescent Relationships in Transgender Young Adult Fiction
141	Chapter 5. Transgender Memoirs for Young Adult Readers
167	Conclusion
173	Appendix
185	Notes
191	References
211	Index

ACKNOWLEDGMENTS

When I came to write my acknowledgments, I realized just how lucky I am to be surrounded by people who believe in me and this monograph. They have enriched my academic career and fueled my desire to see this project through to completion, and I want to mention a few of them here.

I have found a family in the YA studies community, thanks in no small part to the projects I have had the privilege of being involved with since their beginnings. Serving as associate editor, and now co-general editor, of *The International Journal of Young Adult Literature*, I have seen firsthand the wisdom, generosity, and encouragement with which we foster each other's scholarship. My heartfelt thanks to the editorial board of past and present for all that you do, in particular Drs. Alison Waller, Patricia Kennon, Susanne Abou Ghaida, and Nithya Sivashankar. In cofounding the YA Studies Association, I have also been incredibly fortunate to see YA studies continue to blossom into a thriving area of research with dedicated, ambitious, and thoughtful scholars of all career stages. I am grateful to the inaugural executive board, Drs. Leah Phillips, Jennifer Gouck, Rebekah Fitzsimmons, and Emily Booth, for coming together with me to create something special. Leah, you deserve extra recognition for the endless conversations over the years which have nurtured and challenged me to grow as an academic and for being my coauthor of "Ploughing the Field." The opportunity to work with so many talented people has inspired me to think more deeply about Young Adult studies.

I want to thank the excellent colleagues who worked in the Department of English and Creative Writing at the University of Roehampton during the time I was there. Your enthusiasm and sense of community were an immeasurable source of support during the early stages of this project. To Drs. Alison Waller, Andy Kesson, Ian Kinane, Alberto Fernández Carbajal, and Lisa Sainsbury, in particular, thank you for the various ways you have contributed to this monograph. My gratitude is also owed to the Educational Studies Department at Goldsmiths, University of London, where I now reside. Special thanks are given to a few colleagues: Professor Vicky Macleroy, Professor Farzana Shain, Dr. Sarah Pearce, and Dr. Andrew Wilkins.

I am also indebted to Drs. Libe García Zarranz, B. J. Epstein, and other anonymous reviewers. Your thoughtful and thorough feedback has strengthened my abilities as a scholar. To the team at the University Press of Mississippi, thank you for giving a home to this monograph and for doing so much to bring it to fruition.

To my family, I appreciate the love and support you have given freely. Mum, your bedtime stories have inspired a life-long love of reading. Grandma, the sage advice and numerous hours spent proofreading my work across the years have been worth more than you know. Grandad, thanks for always asking whether I'd finished my homework on time, even when I was doing a PhD. Grandad Tom, you reminded me how important it is to give everything in life my all. Madison, you have made every day so much brighter. And finally, Rhys, you have kept me company on the inevitable ups and downs of this project. Your unwavering love and words of encouragement have been a source of comfort for me. Whenever doubt crept in, you were there to remind me that I could do it. Look, it's finally done.

IN TRANSITION

INTRODUCTION

A book about transgender young adult (YA) literature would not have been possible twenty years ago. That is because, although YA literature is understood to have emerged as a discrete category of publishing no later than the end of the 1960s,[1] transgender characters were not explicitly represented in the YA book market until at least forty years later. Though critics sometimes cite Carol Plum-Ucci's *What Happened to Lani Garver* (2002) as the first example of transgender YA literature for the novel's "thoughtful portrayal of Lani, who refuses to conform to gender expectations and doesn't want to be put in a box" (Cramer and Adams 123), this book takes Julie Anne Peters's *Luna* (2004) as its earliest example for Peters's inclusion of a character who is openly and explicitly transgender (a decision I will shortly revisit). Since 2004, transgender representation has become increasingly frequent in YA fiction and nonfiction titles. Collated under the label of transgender YA literature, my research has identified at least 170 novels, short-story anthologies, and memoirs published for a young adult audience in the United Kingdom or United States that include one or more transgender characters—a term I use to encapsulate both fictional characters and the textual figures of transgender people that are represented in nonfiction—in a major role (whether protagonist or secondary).

The field of transgender YA literature has, on balance, changed in myriad ways across its short publication history: in its authorship, trends, characters, conventions, genres, forms, implied readers, and ideologies. Throughout this book, I argue that these changes can be tied to both the changing shape of the YA book market and the sociocultural moment in which the books have been published. As such, transgender YA literature serves as a lens through which to observe the ways that attitudes towards transgender adolescents, and YA literature, have shifted in the twenty-first century. I begin with "transgender problem novels" published from 2007 through 2015, a genre of YA literature that can be largely characterized by the portrayal of transgender identity as a problem to be overcome in a cisnormative society. Subsequent chapters then trace how transgender people—as characters, creators, and intended readers—have come to play a significant role in the production of increasingly nuanced and expansive transgender YA texts. The chapter structure is intended to illustrate a narrative of development, from the cisgender-dominated publishing landscape in the first few years of transgender YA literature to the increasing presence of transgender voices in the last few years.

This book has grown out of a fascination with how the YA book market is adapting in response to the calls for more diversity that have proliferated in recent years. Although the roots of these calls go much deeper in history (as I will come to discuss), diversity has recently become a "buzzword in the Anglo-American publishing industries" (Ramdarshan Bold, *Inclusive Young Adult Fiction* 45). The cultural relevance of conversations about who is represented in YA literature, how they are represented, and by whom has, in fact, grown during the course of researching and writing this book. The global Covid-19 pandemic has caused a renewed interest in books for young people, confirming the importance of reading in their everyday lives. The National Literacy Trust's Annual Literary Survey revealed that 27.6 percent of young people felt an increased sense of enjoyment from reading during lockdown, while 34.5 percent observed they read more during lockdown (Clark and Picton 2). What is more, 59.3 percent of young people felt better because of reading during the pandemic, and 50.2 percent admitted reading was encouraging them to dream about their future (Clark and Picton 2). These figures signal that the significance books have for young people has increased during the last few years (even if they are not all enjoying their increased reading), while other cultural moments have proved that YA literature's capacity to handle important subjects such as equity, equality, and social justice is more necessary than ever.

In an international conversation between eighteen scholars of children's and YA literature, my colleague Leah Phillips and I conducted in 2020, Melanie Ramdarshan Bold made the case that "reading has always been a crucial part of activism" because certain books can "explore issues of racism, discriminations, prejudice, and inequality in a way that's accessible for young people" (qtd. in Corbett and Phillips 4). The viral #MeToo movement; the Black Lives Matter and Black Trans Lives Matter protests that have erupted across the world; the divisive and rampant media racism towards the Duchess of Sussex; and the ongoing battle for trans rights in the face of hatred, ignorance, and discrimination have shaped my research project. At the same time, these cultural movements and moments that signal the ongoing inequalities and injustices in the Western world also serve to remind us how important it is that we interrogate how marginalized teenagers are represented (and misrepresented) in the books young people read. This book maps the growth and development of transgender YA literature as a discrete category of YA publishing in the context of these cultural moves and movements.

Transgender Representation of Past, Present, and Future

If Peters's *Luna* can be considered the first adolescent transgender character in YA fiction, what then is her legacy? Luna is an unfortunate character for whom being transgender causes a significant problem. Being true to her own identity as a girl stands in conflict with the wishes of those around Luna, and her life is messy, uncomfortable, and, at times, pretty bleak. In many ways, *Luna* offers a problematic, though significant, start to transgender representation in YA literature. In a broad-stroke analysis of LGBTQ+ characters in children's and YA fiction, B. J. Epstein remarks how *Luna* "seems to imply that being transgender is necessarily stressful and must involve leaving home, which might suggest to a reader that there are few or even no happy trans stories" (*Are the Kids All Right?* 146) for real teenagers. It makes sense, Epstein argues, that "trans novels can be depressing" (146) because transgender people continue to face unjustifiable hardship in contemporary society—rejection, physical and emotional abuse, and high suicide rates to name but a few—but in her opinion, *Luna* nevertheless "paint[s] a negative picture of transgender people" (145). Reaching a similar conclusion, Catherine Butler points out that *Luna* draws on, and perpetuates, "the assumption [...] that society would never tolerate a person known to be trans" ("Portraying Trans People in Children's and Young Adult Literature" 8). Not all critics have responded to the bleakness of Peters's novel as Epstein, Butler, and I have. Heather Love commends *Luna* for offering "a sensitive account of a transgender adolescent, clearly distinguishing Liam/Luna's experience from homosexuality and portraying the violence of compulsory gender" (160), while Kimberley Reynolds regards the novel as "committed to developing readers' understanding of sex and gender, encouraging them to move beyond the binaries of male/female, masculine/feminine into more nuanced ways of understanding sexual difference and orientations" (129). There is no consensus on whether *Luna* includes a positive or high-quality portrayal of a transgender adolescent (and I am unconvinced judgements of quality are critically useful, especially in a field that, as my first chapter suggests, has been criticized for a perceived lack of quality), but it is patent that *Luna* gives insight into what was considered acceptable in the YA book market at the time of the book's publication.

Subjects that are depicted in children's books and social acceptance are, for Epstein, inextricably linked, with the former revealing the latter. A dearth of transgender characters in YA fiction, in Epstein's words, therefore "implies that transgendered people are not yet accepted as normal" ("We're Here, We're [Not?] Queer" 292). Aside from evidence that not all subjects included in literature for young people are socially accepted, such as the child abuse at the center of Jonathon Todres and Sarah Higinbotham's *Human Rights in Children's Literature*, an association of absence with nonacceptance perhaps obscures a more nuanced picture of the relations and reciprocities between how transgender adolescents are represented in fiction and how they are perceived in the contemporary sociocultural environment. Excellent scholars are working to trace the evolving social, cultural, and legal environment for transgender people in the United Kingdom and the United States: for example, Rachel Mesch's *Before Trans* (2020) explores three individuals who lived before the term "transgender" existed but who nevertheless experienced their gender in complicated ways; Jules Gill-Peterson's *Histories of the Transgender Child* (2018) uncovers a twentieth-century history of transgender children that played a central role in the medicalization of transgender people; and Ben Vincent and colleagues' *TERF Wars: Feminism and the Fight for transgender futures* (2020) examines the politics of feminist, transgender, and transexclusionary movements by way of proposing a more collaborative future. These three examples are by no means a comprehensive account, but they offer a sample of the trans studies work being produced in recent years. My book is informed by sociological and cultural studies work that intersects with transgender phenomena, yet my contribution to this discourse is grounded in YA studies and the analysis of twenty-first-century YA literature.

More precisely, I want to suggest that transgender YA literature has developed as what Lisa Fletcher, Beth Driscoll, and Kim Wilkins would consider to be a "genre world" (997) in the twenty-first century. A genre world broadly encompasses "a sector of the publishing industry, a social formation, and a body of texts" and, as such, "describes the collective activity that goes into the creation and circulation of genre texts, and is particularly focused on the communities, collaborations, and industrial pressures that drive and are driven by the processes of these socio-artistic formations" (Fletcher et al. 997, 998). Elsewhere, Wilkins has argued that "genres are not static, ahistorical categories. Rather, genres are processes. They are formed, negotiated and reformed, both tacitly and explicitly, by the interactions of authors, readers and (importantly) institutions" ("The Process of Genre" n.p.). This book is an attempt to trace the developments of transgender YA literature as a category that is defined and redefined with the introduction of new publications. To this end, the appendix gives a list of a broad selection of the transgender YA texts published from 2004 through 2022 that were identified during the course of my research.[2] A diachronic picture of transgender YA literature—that is, one that is concerned with the ways the corpus has changed over time—charts its evolution "with greater detail and accuracy than would be possible by attempting a singular definition" (McAlister 3).

Based upon Tzvetan Todorov's suggestion that genres "function as 'horizons of expectation' for readers" (18), Alex Henderson delineates what a reader might anticipate from LGBTQ+ YA fiction. They argue that "just as spaceships signal science fiction [and] faeries signal fantasy, [. . .] the presence of queer characters comes with a traditional set of 'horizons' or narrative conventions" ("Playing with Genre" 1). In Henderson's words, a reader can expect "an arc that involves them [the queer character] coming out, their experiences with homophobia and prejudice, and generally revolves around that character's otherness within a heteronormative world" ("Playing with Genre" 1). With narrative moments, themes, and codes forming a familiar set of conventions within the literature, it is possible to conceive of LGBTQ+ YA fiction as a genre (or subgenre, dependent on whether YA fiction is, itself, considered to be a genre), rather than as a corpus united only by its inclusion of common characters.

In their recent *Critical Explorations of Young Adult Literature: Identifying and Critiquing the Canon* (2019), for example, editors Victor Malo-Juvera and Crag Hill suggest "subgenres of YA literature could be considered to have their own canons, such as canons of queer YA literature" (6). Similarly, Christine A. Jenkins and Michael Cart trace "the gradual movement of the genre from the literary margins to the mainstream of literary acceptance and recognition" (*The Heart Has Its Reasons* 114) with their analysis of LGBTQ+ texts. The "instability and incoherence of queer YA as a genre" (18) is a primary interest for Derritt Mason, whose recent monograph explores queer YA fiction's "resistance to easy description, definition, and coherence" (18). Transgender YA literature, too, shares more generic connections than the trans identity of its character(s). The myriad patterns and developments in representation, ideology, and authorship that these connections exemplify are something that I seek to bring to the fore in this book. Wilkins's analysis of YA fantasy fiction suggests that "approaching the study of any genre would imply an analysis of not only the texts, but also potentially its audience, its marketing, its book design, its paratexts, and so on, because these are all part of the complex process by which a genre is formed" (*Young Adult Fantasy Fiction* 3). In this regard, I share Wilkins's all-encompassing approach because an investigation of transgender YA literature that is concerned only with the textual elements would neglect countless other aspects of the books and their publication that can also be read to reveal how the field has developed.

As the first text in the genre world of transgender YA literature, *Luna*'s publication in the early 2000s can be connected to the first of two significant cultural turning points in recent history that have seen transgender people, topics, and issues garner public attention. The first turning point occurred at the beginning of the twenty-first century when, according to Stephen Whittle's observation at the time, "'trans' has become a cultural obsession" (1). Susan Stryker suggests that this moment in trans history can be attributed to a "lot of cultural trends, social conditions, and historical circumstances" colliding to "make trans topics hot" (*Transgender History* 42). In terms of transgender YA literature publishing, however, it can hardly be said that transgender identity became a "hot topic" with only a few published titles becoming available until a publishing boom in the mid-2010s (the second cultural turning point I will come to shortly). This is perhaps attributable to the YA publishing industry's reluctance to represent diverse identity and experiences more broadly. As Ramdarshan Bold notes in her study of 2006–2016 YA literature, "YA, especially bestselling YA, typically feature protagonists who are white or ethnically ambiguous, cisgendered, and heterosexual" ("The Eight Percent Problem" 392). Nevertheless, there is an observable increase in mainstream publishers' interest in transgender representation between 2004 and the mid-2010s.

Alongside Peters's *Luna,* Ellen Wittlinger's *Parrotfish* (2007)—the first YA text to feature a transgender adolescent protagonist—and other texts featuring at least one major transgender adolescent character, including Brian Katcher's *Almost Perfect* (2009), Cris Beam's *I Am J* (2011), Kirstin Cronn-Mills's *Beautiful Music for Ugly Children* (2012), Kristin Elizabeth Clark's *Freakboy* (2013), Lisa Williamson's *The Art of Being Normal* (2015), and Simon Packham's *Only We Know* (2015), were introduced into the catalogs of either major conglomerates or mainstream publishing houses following this first cultural turning point. Arin Andrews's *Some Assembly Required: The Not-So-Secret Life of a Transgender Teen* (co-written with Joshua Lyon, 2014) and Katie Rain Hill's *Rethinking Normal: A Memoir in Transition* (co-written with Ariel Schrag, 2014) also made significant contributions to the YA memoir genre with depictions of transgender teens. Minor adolescent transgender characters were included in titles such as Libba Bray's *Beauty Queens* (2011) and David Levithan's *Everyday* (2012). In addition, titles with one or more major adolescent transgender characters were also published by small, often-queer presses such as Bella Books and Dreamspinner Press, including Rachel Gold's *Being Emily* (2012) and *Just Girls* (2014), Nora Olsen's *Maxine Wore Black* (2014), Jennie Wood's *A Boy Like Me* (2014), and Winter Page's *Breaking Free* (2014). As these aforementioned titles evidence, the "obsession with all things trans*" (*Transgender History* 41) as Stryker puts it, included a correlating increase in the representation of transgender people in the YA book market at the beginning of the twenty-first century.[3]

What unites a significant proportion of early transgender YA titles, as chapter 1 will show, is that transgender identity is employed as a problem for the adolescent characters to overcome because of its divergence from an overarching cisnormativity. A second surge in cultural popularity was then observed in the mid-2010s when Jack Halberstam noted that, "after functioning for at least half a century as the name for bodily disgrace and gender absurdity, 'transgender' (used as an umbrella term for gender-variant bodies) became a household word" (46). As we will see, the second cultural turning point that occurred in the mid-2010s might instead, though far from universally, speak to a recognition of trans people as subjects, with voices, agency, and the right to tell their own stories. The increased visibility of transgender celebrities in popular culture—a moment dubbed the "transgender tipping point" (Steinmetz, "The Transgender Tipping Point" n.p.)—came around the same time as the We Need Diverse Books social media campaign (along with the Own Voices[4] hashtag) became a leading movement in the children's and YA literature world. The two cultural moments coalesced to support a boom in transgender YA literature, fostering the necessary environment for transgender representation to become exponentially more desirable and marketable in YA publishing and thus increasing the demand for transgender stories including, and perhaps especially, stories by transgender authors.

From 2015 to 2022, transgender representation became more plentiful, but also more expansive, as my second and third chapters will show. With more than 150 applicable titles published in these years (see the appendix), here it is most useful to consider how a few specific texts signpost important developments in transgender YA literature. In 2015, Pat Schmatz's *Lizard Radio* was the first speculative YA novel to include an explicitly transgender character as its protagonist. A year later, the first trans YA novel from a conglomerate house to be written by an openly transgender author was published: Meredith Russo's *If I Was Your Girl* (2016). Bells Broussard became the first Black transgender protagonist in the YA market in 2017 in C. B. Lee's *Not Your Villain*, after appearing first as a major secondary character in the first book of the series, *Not Your Sidekick* (2016). The year 2019 saw Akwaeke Emezi become the first Black, openly transgender author to publish a trans YA novel (*Pet*) with a conglomerate house and, relatedly, the first Black, neurodivergent, trans protagonist appeared in the catalog of a mainstream publisher. In 2020, Aiden Thomas's *Cemetery Boys* not only became the first traditionally published Latinx transgender YA novel written by a transgender author, but it also made history when it appeared on the *New York Times* Best Seller List. Two adult autobiographies—Janet Mock's *Redefining Realness: My Path to Womanhood, Identity, Love and So Much More* (2014) and Jennifer Finney Boylan's *She's Not There: A Life in Two Genders* (2003)—have previously been placed on the *New York Times* Best Seller List, but Thomas's *Cemetery Boys* became the first transcentered work of fiction by an openly transgender author to receive the accolade (YA or otherwise). These are only a few of the significant developments that have occurred in my research period, revealing a pattern of innovation, development, and recognition.

Transgender YA literature is a dynamic publishing phenomenon, as the concentrated cluster of pioneering texts suggests. I have identified approximately 50 titles published by the end of 2016, before I began my study in 2017.

The number of publications has grown year on year with a further 120 or so titles published during the course of my research project. Transgender YA texts can, at times, be difficult to locate, source, and access. As Talya Sokoll notes, a number of them are "published by small presses, with little to no marketing" (23) and have, until recently, been largely considered a niche area of YA literature by scholars, publishers, educational establishments, and libraries. A number of these YA texts remain unnoticed and unexplored by scholars, a situation this book seeks to address. Trans titles published in the most recent years of study have generally become easier to locate and access with the increase in the proportion of texts published by mainstream presses and major conglomerates. However, a significant portion of titles still continue to emerge from the sorts of small presses with limited marketing budgets to which Sokoll referred. What is more, with the growing popularity of transgender texts and the growing demands for inclusive fiction, there has been a correlating increase in the number of minor secondary transgender characters in transgender YA fiction.

The sample of titles included in this book illuminate trends and patterns in the YA book market. In her 1996 article "Young Adult Literature Evades the Theorists," Caroline Hunt blamed the fact that "young adult literature is marketed as, essentially, a disposable record of a fleeting moment" (6) for what she perceived to be a focus on social issues, rather than literary theory, in YA scholarship. I do not share Hunt's concerns—concerns which she herself revised in her 2017 article "Theory Rises, Maginot Line Endures"—and I would not suggest YA literature is "disposable" with any of the disparaging connotations that underpin Hunt's observation. Nevertheless, it is true that the field of trans YA literature is rapidly changing, and texts can quickly become outdated, not least because of the speed with which language, social attitudes towards transgender identity, and the authorship of these texts is shifting.

As Karen Coats has suggested, "YA has become such a dominant market force because it corresponds to the way we live now, but that may not be the way we live in three months from now, or next year. [. . .] it's always relational and in correspondence with the world around us" (qtd. in Corbett and Phillips 10). It is in this vein that Coats urges scholars of YA literature to be "constantly attentive to innovation, to follow cool, to take risks, to be unapologetically presentist, to reach strong but always provisional conclusions" ("Young Adult Literature" 322). Tracing how the conventions, themes, genres, characters, narrative arcs, designs, and features have changed over the last decade and a half illustrates the ways (and speed) at which YA literature can grow, develop, and reshape when the conditions are right. To "follow cool" and "be unapologetically presentist" in my examination of the developments of YA literature over time, I have kept pace with the texts that have been published during the course of my research and writing. This book offers the most up-to-date insights into transgender YA literature possible at the time of writing, but its conclusions are, of course, receptive to the reality that there will always be another book published and that trans YA literature is constantly evolving.

In the preface to the second edition of *Merchants of Culture: The Publishing Business in the Twenty-First Century*, John B. Thompson remarks that "writing about a present-day industry is always going to be like shooting at a moving target: no sooner have you finished the text than your subject matter has changed [. . . , and] the industry you had captured at a particular point in time now looks slightly different" (vi). There is "no remedy," for Thompson, "apart from revising and updating the text if and when the opportunity presents itself" (vi). I have leaned into the historicized and historical practice of "presentist" research, and I have taken such opportunity to update and revaluate my analysis until the point it became no longer feasible to do so. While I include references to texts published from 2021 onwards, my analysis is mostly confined to texts published in or before 2020. Yet, irrespective of my efforts to maintain an up-to-date picture, it is vital to understand trans YA literature as a process with a past, present, and future, rather than a static category.

A breakdown of the trans YA literature genre world would look very different ten years ago and (most likely) ten years in the future, signaling some of the same findings that Jayashree Kamblé's epistemology of popular romance fiction uncovered. Kamblé argues that "what may be acceptable as romantic alters over time, not just in terms of archetypes but in terms of the constructed reality in which the relationship can be apprehended/enjoyed, that is, considered 'romantic'" (21). This development, Kamblé suggests, "is made possible because the novel is a form that promotes evolutionary adaptation, linguistically and structurally, allowing the 'romance novel' to be an evolving organism—one that therefore merits regular reevaluation rather than static labels" (21). The diachronic analysis of transgender YA literature offered in this book necessitates an agile approach: responsive to research that has come before, but willing to forge new paradigms for better understanding transgender YA literature as a related, yet discrete, subset of the YA book market.

Transitions in the Twenty-First-Century Young Adult Book Market

Many studies of LGBTQ+ YA fiction, the broader field of literature in which transgender texts are frequently subsumed, are geared towards taking stock of the current state of the literary field and pointing out how future publications can better represent young, queer people. Collectively, Jenkins and Cart's *The Heart Has Its Reasons* (2006) and *Representing the Rainbow* (2018) also analyze an extensive bibliography of YA texts—including novels and short-story collections—published from 1969 to 2016 to trace the trends in LGBTQ+ YA fiction. Epstein's 2013 monograph, *Are the Kids Alright?*, surveys how LGBTQ+ characters are portrayed in English-language picture books, middle-grade books, and YA fiction in order to open up questions about diversity and stereotypes, among other important areas of concern for children's literature and YA studies. Caren J. Town takes a more pedagogy-focused look at the field in her 2017 monograph, *LGBTQ+ Young Adult Fiction*, as a study inspired by her own search for texts that "represented the experiences of gay and lesbian adolescents in ways that weren't tragic or preachy, or filtered exclusively through the perspective of straight narrators" (1) to use in her teaching (I return to the problem of investigations of "LGBTQ+" fiction being limited to gay and lesbian topics shortly). The above examples constitute the most extensive published surveys of LGBTQ+ YA fiction to date, but several shorter studies—in the form of articles and book chapters—also seek to uncover the trends and patterns of the field. Mark Letcher's "Off the Shelves: Celebrating Love in All Shades: YA Books with LGBTQ Themes" (2009), Epstein's "We're Here, We're [Not?] Queer: GLBTQ Characters in Children's Books" (2012), Cady Lewis's "How Far Have We Come? A Critical Look at LGBTQ Identity in Young Adult Literature" (2015), Laura M. Jiménez' "Representation in Award-Winning LGBTQ Young Adult Literature from 2000–2013" (2015), and Robert Bittner and colleagues' "Queer and Trans-Themed Books for Young Readers: A Critical Review" (2016) offer five such examples. While only a sample of the proliferating number of scholarly interventions into the field of LGBTQ+ YA fiction, these examples evidence a growing interest in how the field has developed and can continue to develop in the years to come. These works form a pattern of scholarship seeking to outline categories and frameworks for approaching LGBTQ+ YA texts, establish publishing trends, and highlight areas for growth.

This is book is indebted to the aforementioned scholars as trans texts are a significant part of the LGBTQ+ YA fiction that their studies investigated. Yet the subsummation of transgender YA titles in LGBTQ+ YA literature as a catch-all umbrella can limit our understanding of those texts, and this book draws out the discrete functions, trends, aims, and implied readerships of transgender YA fiction from the broader field. Chapter 1 offers a practical example of why such a project is necessary by demonstrating the ways that all-encompassing claims about LGBTQ+ literature can overshadow the development of transgender representation in the YA book market. The objective of the first chapter—to provide an accurate overview of the early years of transgender YA fiction through an analysis of the transgender problem novel—necessitates that transgender YA texts are differentiated from the umbrella of LGBTQ+ YA fiction that David Levithan claims was entering the market in "unprecedented numbers" ("Supporting Gay Teen Literature" 44) in 2004, despite the fact that the first example of explicitly transgender fiction (*Luna*) was not published until that year. With John Donovan's *I'll Get There. It Better Be Worth the Trip* (1969) introducing the first explicitly gay character into the YA book market thirty-five years before Luna made her appearance, it is clear that general claims about LGBTQ+ YA fiction risk confusing our understanding of transgender YA literature: the history and development of the literary representation of the different identities within the LGBTQ+ umbrella are more varied than one acronym can encapsulate.

Levithan's thought piece does not pose as rigorous quantitative research, but it nevertheless usefully demonstrates how including trans representation under the umbrella of LGBTQ+ YA literature, when it is gay and lesbian literature that is the focus, can obfuscate transgender YA literature's publication history. The conflation of trans representation with other sorts of queer representation via the use of the LGBTQ+ acronym more significantly obscures an understanding of the development of the transgender YA publishing category in the extensive research of Jenkins and Cart. Across their two works, *The Heart Has Its Reasons* and *Representing the Rainbow*, Jenkins and Cart analyze a bibliography of hundreds of LGBTQ+ YA books published between 1969 and the late 2010s with the aim to establish and promote a three-part model for analyzing the portrayal and evolution of LGBTQ+ characters. The categories Jenkins and Cart identify reflect what they find to be the three types of stories with LGBTQ+ characters published for young adults.

Jenkins and Cart's categories derive from Rudine Sims Bishop's work to classify Afro-American children's literature. Bishop's categories—"social conscience" books ("Evaluating Books by and about African-Americans" 17–32), "melting pot" books (33–48), and "culturally conscious" books (49–78)—have been reinvented by Jenkins and Cart as "homosexual visibility," "gay assimilation," and "queer consciousness/community" (*Representing the Rainbow* xiv) to fit LGBTQ+ YA literature. Their homosexual visibility category describes titles where the emphasis is on a character's coming-out story as their identity becomes apparent to other characters. Gay assimilation novels assume the existence of a variety of sexualities and genders and include characters for whom being LGBTQ+ is an incidental part of their identity. These books note differences in passing that are then ignored as "gay/lesbian characters must appear to be no different from the heterosexual norm except for the fact of their sexual orientation" (Jenkins and Cart, *Representing the Rainbow* 272). Finally, in queer consciousness/ community books, LGBTQ+ characters tell their own stories and exist "in the context of a community" (Jenkins and Cart, *Representing the Rainbow* xv). Having the critical language to describe how LGBTQ+ characters appear in YA literature is important to Jenkins and Cart because of their belief in "the indispensability of literature and its power to change the world [that] is foundational to [their] analysis" (xv). Their model is designed both to assess how LGBTQ+ representation appears within YA literature and to consider how these books can have real-world implications as a type of literary activism.[5] Though their use of this model is subjective—it is underpinned by their belief that "what is stereotypic, wrongheaded, and outdated need to be exposed and what is accurate, thoughtful, and artful needs to be applauded" (*Representing the Rainbow* xiii)—the categories are useful both for grounding literary analysis and as a framework through which educators and researchers can choose LGBTQ+ texts and has inspired further investigations of LGBTQ+ fiction.[6]

Jenkins and Cart's terminology is especially useful for large-scale categorizations that allow us to trace the evolution of LGBTQ+ literature. For example, they observe that the majority of titles with gay and lesbian characters in the 1970s and 1980s shared the features of homosexual visibility literature (Jenkins and Cart, *Representing the Rainbow* xiv). Their model is also helpful for making observations about how trans literature follows in the wake of the development of nonheterosexual representation in YA literature. Where the terminology they have devised falls short, however, is in its scope to accommodate an increasingly diverse spectrum of identity in LGBTQ+ YA literature into the categories. First published in *The Heart Has Its Reasons* and replicated twelve years later in *Representing the Rainbow*, Jenkins and Cart's three categories were adapted from Bishop's work specifically for the evaluation of gay and lesbian characters and remain most suited to those identities. For instance, the "homosexual visibility" category (even the title of which excludes other LGBTQ+ identities) is used to identify books that contain "'coming-out' stories, in which a character who has been assumed to be heterosexual 'comes out' as gay/lesbian" (Jenkins and Cart, *Representing the Rainbow* 272). In their later title, which traces LGBTQ+ literature published by 2016, Jenkins and Cart group several transgender titles in the category of homosexual visibility literature despite the characters never coming out as gay/lesbian. The categories do not offer the necessary language or tools to analyze the nuances of transgender representation nor to trace how the publishing category has developed.

As trans studies scholars frequently show, the conflation of transgender narratives with LGBTQ coming-out stories wrongly implies that the processes of recognizing nonnormative gender identity and sexual orientation are analogous. Lal Zimman cautions scholars to "take care not to treat coming out as though it were practiced and regarded homogenously across queer communities" (54), while Evan Vipond suggests "the process of understanding who you are (subjectivity) and how you want to live in the world (embodiment) and the process of developing and understanding sexual attractions, desires, and behaviors are distinct" ("Becoming Culturally [Un]Intelligible" 31). Trans studies and YA studies are not, however, in regular dialogue. In 2013, Epstein pointed out that though "recent years have seen an increase in research into both children's literature and queer studies, there has been little overlap of this research" (*Are the Kids All Right?* 2). The situation has improved since the publication of Epstein's 2013 monograph, with works such as Kenneth Kidd and Derritt Mason's edited collection titled *Queer as Camp: Essays on Summer, Style, and Sexuality* (2019), Mason's *Queer Anxieties of Young Adult Literature and Culture* (2021), and Paul Venzo and Kristine Moruzi's edited collection titled *Sexuality in Literature for Children and Young Adults* (2021). Most recently, Tom Sandercock's *Youth Fiction and Trans Representation* (2022) has turned the spotlight onto trans YA fiction within a broader project that includes consideration of picture books, short, animated cartoons, live-action television, and young adult films.

This book focuses on transgender YA texts, drawing them out as a discrete publishing category from their eclipsed position behind gay and lesbian YA literature (in both popular and academic discourse), and I therefore engage with questions of absence, as well as presence, when it comes to the variety of transgender representation available in the YA book market. The gaps and omissions in YA literature's queer representation are being noticed by scholars by way of highlighting how a lack of specific representation can lead to a lack of cultural recognition for people who are "otherwise queer" ("We're Here, We're [Not?] Queer" 272; "'The Case of the Missing Bisexuals'" 1), as Epstein puts it. Epstein's earlier articles asks: "What happened to the BTQ in GLBTQ?" to point out that, at the time, books "tend[ed] to ignore other colours in the queer rainbow, which may mean that authors, publishers, and members of society in general are able to accept non-heterosexuals as long as they are monosexuals and as long as they are not too queer" (292). Her more recent article then makes the case that a paucity of bisexual characters in books for young people is problematic, especially when literature for young people is relied upon as a means for teaching them about sexuality and relationships because it implies bisexual people are not accepted or simply do not exist. Henderson's "*Let's Talk about Love, Tash Hearts Tolstoy*, and the Asexual Coming-of-Age Story" (2019) shares a similar objective by aiming to show why "it is important to represent and normalise asexuality within the media and within fiction, particularly fiction aimed at young people" when "on the rare occasion that it can be found, the representation of asexuality [. . .] is largely based in negative stereotypes and tropes drawn from misconceptions" (2). My own work argues that transgender young people need representations of their lived experiences that are nuanced, varied, and have intersectional inclusivity.

The process of distinguishing trans texts from their fellow LGBTQ+ titles necessitates a clear working definition of what transgender identity means in the project's contemporary sociocultural and book-market contexts. I use "trans-ness," in line with Russo's use of the term in *If I Was Your Girl*, as the noun form of transgender, and I use "transgender" or "trans" (as a shortened form of "transgender") interchangeably as inclusive adjectives to describe people and characters whose gender identity differs from that which they were assigned at birth, including those whose gender falls within, between, and beyond the binary.⁷ While "trans*" (with the asterisk) has sometimes been favored by trans studies scholars for "draw[ing] attention to the word, indicating the possibility of a deeper meaning than the prefix itself might suggest" (Tompkins 27) and "mak[ing] trans* people the authors of their own categorizations" (Halberstam 4), I have chosen to use "trans" (no asterisk) to align with the most frequently used terminology in my primary corpus. Moreover, by way of promoting the importance of respecting transgender people's right to define their own identities, my analysis always refers to characters with the name, pronouns, and gender that align with their identity (as opposed to their assigned sex) unless my purpose is to directly replicate a reference to the character in a primary text. Vocabulary is always developing, and this is true of the trans lexicon. For example, K. J. Rawson and Cristan Williams's 2014 attempt to map the rhetorical landscape of the term "transgender" concludes with the admission that their insights are "just another contour in its [the term's] ever-growing complexity" (6). Where other critical texts I engage with use the term "transsexual," for example, I have chosen to use "transgender" as more inclusive and updated. Nevertheless, I recognize that the language people identify with is a very personal choice and is likely to continue to evolve. I have chosen to use what is generally agreed to be the most appropriate and respectful terminology at the time of writing, but I wish to acknowledge that any written account is inevitably a snapshot of a specific moment in our history, and that time continues to reshape our communication.

The type of representation that my project focuses on is YA texts in which the character's trans identity is made explicit, but my own approach to identifying LGBTQ+ representation as that which is named in the texts is not universally shared. The introduction to Michelle Ann Abate and Kidd's *Over the Rainbow: Queer Children's and Young Adult Literature*, for instance, argues that "understanding children's literature as queer rather than more narrowly as gay/lesbian broadens interpretive possibilities" (4) because queer literature for young people "predates and may outlast the LGBTQ movement" (3). Abate and Kidd's critical approach to identifying queer representation is aligned with the practice of queer reading, a method of reading queerness *into* a text that does not, itself, offer explicit signals to LGBTQ+ content. Building on Eve Kosofsky Sedgewick's definition of "queer" as "the open mesh of possibilities" (qtd. in Abate and Kidd 3), *Over the Rainbow* includes discussion of literature from the nineteenth and early twentieth centuries where the term is used synonymously with "odd, eccentric or singular, often but not always negatively so" (4). Roberta Seelinger Trites's "Queer Performances: Lesbian Politics in *Little Women*" and Robin Bernstein's "The Queerness of *Harriet the Spy*," both included in Abate and Kidd's edited collection, offer useful illustrative examples of such queer reading practice.

A more specific example of trans reading—reading trans-ness into a text—can be found in Leland G. Spencer's "Performing Transgender Identity in *The Little Mermaid*: From Andersen to Disney" (2014). Spencer argues that "a close transgender reading of the texts brings different parts of the narratives into focus" (115), such as reading the "mermaid's fascination with humans" as a mirror for "many transgender people's fascination with transgender role models" (116). According to Jody Norton, the method of trans reading involves "intuiting/interpreting the gender of child characters as not necessarily perfectly aligned with their anatomies" (299). Trans reading "may involve as simple a move as locating a male identity in a female body," or it may take the form of "a much subtler imaginative enactment of a much wider range of identities" (Norton 299). As a practical example, Leah Phillips makes a compelling argument that the protagonist of Tamora Pierce's The Song of the Lioness series (1983–1988) can be read as being "neither boy nor girl but, rather, both" (*Female Heroes in Young Adult Fantasy Fiction* 64). Phillips's interpretation is buttressed by Pierce's own epitextual announcement that "Alanna has always defied labels. She took the best bits of being a woman and a man, and created her own unique identity. I think the term is 'gender-fluid,' though there wasn't a word for this (to my knowledge) when I was writing her" (@TamoraPierce). Yet both Phillips's and Pierce's interventions are ultimately acts of trans reading, making trans identity explicit where it was only, at most, implied in the original text.

If you apply this method of reading, transgender representation has a far larger basis in children's and YA fiction. R. Anthony Slagle argues that "queerness is pervasive in texts, even those that are not intentionally queer" (132), and it is reasonable to draw a similar conclusion about trans-ness. Sandercock's recent *Youth Fiction and Trans Representation* does just that, adopting Norton's trans-reading approach to examine a broad corpus of YA novels, graphic narratives, television, live-action film, children's picture books, and animated cartoons by way of "offer[ing] a sense of the scope and diversity in contemporary trans representation for young people" (4).

Sandercock's corpus includes trans novels such as Wittlinger's *Parrotfish* and Beam's *I Am J* discussed here, but it also includes, for example, YA body-swap films, such as *The Hot Chick* (Brady, 2002) and *All Screwed Up* (Stephen, 2009) where Sandercock states the cross-gender swap "is not desired by either character" (150). Sandercock's approach challenges the impulse to label characters as trans or nontrans and encourages readers to explore expansive, imaginative interpretations of gender while offering myriad insights into a broad range of gender-variant characters and phenomena for young people. Yet, the growing wealth of trans representation—that which is named as such—in recent YA texts warrants the dedicated attention that is given in this book.

The importance of clear and recognizable language to signal a character's trans-ness in literature for young people cannot be overstated. As Gabrielle Owen recognizes, there is power in "naming and knowing the self" (*A Queer History of Adolescence* 131) with language that enables us to be seen by others. In the author's note for Miles McKenna's YA transgender memoir, *Out! How to Be Your Authentic Self* (2020), Mckenna proposes that "labels, as I have come to understand them, are just tools that we use to define ourselves for other people. To have a sense of belonging or exclusion from a pack" (11). In everyday life, labels are tools that create that "sense of belonging," but in literature they are a vital means of connecting readers with illustrations of their own identity. A focus on explicit representation underpins both the textual selections and arguments I make, for reasons that I continue to discuss throughout. In short, I am interested in interrogating how books are constructed when they explicitly identify a major character as transgender, and my second chapter perhaps most strongly makes the case for the importance of such overt visibility. Dividing a broad selection of primary texts into categories based upon how trans-ness is signaled in their peritextual materials, I argue that naming a character's trans identity is the most effective way of ensuring trans characters are locatable within the extensive catalog of YA fiction published each year. By providing potential readers with easily recognizable (and searchable) information that trans identity is represented in the book, texts are performing the vital task of assisting readers to connect with a "community on the page" (*Representing the Rainbow* xiii), as Jenkins and Cart put it, as well as bringing marginalized identities into the mainstream book market.

Approaching Transgender Young Adult Literature

Representation—who is represented, how are they represented, and by whom—is among the most fervently debated topics in YA literature studies at the moment. Representation is a term and concept that runs throughout this book and, relatedly, through children's and YA literature criticism of past and present. In "Ploughing the Field: A Discussion about YA Studies" (2020), Alison Waller points out that YA literature studies "is a discipline with a history that needs to be considered as much as the innovative contemporary moment" (qtd. in Corbett and Phillips 16), and it is in that vein that I now offer a historical grounding to my discussion of representation in twenty-first-century texts. In 1990, Bishop argued that "literature transforms human experience and reflects it back to us, and in that reflection, we can see our own lives and experiences as part of the larger human experience" ("Mirrors, Windows, and Sliding Glass Doors" xi). The ensuing claim—that all children need and deserve inclusive fictional representation that acts as mirrors, windows, and sliding glass doors through which they can encounter their own and others' lived experiences—has provided the critical language that has underpinned many subsequent calls for more diversity in children's and YA literature. Put simply, "mirrors" reflect aspects of readers' multilayered and complex identities; "windows" show readers identities and cultures that are different from their own; and "sliding glass doors" enable readers to enter creative worlds using their imagination. Bishop was writing specifically about race and ethnicity in children's books, and the legacy of "Mirrors, Windows, and Sliding Glass Doors" can be traced through work that is concerned with calling out a lack of racial diversity in YA literature. Ebony Elizabeth Thomas locates Bishop within a "protest tradition launched decades ago by leaders in the multicultural children's literature movement such as Augusta Baker, Pura Belpré, Nancy Larrick, Jella Lepman, Charlemae Hill Rollins, and Rudine Sims Bishop, as well as many other authors, librarians, educators, and community activists" (*The Dark Fantastic* 4–5) that preceded "more recent efforts" (4) on social media in the past few years.

Bishop's metaphor predates the primary corpus of this study by nearly a decade and a half, but the ongoing critical relevance of mirrors, windows, and sliding glass doors as an analytical concept speaks to the fact that more work is needed to align the reader identification opportunities of marginalized young people with those of their white, straight, cisgender, able-bodied, middle-class peers. For example, Mary Catherine Miller claims literature should offer young transgender readers "reflections of their own feelings about gender and personal identity" (84); P. L. Thomas and colleagues situate LGBTQ protagonists as a "potential opportunity to see 'someone like me'" (78); and Epstein argues that literature should "show GLBTQ children reflections of themselves" ("We're Here, We're [Not?] Queer" 290). The first chapter of this book changes the terms of the discussion from whether marginalized identities are represented in my primary corpus to asking *how* they are represented and by whom.

There is repeated evidence that young people benefit from the opportunity to identify with the literature they read. Aidan Chambers's scholarly intervention argues that "until you encounter in stories a self that's recognisably yours [. . .] you do not believe you exist or, at the least, believe you are subservient to a dominant group who do possess an identifying body of stories—a literature" ("Finding the Form" 273). Personal testimonies from transgender people including Jennifer Finney Boylan also suggest that searching "the library in vain for the story of a person I might resemble" to no avail led her to feel "as if [she] did not exist" (qtd. in Mesch 12). Both together and separately, these perspectives make a strong case for the importance of representation. These perspectives are particularly formative in my fourth chapter, where I argue that contemporary trans YA fiction can offer useful spaces for trans YA readers to explore their own experiences of home, experiences that have become all the more significant during the Covid lockdown measures, by offering windows and mirrors of ordinary family life. However, not every critic is convinced by the importance of representation. For Maria Nikolajeva, the idea that readers are expected to identify with a character is a "fallacy" (*Power, Voice and Subjectivity in Literature for Young Readers* 185) because "as mediators of literature, we want children to be able to place themselves in other people's life situations, to develop understanding and compassion, to be self-reflective, and not least, to be able to assess ideology" (202). None of Nikolajeva's claims work to directly counter calls for more inclusive representation in literature: not only do marginalized readers also need the opportunities to develop the critical reading skills that Nikolajeva outlines, but having insights into "other people's life situations" necessitates more diverse characters. Yet Nikolajeva's stance appears to overlook the experiences of marginalized readers for whom opportunities for identification are in short supply. It is a stance that has caused controversy.

In February 2021, the *School Library Journal* used the illustration of a white child reading a book with a Black child's face as its cover image with the title "Why White Children Need Diverse Books," suggesting that diverse books are an important tool for teaching white children about the experiences of people of color. The journal was criticized for centering whiteness (Forest Park Public Library n.p.). In a similar vein, "Nonfiction Windows So White," an article written by Marc Aronson and published online by *The Horn Book* in March 2021, agrees that the mirrors, windows, and sliding glass doors framework "has become a central part of our vocabulary as we evaluate books for children and teenagers" (n.p.). However, it is how the article makes use of the metaphor that is useful here for thinking about how the charged conversations regarding representation can offer important insights into the various portrayals of trans adolescents. Aronson's article takes an approach to representation that is reminiscent of the "color blind" or "all lives matter" rhetoric that has been critiqued by scholars and activists alike who have pointed out the necessity of recognizing the specific plights and needs of marginalized people.[8] Aronson uses Bishop's metaphor to underpin the argument that "when a writer from any and every background believes that every topic is theirs to explore [. . .] we will have a true blossoming of the promise of diversity" (n.p.). As Ramdarshan Bold points out, "there have been numerous cases, across the decades, of authors from dominant groups writing damaging and stereotypical depictions of socially marginalised people whose identity they do not share" ("The Thirteen Percent Problem" 4), citing John Boyne's afterword in his transgender YA novel, *My Brother's Name Is Jessica* (2019), among her recent examples. The peritextual materials of Boyne's novel are discussed in greater detail in my second chapter, but here the afterword offers a useful entry point into a discussion of how questions of authenticity have shaped my project as a whole. Boyne boldly declares that "the worst piece of advice anyone can give a writer is to write about what they know" (Afterword). Whether or not it is ethical for an author to tell stories about a marginalized community, culture, or identity that they do not participate in or share is arguably one of the most contentious questions in contemporary debates about diverse literature.

It is a commonly taken critical stance that the act of reading creates meaning that exceeds the author's intentions for the text's interpretation. Meaning and interpretation can most certainly exceed, or simply differ, from that intended by the author, but I want to demonstrate an alternative way of conceptualizing the relationship between the author, text, and reader that does not necessitate the author be metaphorically killed by the readers, as Roland Barthes would advocate (*Image, Music, Text*). Insisting on the author's role in the interpretation of texts forms an important aspect of this project for two reasons. First, the social-media–dominated context into which my later primary texts have been published opens up new channels of communication between author and reader that inevitably play a part in shaping how texts are interpreted. This is especially relevant to chapter 5's investigation of the connections between transgender YA memoirs and digital transgender youth culture that I argue are born from the multimedia storytelling of the memoirists. Second, when it comes to the depiction of marginalized identities, it is important to consider who is writing. According to Jonathon Gray, "authorcide risk[s] silencing previously marginalized writers and creators just at the point when they were becoming especially visible and audible" ("When Is the Author?" 91). Chiara Pellegrini writes that "despite post-structuralist assertions about the death of the author, historically marginalized subjects have proven to be less enthusiastic about dispensing with authority over their texts" (53–54). That is because marginalized authors "have fought to obtain their status as viable subjects and [. . .] their ability to control their narratives remains precarious because of their subordinated position in social hierarchies" (Pellegrini 54). To a similar end, Ramdarshan Bold suggests that "authorial identity is of particular importance to those that write within the margins, i.e. writers that do not have white, upper middle class, male, heterosexual, able-bodied, cisgendered, Western privilege/s" (*Inclusive Young Adult Fiction* 109). My work is informed by the perspective that, although the identity and intentions of the author do not supersede textual effects, they are nevertheless a part of deciphering the text's function. The genre world concept and the analytical method it prompts—reading texts alongside authorial identity and authorial interventions (as well as publishing data)—have the potential to "yield new insights and a fuller, richer understanding" (Fletcher et al. 998).

Relatedly, my project is also an attempt to trace how authors of trans YA literature have changed, and it is an objective that shapes the trajectory of this book. Cisgender writers continue to author trans YA texts with varying levels of critical reception: Boyne's controversial *My Brother's Name Is*

Jessica (2019) is one particularly ill-received example among a corpus of texts including Eric Devine's *Look Past* (2016), Sonia Patel's *Jaya and Rasa* (2017), Alice Oseman's *I Was Born for This* (2018), and Amber Smith's *Something Like Gravity* (2019). However, the balance of authorship has shifted towards transgender authorship during the course of this research project. How transness is represented on the page is, of course, vital to my project, but so, too, is drawing attention to whose voices are being represented in the production of these books. In *The Hidden Adult* (2008), Perry Nodelman argues that children's literature (a term he uses to group both children's and YA texts) "is a literature that claims to be devoid of adult content that nevertheless lurks within it" (*The Hidden Adult* 341) because adults are inextricably implicated in its production, distribution, and consumption. Nodelman's work sits among a prominent subset of scholarship across the fields of children's and YA literature studies by, among others, Jaqueline Rose, Maria Nikolajeva, and Clémentine Beauvais that seeks to interrogate this so-called hidden adult; that is to say, the adult who is involved in creative roles such as author, editor, publisher, and illustrator, as well as those responsible for putting the book into the young person's hands, including guardians, teachers, and librarians. I am interested in the hidden adults, but also in the hidden cisgender people (as creators and readers) lurking beneath the surface of ostensibly transgender exteriors.

Given that cisgender researchers have also historically lurked in trans scholarship with "few [making] their positionality explicit in their research" (Schiffer 700), I want to directly acknowledge my position as a cisgender scholar who has not shared the transgender lived experiences depicted in my primary corpus and who writes from a position of privilege as white woman in the UK. My purpose in this book is to critically investigate how trans identities are represented, marketed, and sometimes commodified in the twenty-first-century YA book market, not to claim authority to speak about transgender and other marginalized experiences as if they were my own. I aim to create awareness about the importance of supporting trans narratives, especially in a climate where book banning and censorship of LGBTQ+ children's and YA literature is increasingly prevalent. I join Sandercock in "oppos[ing] the censorship of literature and media as much as I encourage robust and nuanced analysis of such texts to understand the kinds of meanings that are being communicated to youth about trans and queer ways of being" (*Youth Fiction and Trans Representation* 3). Indeed, I view this research project as a means to make space for more marginalized people to narrate their own experiences, both in the YA book market and in YA scholarship. When prominent cisgender individuals continue to use their voices to attack, limit, or deny the lived experiences of trans young people, it becomes even more important to provide a counterbalance by celebrating and amplifying trans authors, while challenging cisnormative approaches to trans representation.

Transgender YA texts, especially (but not exclusively) early texts written by cisgender authors, often take a pseudoanthropological approach to trans-ness. Books are marketed to the cisgender teenagers who are signaled as their implied readers in ways that will continue to become clear throughout my substantive analysis. The implied reader—a concept I use in line with Wolfgang Iser's formulation of an intermediary between the author's and reader's consciousness—signals the vantage point and approach a reader is asked to take when reading a text. In Iser's words,

> reading sparks off an ideational activity in the course of which each individual reader will have to discard and replace the ideas formed through information provided and knowledge invoked; it seems to me that this process, always active as the reader travels inside the text and executes the instructions given to him, actually gives shape to his identity. (63)

Put simply, it is how readers are expected to interact with the text that reveals their implied identity. There are examples I consider in my analysis whereby specific readers are named in the paratextual materials of a book as its intended recipients, such as Russo's addresses "to [her] cisgender readers" and "to [her] trans readers" in her author's note for *If I Was Your Girl*, but these instances do not necessarily signal the same reader as the implied reader. The various implied readers I refer to in my chapters have, instead, been inferred by posing a number of my own questions to readings of the texts: What knowledge of trans-ness is a reader expected to bring to a book? What subject position does the narrative encourage a reader to identify with? How are other characters' attitudes to trans-ness dealt with in the narrative? What approach to trans-ness do the peritextual and textual materials signal?

Chambers argues that the implied reader concept offers a means of determining "what kind of book it is, and what kind of reader (or, to put it another way, what kind of reading) it demands" ("The Reader in the Book"

11). The implied readers of the primary texts identified in this project have informed my approach to analysis in myriad ways, not least in my aim to interrogate how these texts function in their sociocultural and book market contexts. I am interested in how the implied readers of transgender YA texts shift dependent on a number of factors including the identity of the author, genre, type of publisher, and year of publication. Importantly, I am interested in what shifting patterns in the identities of the implied readers I have observed through comparative analysis of several texts in the category can tell us about how the representation of trans-ness is changing across the twenty-first century.

Tracing the Development of Transgender Young Adult Literature

This book locates the emergence of trans representation as a relatively recent development in YA literature through the lens of YA studies. However, I want to give explicit recognition to the reality that the existence of transgender youth predates this newfound, explicit visibility in the YA book market. Gill-Peterson's *Histories of the Transgender Child* challenges the widespread myth that transgender children are a twenty-first-century phenomenon by demonstrating that "trans children have a documentable past stretching the *entirety* of the twentieth century, long before today's trans and gender-variant adults were even born" and that "trans children outright precede the category of 'transsexuality' and the contemporary medical model" (8). In this regard, the concern raised by Abigail Shrier in *Irreversible Damage* (2020) that "[t]he Western world has seen a sudden surge of adolescents claiming to have gender dysphoria and self-identifying as 'transgender'" (n.p.) represents an example of a problematic and frankly dangerous tendency Owen recognizes to dismiss adolescent forms of knowing as "a whim or drama, hormonal or identity instability surrounding a new teen trend" (*A Queer History of Adolescence* 93). I recognize the long and complex history of trans young people, and my purpose here is to trace the related, but distinct, emergence and development of transgender representation as a literary phenomenon. Each chapter plays a part in mapping the changing shape of YA literature and transgender representation in the twenty-first century. Chapter 1 establishes the "horizons of expectation" (Todorov 18) for transgender YA fiction by outlining how the literature developed in the popular presses and how trans-ness was represented in the mainstream market. I show how the generic conventions of a selection of early trans YA novels featuring teenage trans protagonists, written by cisgender authors, overlap and depart from the precedents set by problem novels (especially queer problem novels) and establish a prehistory for trans-authored transgender YA fiction. I extend existing criticism that has highlighted how trans identity is yoked to being "born in the wrong body," arguing that the shared notions of liminality and arrival of trans-ness and adolescence shape this body of fiction. While the protagonists mostly desire to enter adulthood in culturally cohesive bodies, transition is not available to them within the narrative timelines. I complicate the critical assumption that transition is the resolution presented in these problem novels by showing that, instead, social acceptance serves this function. With these novels, cisgender authors created a protocanon and set expectations for trans representation in YA fiction that are still influencing publishing decisions. Subsequent chapters refer back to and complicate the precedents set out in this opening chapter to show how the market has since expanded and developed.

A chronological sequel to chapter 1, chapter 2 transforms the picture of trans YA publishing by showing how the field has developed from 2015 to include trans authorship, more variety, and greater intersectional diversity and situates these developments in the context of the We Need Diverse Books movement and the "transgender tipping point" that coincided in the mid-2010s. This chapter then examines the peritextual materials of a broad range of these trans YA titles that proliferated from the mid-2010s to determine how books are pitched to potential readers. In particular, I focus on how books signal that trans characters or themes are included in their narratives and how peritextual features are used to construct authorial identities, bringing readers' attention to authors' various knowledge, expertise, and relevant experience to write trans characters in order to ascertain their intended readership. The peritextual focus offers an alternative approach to the study of transgender YA fiction, where existing research has mostly focused on the stories or their pedagogical function for teenage readers. I argue that the choices made by authors, illustrators, editors, and publishers regarding books' peritextual features can signal the spaces the books are intended to occupy within their contemporary market. My findings reveal that trans YA novels are often marketed to cisgender readers by cisgender-dominated publishing houses at the expense of trans adolescents who are seeking reflections of their lived experiences.

Chapter 3 explores alternative strategies of representation, bringing together a group of socioculturally engaged speculative stories from my primary corpus that blend the generic conventions I set out in chapter 1 with the tropes and possibilities of fantasy. These texts are frequently underpinned by an attempt to challenge discrimination and show trans young people navigating their various worlds in ways that are entertaining, enlightening, and/or informative, depending on the lived experiences of individual readers. Realism and fantasy have many common traits (not least that they both offer fictional worlds), but this chapter asks whether the latter's distance from consensus reality, propensity for exaggeration, and freedom from the confines of feasibility afford authors greater scope to draw attention to, and critique, the normative structures that inflect the lives of trans teens. In particular, I show the various ways that the world-building strategies of some of the fantastic texts function as commentaries on quotidian issues and suggest extraordinary adolescent characters can offer ordinary readers opportunities to explore two key subjects of relevance to trans teenagers—identity and empowerment—through allegory and metaphor. Not all speculative texts challenge the status quo, just as not all contemporary realist texts maintain it. Rather, I contend that a growing market of speculative trans YA fiction has opened up new fictional avenues for readers to creatively engage with the lived experiences of trans people, while expanding the imaginative possibilities for trans teen readers looking for empowering reflections of their own lives in fiction.

Chapter 4 develops the previous chapter's insights into the empowerment of transgender teens by asking if transgender YA fiction offers a useful, newly politicized space to update and transform Nikolajeva's observations regarding power in adult-child relationships. Identifying a thematic connection across the different genres I examine, this chapter interrogates how parent-adolescent relationships and domestic spaces are reflected in a selection of YA texts, a focus that has become all the more pertinent owing to recent sociological research suggesting that the lockdown measures of the Covid-19 pandemic resulted in declining mental health for many trans teenagers forced to isolate with unsupportive relatives. Home and family are focal points in most young people's lives. I argue that the depiction of relationships between cisgender parents and transgender teenagers disrupts the notion of "parent-as-authority-figure" (Trites, *Disturbing the Universe* 54) and that the representation of transgender teenagers' authority reflects (and contributes to) the contemporary cultural zeitgeist's recognition of marginalized people's authority on their identities, experiences, and stories.

Further exploring the authority of transgender young people, chapter 5 pushes the boundaries of transgender YA literature by offering a "snapshot" (McAlister 4) examination of trans YA memoirs that traces how the genre has been established and developed in my research period to recognize trans young people as authors. Creating two chronological snapshots (2014–2016 and 2017–2020) with my primary texts, I argue that trans YA memoirs were first conceived as a form of trans autobiography—a genre of transgender (or transsexual) autobiography for adults—for a young adult readership but, over time, have become increasingly connected to trans digital youth culture. Online spaces have had a significant impact on trans teenagers' ability to access supportive communities. My aim is to demonstrate that transgender YA memoirs have responded to the changing sociocultural, multimedia context by building connections between what is available online and what is available in print. The life writing in my primary corpus can be thought of as related to, yet separate from, the fiction explored in earlier chapters, and I hope that this final chapter lays some foundations for future investigation into trans YA memoirs, their place in a tradition of autobiography, and the development of the genre as part of a multimedia landscape for transgender youth in the coming years.

Abate and Kidd's question as to whether "queer literature for young readers [can] effect, as much as document, change" (146) is one that I take on and revise by asking: Can transgender representation in YA books effect, as well as document, the changing sociocultural environment for transgender teens? The rest of this book sets out my argument that trans YA literature offers significant reflections of trans-ness and adolescence as overlapping subject positions, reflections that are in dialogue with the sociocultural and publishing moments of the texts' production and have changed over time in ways that are revealing and enlightening.

Chapter 1

THE TRANSGENDER PROBLEM
A New Subcategory of Young Adult Fiction

The influence and endurance of Rudine Sims Bishop's mirrors, windows, and sliding glass doors metaphor as a means of stressing the importance of books representing identities and experiences that have been historically and culturally marginalized cannot be overstated. In the introduction, I briefly demonstrated how the metaphor has shaped critical enquiry into LGBTQ+ representation in literature for young people, referencing examples such as P. L. Thomas and colleagues (2010), B. J. Epstein (2012), and Mary Catherine Miller (2014). With transgender representation undeniably present in the current YA book market, it is necessary to build on earlier calls to action with a critical stance that interrogates the types of representation available to teenage readers. In this chapter, I analyze early trans YA novels in relation to the precedents set by problem novels, and especially queer problem novels, in order to establish a history of the field and interrogate the conventions that later works disrupt or extend.

Karen Coats points out that "when we think of mirrors, we think of them as reflecting what is in front of them in a straightforward way; that is, we believe that what we see in a mirror is an accurate imitation of the real world" (*The Bloomsbury Introduction* 1). Reflections can be deceiving though, and Coats invites us to "think more carefully about the qualities of the mirror itself, rather than what it reflects" (1). In particular, Coats points to the "fun house mirror [. . .] that elongates and shortens part of the body, or a dressing room mirror that makes us look thinner than we expected, or a broken mirror that breaks apart or doubles parts of our face" as a metaphor that she uses to consider the mirror's occasionally distortive properties and the "edges or frames that limit, focus, and contain the field of what they reflect" (1). In destabilizing the mirror's accuracy, Coats encourages us to "come up with some new ideas about seemingly realistic or even nonfiction literature" and how it "doesn't fully reflect or represent reality in a transparent and unproblematic way" (1). For my purposes, Coats's questions can usefully be brought into dialogue with Bishop's metaphor by way of interrogating how transgender adolescent identity is reflected, focused, contorted, distorted, and limited by the mirrors (that are also windows and sliding glass doors) in my primary corpus.

I show how trans-ness was represented by trans protagonists in early realist YA fiction published between 2007 and 2015 and how the fiction developed through mainstream publishing houses in these years. As Heather Love points out, "Establishing a transgender tradition means addressing the crucial distinction between literature about transgender people and literature by transgender people" (150), and I begin my contribution to that work by offering insights into the first decade or so of trans YA fiction. This could be called a prehistory of trans YA literature by transgender authors because it is almost exclusively about, rather than by, trans people. YA novels featuring transgender adolescents published by the major conglomerate houses—Penguin Random House, Macmillan, Hachette, HarperCollins, and Simon & Schuster—were exclusively authored by ostensibly cisgender writers until the publication of Meredith Russo's *If I Was Your Girl* by the Flat Iron imprint of Macmillan in 2016 and, at the same time, were almost always written from the perspective of the transgender teen.[1] When the first trans-authored stories were later published (leading up to the boom in trans-authored fiction that I come on to explore in the next chapter), it was by small, independent, and usually cisgender-dominated queer presses with limited reach. For example, Bella Books, a press devoted to "fiction for and about women-loving-women" ("About Us" n.p.), published Rachel Gold's *Being Emily* in 2012 and *Just Girls* in 2014. Harmony Ink, the LGBTQ+ teen and new adult literature imprint of Dreamspinner Press (a publisher of gay romance), also published Christopher Hawthorne Moss's *Beloved Pilgrim* in 2014 (first published by the now obsolete Shield-Wall Books in 2011). As I suggested in the introduction, transgender YA novels from small presses, especially those such as the above titles that were published prior to 2015, are particularly challenging to discover. Transgender characters written

Table 1.1: A selection of transgender YA problem novels published in the US and UK from 2007 through 2015.

Author	Title	Publisher	Country	Year
Ellen Wittlinger	*Parrotfish**	Simon & Schuster	US	2007
Cris Beam	*I Am J*	Hachette	US	2011
Kirstin Cronn-Mills	*Beautiful Music for Ugly Children*†	North Star Editions	US	2012
Kristin Elizabeth Clark	*Freakboy*	Macmillan	US	2013
Lisa Williamson	*The Art of Being Normal*	David Fickling Books	UK	2015

* I refer to two different editions of *Parrotfish*. Unless otherwise stated, the citations given refer to the 2015 edition.

† I refer to two different editions of *Beautiful Music for Ugly Children*. Unless otherwise stated, the citations given refer to the 2012 edition.

by cisgender authors (or, at least, authors who do not publicly identify as trans or nonbinary) were most visible in the mainstream market in these years. In this chapter, I focus on five YA novels, selected to give insights into how cisgender-dominated conglomerate publishers introduced adolescent trans protagonists into their catalogs (see table 1.1).

The primary material considered in this chapter could be deemed less relevant to today's adolescent reader than more recent publications (as Rebekah Fitzsimmons has suggested, the YA book market progresses rapidly because "young adults are a renewable resource" [qtd. in Corbett and Phillips 3]). However, beginning my investigation in the years before the boom in transgender YA literature is important for two reasons. First, my diachronic approach to scrutinizing transgender YA fiction at various points in time offers "greater detail and accuracy than would be possible by attempting a singular definition" (McAlister 3). Second, these early texts created a protocanon and solidified expectations for transgender representation in YA fiction that are still influencing publishing decisions in the "genre world" (Fletcher et al. 997) and thus warrant further critical attention.

Wittlinger explains that the impetus for writing the first YA novel to feature an openly trans protagonist came from meeting her daughter's transgender friend, Toby, and realizing that "for my daughter and her friends, being transgender was a completely reasonable idea, not in the least weird or unnatural. It was a difference no more unusual than any other" ("Parrotfish Needed an Update" n.p.). Following Wittlinger's encounter with Toby, she determined "the time seemed right for a book that shared that opinion" (n.p.). There was a disconnect between the ordinary, everyday reality of Wittlinger's daughter and the world as it was reflected in the YA book market. Wittlinger's commentary reveals a desire to bring transgender people, topics, and issues into the mainstream reading of an implied teenage audience, which she achieved by creating the novel's transgender protagonist, Grady.

Wittlinger was, in fact, successful in leading the charge for including trans protagonists in mainstream publishing. All of the major conglomerates have now published YA fiction that features trans characters, and I have identified at least eighty titles with trans protagonists (approximately half of those by conglomerate publishers), including the novels I have already specified by name. Wittlinger's description of transgender identity as "a completely reasonable idea" and "a difference no more unusual than any other," however, reiterates her position as a cisgender author otherwise unfamiliar with trans-ness, and hints at a cisnormative gaze within *Parrotfish*. The novel's function, at least as Wittlinger sees it, was to introduce and explain trans-ness to implied, unknowing teenage readers. *Parrotfish*'s publication marks an important moment in the development of YA fiction. At the same time, it is clear that Wittlinger's imaginative act was the latest iteration of a Western fascination with social issues.

Using Coats's concept of the distorted mirror, I examine how being transgender inflects characters' experiences of being adolescent and vice versa in these fictional representations. I also ask whose readerly needs were at the center of the decision-making processes in the books' creation and production. These dual research questions help me to uncover trends that positioned trans adolescents outside of the mainstream (even as their representation was brought into the mainstream book market). I extend existing criticism, which has focused on YA fiction's representation of trans-ness as a corporeal problem. In particular, Jennifer Putzi argues that trans identity is yoked to being born in the wrong body for transgender girls. I show that the transgender girls, boys, and nonbinary teenagers in these protocanonical texts are almost all portrayed as desiring to enter adulthood in culturally cohesive bodies. I then complicate the critical assumption that transition is the resolution presented in these problem novels by showing that, instead, acceptance dénouements in which trans characters receive validation from cisgender characters serve this function. Though it is at least partly a practical decision not to feature bodily transition as most of the protagonists do not reach the age of majority by the novels' conclusions, I argue acceptance dénouements also signal an implied cisgender reader. They do so by prioritizing cisgender readers' opportunities to learn about, and come to accept, trans-ness alongside cisgender characters. The consequence is that trans problem novels have historically established a link between trans identity and rejection that solidifies trans-ness as a social issue.[2]

In the rest of this chapter, I set out some of the key conventions of the problem novel genre, and particularly the queer problem novel subgenre, in order to assess how YA fiction has framed transgender adolescence in ways that typically "limit, focus, and contain the field of what they reflect." Following that, I show how the representations of trans-ness across the transgender problem novels are shaped by cisconstructed wrong-body rhetoric, serving as metaphors for the developmental concerns of the mainstream teenage readership while recapitulating binary notions of gender. Then, I demonstrate how scenes depicting the trans protagonist being accepted by cisgender family members and/or friends function as problem-solving dénouements in almost all of the novels, and ultimately serve the educational needs of cisgender readers. I end the chapter by briefly considering the developments that occurred from 2007 through 2015 through the lens of two republished novels, with the aim of showing how sociocultural discourses about trans-ness had really started to shape the publishing market by mid-2010s. The conventional features of trans YA fiction unpacked in this opening chapter are referred to and complicated in subsequent chapters that foreground how the market has expanded and developed. Indeed, this book reflects a broader cultural project to push back against the precedents that the early trans YA fiction established, and chapters 2 through 5 explore the various means with which this work is taking place.

(Queer) Problem Novels

Emerging as a genre of YA fiction in the 1960s and 1970s (see, for example, Cart, *From Romance to Realism* 26; and Reynolds, *Radical Children's Literature* 2), problem novels conventionally "place a social issue at the centre of the plot" (Kokkola 16) that is considered to be relevant to their implied teenage readers. These sorts of novels often include "candor, unidealized characters and settings, colloquial and realistic language, and plots that [portray] realistic problems faced by contemporary young adults" (C. A. Jenkins 43), and they do so in such a way as to foreground the problem as something to be resolved in the narrative. As Cart rather wryly puts it, "subject (think 'problem') and theme [are] the tail that wags the dog of the novel" (*Young Adult Literature* 35). Since problem novels began to be published more than half a century ago, their adolescent protagonists have dealt with a host of contemporary issues, including drug abuse, teenage pregnancy, familial conflict, and eating disorders, to name but a few.

The problem-novel genre has not received much critical acclaim from YA studies scholars who regularly demean it for a perceived lack of "quality." For example, Lydia Kokkola notes that the term "problem novel" "is derogatory" (16), while Cart suggests the problem novel "is to young adult literature what soap opera is to legitimate drama" (*Young Adult Literature* 35). Though I step beyond debates of quality here, it is important to acknowledge that the field of YA literature has a history of being dismissed by critics who perceive it to be inferior. A popular (and inflammatory) example can be found in Ruth Graham's notorious online thought piece "Against YA," which claims that if adults are "substituting the maudlin teen dramas for the complexity of great adult literature, then they are missing out" (n.p.). Scholars have pushed back against this sort of mistreatment of the field. In the mid-1990s, Peter Hollindale argued that a YA book had come to be identified as a "simple children's book with added sex, violence, and family collapse" (85), when it should be understood as part of a complex field of literature. More recently, Rebekah Fitzsimmons and Casey Alane Wilson also lamented that, "despite the complexity and depth of the YA category, much of contemporary culture still views YA literature as an overly simplistic genre filled with superfluous melodrama and silly, overused plot devices" (xiii). Other critics have stressed the intricacy of problem novels, suggesting that "young adult problem novels are especially complex, even when their didactic messages are obvious" (Lefebvre 292). The question of whether problem novels are "quality" literature—or even what "quality" means—has not been resolved, but we will see that the genre's conventions have shaped YA fiction's depiction of nonnormative identities.

Authors have repeatedly mobilized the problem-novel genre to introduce culturally marginalized identities to mainstream teenage readers. The texts are written in such ways as to mimic "the frisson of reading about darkness from the comfort of a clean, well-lit room" (Cart, *Young Adult Literature*

36), presenting different identities as problems in and of themselves for a mainstream readership. As Kokkola points out, "problem novels often inadvertently imply that aspects of identity—for instance, the character's ethnic heritage or sexual orientation—are 'problems' the character has to struggle with, and come to terms with. [. . .] The problem novel genre is a celebration of the myth of the troubled teen" (16). In other words, "the overarching 'problem' of the problem novel is that the teenager is filled with angst about an aspect of their lives they cannot control" (Kokkola 16) but that is nevertheless presented as somehow controllable. This is particularly true of novels featuring nonheterosexual characters for whom the identification of their nonheterosexuality in adolescence is often positioned as resolvable.

Owing to hetero- and cisnormativity in the YA book market and its contemporary social context, queer identities have often been presented as an issue, or problem, to overcome. Epstein argues that despite the fact being queer is an identity, "many who write, publish, market, sell, stock, and use these books do not see it that way. Rather, to them, queerness is not an identity but an issue" (*Are the Kids All Right?* 28). In fact, over 70 percent of the YA novels surveyed in Epstein's 2013 study "suggest that queerness is a problem or causes problems" (75). Queer problem novels—what Christine A. Jenkins and Cart alternatively label "homosexual visibility" novels (*Representing the Rainbow* xiv)—typically represent the experiences of a teen recognizing their queer identity, coming out to family and friends, and navigating the issues that being queer brings about in their life. That homosexuality was (and is) viewed by many in the contemporary sociocultural environment as a social problem "only exacerbated the tendency to regard literature with gay content as belonging in the 'problem novel' category, which robbed homosexuals of individuality and perpetuated stereotypes" (Jenkins and Cart, *The Heart Has Its Reasons* 18). Among the most harmful of stereotypes presented in queer problem novels is the suggestion that "it is close to impossible to be an out queer who is happy and healthy" (Epstein, *Are the Kids All Right?* 63). Queer people are repeatedly depicted as "unfortunates doomed to either premature death or a life of despair lived at the darkest margins of society" (Jenkins and Cart, *The Heart Has Its Reasons* xvi).

Though queer problem novels deal with a specific identity group, they are often positioned as didactic tools to address broader developmental and cultural concerns about adolescence, normative adulthood, and the relationship between the two. At their most extreme, Katelyn R. Browne claims, queer YA problem novels have depicted adolescence with "two natural ends: successful, heteronormative adulthood, or the grave" (4) by way of disciplining readers. Similar to other novels where death and trauma can be employed "to threaten [young people] into subjection and to show them the unpleasant realities of life and the consequences of defying the rules and norms of American culture" (Tribunella xxiii), the "bury your gays" trope frequently "tokenize[s] queer death for the heterosexual characters' growth" (Browne 2). The death of queer teenagers functions as a didactic tool aimed to encourage or enforce teenagers' development into normative adulthood. In other words, heteronormativity embedded in the storyworlds of these problem novels "kills or threatens queer characters for the developmental benefit of the nonqueer characters left behind" (Browne 18). The death is not always literal, though it is in many cases. In some queer problem novels, queer teens survive "in body" but "coming out as queer is presumed to lead to social death" (Browne 7). Queer problem novels regularly suggest to readers that being a queer teenager leads to rejection and ostracization from heteronormative families, peer groups, and communities.

The problem novels that have influenced and informed the introduction of marginalized identities in the YA book market are "really about how their readers will think and act after finishing the book" (Nodelman, *The Pleasures of Children's Literature* 200). They are designed to explore the identities and lived experiences of those who are deemed to be cultural outsiders as a metaphor for more mainstream teenage concerns. Browne argues that, for YA fiction, "a queer character serves as a useful developmental surrogate, the epitome of frantic, fumbling, uncertain adolescence" (6). Perhaps to an even greater extent, trans-ness and adolescence have much in common in terms of how they are perceived. Putzi proposes that "the interrogation of adolescence is particularly important for trans studies in that the experience of determining one's gender identity and receiving medical treatment is often figured by both medical discourse and transgender individuals themselves as a type of adolescence (or second adolescence)" (429). I add that trans-ness has also offered (and continues to offer) YA texts another means of exploring the sense of in-between-ness, otherness, and of being outside of the norm that is common to adolescents, demonstrating that the interrogation of transgender representation is fundamental for YA studies as well. Considering how authors of transgender YA problem novels adhered to, or disrupted, the precedents set by queer problem novels can reveal the ways that early texts frame transgender adolescence as a resolvable problem.

Transgender Identity as the Problem

The protocanonical trans YA texts participate in the problem-novel genre with plots that are preoccupied with a central issue. Each of the storylines revolves around what trans-ness means in the context of the adolescent protagonists' identities and contemporary US and UK communities and employs trans-ness as an obstacle to happiness from a cisgender point of view.[3] *Parrotfish* is about teenage Grady coming to terms with being a boy, having been assigned female at birth, and grappling with the fact that his gender is not widely accepted amongst his family and friends. Cris Beam's *I Am J* features transgender boy J coming out, dealing with rejection, and attempting to begin a process of medical gender affirmation treatment. Kirstin Cronn-Mills's *Beautiful Music for Ugly Children* introduces Gabe, another male transgender protagonist. Gabe has been openly transgender to his family for a while, but the novel shows him coming out to a mentor figure, dealing with prejudice and transphobia, and attempting to fully embody his gender. Kristin Elizabeth Clark's *Freakboy* and Lisa Williamson's *The Art of Being Normal* each feature two transgender protagonists at different stages of their respective journeys. The first narrative strand of verse novel *Freakboy* is narrated by adolescent Brendan, who is attempting to identify and come to terms with their genderfluid identity, and the second strand is narrated by Angel, a transgender woman in her midtwenties, who retrospectively unpicks her childhood and teenage experiences as she mentors Brendan. A third strand is narrated by Brendan's girlfriend, Vanessa, and deals with Vanessa and Brendan's relationship, and particularly her response to Brendan's recently shared genderfluid identity. In *The Art of Being Normal*, Kate's narrative arc shows her coming out to her parents and grappling with her identity as a teenage girl who was assigned male at birth, while Leo has gone stealth[4] in a new school and explores the difficulties of beginning an intimate relationship as a trans person and attempting to reconnect with his estranged father. The novels share a number of common conventions, including the characters dealing with gender dysphoria, coming out, familial rejection, abuse, and discrimination, as well as more localized problems such as the prohibitive cost of gender-affirming medical treatment for US trans adolescents and the long waiting lists for appointments with the Gender Identity Clinic that trans teens are facing in the United Kingdom.

It is also worth observing two novels with major secondary characters published around the same time as the above novels, in which the trans character's identity is presented as a social problem. Julie Anne Peters's *Luna* stresses the disruption that Luna's trans identity causes to her cisgender sister's life. The novel addresses both "the difficulties of being trans (and, in this case, in the closet) and of being intimate with someone who is" (Love 159). Brian Katcher's *Almost Perfect* also shows problems relating to transgender identity, this time from the perspective of cisgender protagonist Logan. Logan is thrown into a sexuality-questioning turmoil upon finding out that his girlfriend, Sage, was assigned male at birth (see Gouck for a compelling investigation of *Almost Perfect* as "both a trans problem novel and MPDG [Manic Pixie Dream Girl] text" that "serves to intensify the typical Pixie narrative" [93]). Each of these novels "fixes" the problem by removing the transgender character. Both Luna and Sage leave before the end of the stories: the former exits to live full time as Luna, while the latter departs to detransition.

In 1998, Kenneth Kidd argued that "the young adult genre has been extraordinarily receptive to lesbian/gay themes, largely because coming out is often described in the idiom of adolescence as an intense period of sexual attraction, social rebellion, and personal growth" (114). Trans-ness also lends itself to the plots of YA fiction. Trans-ness and adolescence are both linked by liminality, in-between-ness, and a sense of journeying towards a preconceived destination, the arrival at which offers a solution to the problems that have been encountered along the way. According to Alison Waller, adolescence is portrayed across YA literature as "'other' to the more mature stage of adulthood, often perceived as liminal, in transition, and in constant growth towards the ultimate goal of maturity" (*Constructing Adolescence in Fantastic Realism* 1). Angel Daniel Matos, too, observes how adolescence is "approached as a moment of budding promise" because it is the temporal period during which teenagers are supposed to become "productive" or, rather, *re*productive adults ("Adolescence" 10). The developmental trajectory of adolescence has led scholars including Owen to suggest that it "bears the ideological weight of all transitory and contingent moments of self-making so that adulthood can represent a final arrival at selfhood" ("Adolescence, Trans Phenomena" 563). Transgender people are also often perceived to be transitory subjects. Their journey is understood to move them from living as one gender to another, whether within or beyond the binary (Wilson 427). As they are both adolescent and trans, the protagonists of transgender problem novels appear doubly transitory.

Across the protocanonical novels discussed in this chapter, the goal of reaching adulthood, and doing so in culturally cohesive bodies, is what drives the narratives forward. Trans-ness is shown to be the social problem that has disrupted otherwise mostly normative lives. While my next chapter reveals that a shift towards intersectionality has occurred since the mid-2010s, the protagonists of these early transgender problem novels are usually white, middle class, straight, aged between thirteen and eighteen, living with their parental guardians, and in education, though there are a few exceptions: J is born to a Puerto Rican mother and a white Jewish father in *I Am J*; *The Art of Being Normal*'s second protagonist, Leo, is from a working-class, single-parent family; and the second protagonist of Clark's *Freakboy*, Angel, has a Mexican mother and is in her early twenties. The apparent predominance of whiteness in early transgender YA literature is hardly surprising, given that children's and YA literature have long histories of being overwhelmingly white, and the term "transgender" "originated among white people within Eurocentric modernity" (Stryker and Currah 8). The imbrication of whiteness and ideas of transgender normativity (Vidal-Ortiz 266) has caused very real harm to Black and Brown transgender young people, who have historically been "frequently misdiagnosed as either homosexual or schizophrenic and then institutionalized or imprisoned," while their white counterparts were "often offered 'curative' medical support" (Owen, *A Queer History of Adolescence* 74). As Gill-Peterson argues, "not only does the whiteness of medicine interfere with the intelligibility and livelihood of black, brown, indigenous, and other marginal trans people, but it substitutes for them a point of view rendered detached and transcendent through their exclusion" (28). The influence of whiteness in shaping medical and social understandings of trans identity has also led to the establishment of narrow and limited definitions of trans embodiment. This historical legacy is clearly discernible in YA literature's representation of trans adolescents.[5]

Almost without exception, early transgender problem novels present their protagonists as having been "born in the wrong body" (as we will see, only Clark's older transgender protagonist, Angel, rejects this conceptualization). The characterizations of transgender teenagers in Wittlinger's, Beam's, Clark's, Cronn-Mills's, and Williamson's novels draw on this sense of an estrangement between the inner and outer selves of transgender people that trans studies scholars have referred to with phrases such as a "discomfort with their skin or bodily encasing" (Prosser 68) or a "deeply felt sense of being in the wrong flesh bag" (Halberstam 29). In the case of trans YA fiction, wrong-body discourse functions to set up trans-ness as a solvable problem—via transition to a right body—that complements the conventions of the problem novel genre. Bodily transition is not achieved by the adolescent protagonists within the novels' timelines at least in part because of the practical limitations of being a teenager (more on that later), but wrong-body discourse presupposes that transition will eventually provide a resolution that delivers nonnormative adolescents into cisnormative adulthood.

In this sense, wrong-body discourse lends itself to a new manifestation of the bury-your-gays trope seen in nonheterosexual problem novels. Rather than the "boundary-policing, maturity-enabling death" (Browne 4) in many of the problem narratives with nonheterosexual teenagers, trans characters can expect a metaphorical death of their misaligned bodies and a rebirth into normative adulthood through gender affirmation treatment. Interrogating the prevalence of wrong-body discourse in YA texts featuring transgender girls, Putzi argues that "the problem for the transgender individual [. . .] is that body and gender do not correspond" and that, to solve this problem, "gender is seen as immutable, and therefore the body must change" (424). In spite of the fact that Putzi confines her analysis to transgender girls, the observations she makes can also be applied to other gendered characters.

Early trans problem novels reveal a shared pattern of wrong-body discourse, even though the majority of characters represented are transgender boys. In *Parrotfish*, Grady describes feeling like "inside the body of this strange, never-quite-right girl hid the soul of a typical, average, ordinary boy" (Wittlinger 9). Grady's "body" is gendered female, while his "soul" is gendered male. In *I Am J*, prompted by a question he heard on the radio, protagonist J contemplates whether he would rather have the ability to fly or to be invisible. The choice is obvious to J: "Of course he'd be invisible. [. . .] He wouldn't have this body that betrayed him all the time" (Beam 185–86). That his body is portrayed as a betrayal of J's identity sets up a conflict that suggests, like Grady's, J's body must be changed. In *Beautiful Music for Ugly Children*, a similarly incongruous relationship between the protagonist's mind and body is created to explain trans-ness to readers. Protagonist Gabe divulges that he wishes he had "been born a vampire or a werewolf instead [. . .] because that stuff would be easy," whereas "having a brain that doesn't agree with your body is a much bigger pain in the ass" (Cronn-Mills 8). Cronn-Mills employs humor and sarcasm to make light of Gabe's situation, perhaps making him more relatable and charismatic as a protagonist whose comical preference for being born a vampire or werewolf nevertheless dehumanizes transgender people. For Kate—the protagonist of Williamson's *The Art of Being Normal* and the only female adolescent trans protagonist represented in these texts—being transgender is similarly dehumanizing. Kate's trans-ness is portrayed by the image of her looking in the mirror and "the kid who looks back; he's like a stranger to me, an alien even. It's like I know the real me is in there somewhere, but for the moment I'm trapped in this weird body that I recognise less and less every day" (Williamson 197). With images of Kate's body as "stranger," "alien," and "weird," the novel conceptualizes being transgender as a problem rooted in Kate's corporeality.

In all of these examples, wrong-body rhetoric invokes binary approaches to gender, such as male/female, mind/body, wrong/right bodies. Despite differences in their narrative methods, which range from serious to speculative to humorous, the above scenes work by creating schisms between these binary oppositional pairs. The juxtaposition of Grady's "strange" female body and his "typical," "average," and "ordinary" male inner-self constructs a fractious relationship between male mind and female body in much the same way as Gabe's amusing, "pain-in-the-ass" dilemma of having a brain that "doesn't agree" with his body. Kate's inner self is "trapped" in a body that obscures the "real" her in the same way as the female-coded body that J longs to be invisible (if it cannot become the "right" body) misrepresents him. The reflection of trans-ness in these descriptions is distorted by the sense that trans bodies are abnormal by cisnormative standards, and even nonhuman ("alien," "vampire," "werewolf," or "invisible"). Resolution is promised through a "teleological trajectory [. . .] toward the achievement of one's true self, which necessitates that a character be able to pass successfully as the gender of their choice" (Putzi 426–27). In turn, transition to a supposedly right body (read: acceptable cisnormative body) is heralded as a liberation of a true, inner self.

A particularly poignant scene in Williamson's novel delves deeper into Kate's sense of "wrongness," using a trope that has historically appeared in transgender texts for adults, as well as in other categories of YA fiction. The mirror—this time an object within the text, rather than a metaphor for the text itself—plays a role in many imaginative discourses pertinent to young people. Based upon Lacanian and Bakhtinian theories of the individual's relationship with the mirror, Robyn McCallum argues that the mirror is used in fiction for young people to "describe the relation between self and other" (97). In adult transgender texts, mirrors are used either (or both) to "convey the psychological sense of splitting and disconnection from the body" and offer "objectifying access to the transgender body as well as a sympathetic experience of universalized dysphoric affect through which the audience is entreated to understand and discharge transgender difference" (Keegan n.p.). In Williamson's novel, where the mirror trope is most prominent, the mirror functions to give readers a sense of what trans-ness might feel like (per Williamson's definition), at the same time as exposing Kate's body as "other" and establishing a clear sense of how that body might change.

The dissonance between Kate's mind and body is brought to the fore with weekly inspections that consist of her standing in front of the mirror and observing, measuring, and recording (in her inspection notebook) how her body is growing and developing. After retrieving a tape measure and a "small purple notebook" (11), Kate describes: "I position myself in front of the mirror on the back of my bedroom door, pull my T-shirt over my head and step out of my jeans and underpants. An inspection is due" (11). Her inspection includes pressing her palms to her chest in the hopes that it will be "soft and spongy" (11), observing that her penis has "grown an entire two millimetres since last week" (11), and moving close enough to the mirror that she struggles not to go cross-eyed so that she can inspect the masculinization of her facial features. Jay Prosser posits that, when exposed via the mirror trope, "the [transgender] material body can be approached in bits and pieces—an assembly of parts to be amputated and relocated surgically" (100). Kate's nudity displays her "bits and pieces" as a series of sexualized, dysphoric objects that she, along with readers, can scrutinize. Taking "one last look in the mirror, at the stranger looking back at [her]," Kate "shiver[s]," glad that this week's inspection has reached its conclusion (Williamson 12). The uncanniness of Kate seeing a "stranger" in the mirror instead of her own (albeit undesired) reflection—an image that repeats one already seen in Williamson's novel—destabilizes trans embodiment as a way of being human.

Leo, the second transgender protagonist of Williamson's novel, functions differently from Kate and the other adolescent protagonists of these problem narratives because he is at a later stage in his trans journey. The variations between Leo and Kate, as C. Butler points out, are perhaps designed to cover as many diverse issues relating to transgender adolescence as possible within one novel ("Portraying Trans People in Children's and Young Adult Literature" 9). In addition to being of a different gender, age, and social class to Kate, Leo has already socially transitioned (and has begun medical treatment with hormone blockers), serving as a relatively experienced mentor. Leo's inner felt trans-ness has a less prominent role in the narrative precisely because he is not exploring his identity and learning to come to terms with his gender in the same way as Kate. Nevertheless, Williamson portrays the trans-ness of her second protagonist as a problem rooted in the body. When Leo shares his transgender identity with Kate around two-thirds of the way into the novel, it is a physical and corporeal, as opposed to verbal, declaration. Leo strips off his hoodie, sweatshirt, shirt, and T-shirt in front of Kate until his chest binder is visible by way of revealing his identity (Williamson 199). Leo's bound chest is a metonym of his transgender identity, one that the reader can decode owing to an earlier scene that shows Kate watching a YouTube video of a transgender person that conveniently foreshadows Leo's revelation: "You'd never guess in a million years that he [the YouTube video star] used to be a girl until he pulls up his T-shirt and shows you something called a chest binder that looks like a white crop top and flattens down his breasts" (158). Leo's narrative strand does not unpack transgender embodiment in the same detail as the above examples, but the revelation of Leo's trans-ness to Kate emphasizes his corporeality and the physical binding of Leo's breasts provides a temporary solution to the fact that he was also born in the wrong body.

 The "problem" with the problem genre and its representation of marginalized identities is that it "implies that the issue can or should be resolved" (Kokkola 16). A more specific problem with the trans problem novel subgenre is that its depiction of trans-ness as a resolvable issue recapitulates an essentialist approach that undermines the complexities of gender identity and disregards nonbinary experiences. As Ulrica Engdahl points out, wrong-body discourse presupposes that "the body is [. . .] wrong in relation to an inner, real, and authentic gender identity" (267). The consequence of this is "the impression of an essence that the body constrains, producing a reified image of both body and self as static and separate entities and thereby correlating an essentialism of genital materiality that disputes the realness of transgender experience" (Engdahl 267). The identification of a wrong body that inherently contradicts the protagonists' sense of inner gender in the earlier scenes erases the possibility of alternative forms of gender embodiment that are not cisnormative, culturally cohesive bodies. Talia Mae Bettcher notes that "in the wrong-body model, to become a woman or a man requires [. . .] the correction of wrongness" and the acceptance of "a dominant understanding of what a man or woman is" (390). The fictional narratives both imply the necessity of "correction" and promote restrictive, cisnormative ideas about gender that rely upon a correlation between sex and gender, body and mind.

It is for this reason that UK transgender youth charity Mermaids distanced themselves from the use of wrong-body discourse in September 2020. Their decision was based on the belief that "transgender people shouldn't be expected or encouraged to reject their entire amazing, intelligent, beautiful, creative bodies, simply because of gender incongruity" ("Do You Use the Phrase: 'Born in the Wrong Body'?" n.p.). There was a time, the statement suggests, when the phrase "seemed helpful" as a way of explaining trans-ness as a new concept that catered to "a collective lack of experience" (n.p.). But, by 2020 the decision was made to favor more inclusive language that prioritized "people who might be struggling with their gender" (n.p.). A similar shift occurs in the texts examined later in this book when publishers became more invested in stories that are written for, and by, trans people. In its earliest form, though, trans YA fiction can be seen to accommodate unknowledgeable cisgender readers via wrong-body discourse that does little to disrupt or complicate a cisnormative approach to gender.

The arguments I have been making about wrong-body discourse in binary depictions of trans-ness can, to an extent, also be leveled at Clark's depiction of nonbinary identity in *Freakboy*. The idea that Brendan was born in the wrong body also underpins their sense of identity. For example, a short poem within the verse novel titled "On the Wall," a reference to *Snow White*'s truth-telling magic mirror, depicts Brendan unwilling to look at their reflection and asking "How do you deal when / what you see just *doesn't* / reflect your soul?" (Clark, *Freakboy* 216). They also grapple with an "[i]nsideous sensation" of being "in the wrong skin" (335). Notable differences between *Freakboy* and the other protocanonical novels, however, hint at a more nuanced approach than I have observed in early binary depictions. Clark's more nuanced approach can perhaps be attributed to her experience, knowledge, and perspective as the mother of a transgender child, an observation that will become more pertinent in subsequent chapters. In any case, "wrongness" is central to Brendan's relationship with their body, but Clark explores how wrong-body discourse applies to nonbinary gender identities to challenge the assumed healing properties of transition that are perpetuated by other early novels. Brendan laments: "I'm in the wrong skin / but there's no way to make it right / because I'm not into / long fingernails, / high heels, or skirts / either" (*Freakboy* 377). The self-reflective commentary functions to convey an ambivalence to the prescriptive gender norms that characterize the majority of binary transgender representation. Second protagonist Angel also decries the "'trapped-in-a-man's-body' bullshit" (59) that Brendan feels fits their sense of self. Angel's reasoning is that before she was a woman, she was a little girl, in spite of her sex being read differently by those around her. The perspectives Clark delivers through Brendan and Angel are refreshing interventions in early YA transgender fiction's conceptualization of trans-ness, a conceptualization that so often hinged upon the idea of becoming a gender through transition, suggesting Clark's text was already beginning to push back on some of the transgender problem novel's conventions.

When the reflection of trans-ness is almost universally distorted to equate it with wrong-body discourse, it limits the fictional mirrors (as well as windows and sliding glass doors) available. This cisnormative "fun house mirror" (Coats, *The Bloomsbury Introduction* 1) denies readers "the space in which to think about the complexity of gender, space in which many of them might see themselves" (Putzi 445). Transgender author T. Cooper notes in his comic-book exploration of masculinity that "most people understand mistakes" like being born into the wrong body, but "anything else is too complicated. Demanding. Not black-and-white enough. Too gray. Too man-without-a-penis. Too woman-with-one. Does. Not. Compute" (211). In this sense, trans-ness is most legible in mainstream culture and to cisgender readers as a "bridge, or part-way stage which will lead to the transgender person's eventual inhabitation in both body and soul, of a stable and traditional binary gendered subject position to which they felt they belonged all along" (Lovelock 682). Adolescence is likewise perceived to function as a transitional stage between childhood and adulthood, and YA literature mostly concerns narratives of coming of age, with adolescence representing a stage of evolution, development, and growth. The trans adolescent protagonists of these novels serve as developmental metaphors that reinforce the ideological imperatives embedded in trans-ness and adolescence to strive towards cohesion and stability, as opposed to the "instability" and "unfinishedness" of queer adolescence (Owen, *A Queer History of Adolescence* 62).

While "transgender theory is methodologically invested in disrupting notions of identity" (Owen, "Adolescence, Trans Phenomena" 555) that concepts such as adolescence buttress, early transgender problem novels guide their adolescent teenage characters towards normative adulthood. The perceived extent to which medical treatment features as the culmination of trans adolescence and the means with which trans adolescents develop, grow, and become "normal" adults in her primary corpus is a concern for Putzi, who is both a literary critic and the mother of a transgender child. As I suggested earlier, Putzi's analysis aims to demonstrate that YA novels privilege gender reassignment surgery as a necessary step for transgender adolescents to become adults. Using case studies from texts, including Gold's fictional *Being Emily*, Katie Rain Hill's *Rethinking Normal*, and Jazz Jennings's *Being Jazz* (two memoirs I consider in chapter 5), Putzi evidences her claim that "transgender experience and embodiment [in YA literature] is only momentarily disruptive because it is resolved—even overcome—by the treatment of medical professionals" (427). Yet problem novels have not historically concluded with their teenage protagonists' arrival in adulthood, the age at which gender affirmation medical treatment becomes legally available (though not easily accessible) to transgender people. As Trites has pointed out, "many of the novels that emerged in the 1970s that have subsequently been referred to as 'problem novels' are *Entwicklungsromane*: the character grows as s/he faces and resolves one specific problem" (*Disturbing the Universe* 14), ending before the protagonists come of age. With the exception of J, who turns eighteen by the end of *I Am J* and starts his journey with testosterone treatment, the adolescent protagonists in these problem novels do not come of age either. Unlike in Putzi's article, the novels examined in this chapter's primary corpus do not culminate with the stability of culturally cohesive bodies, only with the intimation that bodily transition will happen in a future beyond the novels' timelines. I want to show how YA problem novels create the conventional resolution of the problem-novel genre when the desired "fix" for the wrong-body problem is logistically out of reach. In doing so, I propose that it is an additional, subtextual problem that is solved instead, one that also signals an implied cisgender reader.

Problem Solving

YA literature scholars have been arguing for a long time that the archetypal YA protagonist's goal is to grow up: to take a step towards adulthood having gained the associated knowledge, experience, and authority. In *Disturbing the Universe*, Trites expresses her surprise at the "number of YA novels that imply the same ideology to adolescent readers: stop being an adolescent and become an adult" (79). Take, for example, Donovan's ground-breaking LGBTQ+ YA novel, *I'll Get There. It Better Be Worth the Trip*. Kokkola has pointed out that the "'There' of Donovan's title is presumably adulthood. 'Getting There' is presented as the reward for the terrible trip one must take through adolescence to achieve this goal" (110). It is to this end, Trites argues, that "[b]ooks for adolescents have many ideologies. And they spend much time manipulating the adolescent reader" (*Disturbing the Universe* x) towards an adult way of thinking. Trites's claim of manipulation is a pessimistic one compared to the more broadly made contention that YA fiction, and problem novels especially, tend towards didacticism. Nevertheless, it usefully opens up the question of how far the narrative arcs of trans YA narratives function to move characters and readers alike through the various situations designed to encourage adolescents to grow up into adulthood.

The narrative resolutions of early trans problem novels focus on acceptance. In a 2016 critical survey of queer-themed books for young people, Robert Bittner and colleagues observe that "YA novels often come pre-loaded with stereotypes and half-truths about trans people that need to be dismantled in order for the characters to find the acceptance they strive for" (955). I argue that scenes that depict the transgender protagonists gaining acceptance from cisgender family members, friends, and/or peers, after a period of rejection or misrecognition, function as the problem-solving dénouements of almost all of the novels. In these dénouements, recognition and validation of the protagonists' genders from cisgender characters propel the transgender teenagers towards culturally cohesive adulthoods by paving the way for bodily transition to occur in the future. At the same time, these endings work to reveal growth and development amongst cisgender characters. As I showed earlier, being trapped in the wrong body is the central problem established by early transgender problem novels. However, the resolution provided in these novels is mostly the acceptance and accommodation of difference. It is "the capacity of literature to change us, to change our perspective on the world, that makes it a powerful vehicle for understanding cultures and experiences different from our own" ("Windows and Mirrors: Children's Books and Parallel Cultures" 8), Bishop argues. Stephen M. Zimmerly points out that YA fiction has shown a trend towards "recognizing the particular power the secondary character can have for adolescent readers in experiencing growth and finding one's place in the world" (3). Wittlinger, Beam, Cronn-Mills, Clark, and Williamson each use secondary characters to deal with the impact that transgender identity has on the peers, families, and community of trans teens (and vice versa) in their fiction. In solving the problem with acceptance, the didactic messages of early trans problem novels are geared towards the learning and development of cisgender readers.

Epstein argues that *Parrotfish* "shows that it is possible to be transgender and to receive support, encouragement, and respect, and to have a positive life" (*Are the Kids All Right?* 146). In particular, Grady's father has tried to embrace Grady's identity from when he first learned of his gender. Other characters, including Grady's mother and estranged best friend, Eve, are less immediately accepting. Both characters continue to refer to Grady by his given female name and often use female pronouns to refer to him, persistently challenging his male gender identity. Their rejection paves the way for the resolution scene in which Grady's loved ones come together to perform the Katz-McNair's annual period Dickensian Christmas show. In an updated version of their familiar production, Grady has amended the script to include a recognition of his male identity. Grady's father, playing Mr Cratchit, delivers the line: "Things are just as they should be" (Wittlinger, *Parrotfish* 267). Eve responds: "Yes, this year has seen your Angela become your Grady and exchange her long dresses for his sturdy trousers" (267). Though the lines are scripted, their performance by Grady's family and friends serves as a blessing for Grady's identity. Knowing he has gained their acceptance, Grady begins to contemplate questions including "[H]ow far would my transition go? Did I want to take hormones? Would I eventually have surgery to make my body fit my soul?" (285). He realizes: "I'd need more help than my family and friends could give me to figure it all out, but at least now I knew they were on my side. And that was a huge gift" (285–86). Whether or not Grady ultimately chooses to transition is not revealed. The novel ends with Grady and his family enjoying their Christmas dinner together, and so it is with acceptance and support that the problem is resolved.

The resolution in *I Am J* is less affirming of J's identity than the theatrical performance put on by Grady's loved ones, but his journey through the trials and tribulations of transgender adolescence is nevertheless rewarded with a somewhat accepting relationship with his mother. J's mother has always referred to J as "m'ija" (Spanish for "my daughter"), but the reconciliation scene at the end of the novel shows J's mother stop herself: "'I'm sorry, m'— Carolina paused. 'M'ijo [my son]. I love you'" (Beam, *I Am J* 320). Their relationship does not fully recover from the conflict that has occurred throughout the novel (conflict that I return to in chapter 4's investigation of the parent-adolescent relationships represented in transgender YA fiction). After leaving his family home because of his father's rejection, J chooses to continue living with his best friend and, instead, visit his parents during weekends (323). This ending is, for Epstein, perhaps particularly relatable because J provides a representation of a more realistically "typical teenager" (*Are the Kids All Right?* 148). The ending is imperfect, but J's mother's change to referring to J as her son, rather than her daughter, is used to promote understanding and acceptance of J's identity and create a somewhat fulfilling emotional resolution before J is accepted to university and departs for his adult life, during which he will continue his physical transition.

The narrative arc of *Beautiful Music for Ugly Children* is also mobilized to steer readers towards acceptance of its transgender protagonist's identity in a cisnormative society, although the novel offers a notably different version of the acceptance story than plays out in other novels. Gabe has been out to his family as transgender for some time, and he, instead, struggles for acceptance from a cisgender majority that includes his school peers and his elderly neighbor-cum-mentor, John, the only major character to still know him as female. Gabe is an aspiring radio DJ, with a late-night community radio show (supported by John) from which the novel's title is derived. Gabe and his show have gained somewhat of a large fan group, affectionately named the Ugly Children Brigade, who are unaware that much-loved Gabe is the same person that they dismiss or even bully at school as Gabe is not "out" there either.

Bittner and colleagues have pointed out that Cronn-Mills tries to "subvert the coming-out drama" (955) by beginning the novel with both Gabe and his parents already aware of his trans-ness. Yet Gabe is afflicted with the belief that his "parents think [he's] gone crazy and the rest of the world is happy to agree with them" (Cronn-Mills, *Beautiful Music for Ugly Children* 8) and comes out multiple times—to John and the Ugly Children Brigade—in a narrative that revolves around transgender identity and the pursuit of acceptance. In Gabe's solo radio show at the conclusion of the novel (John has been severely injured defending Gabe from a transphobic attack), Gabe delivers an emotional address that provides a reflective commentary on the novel and centralizes the objective of receiving acceptance from Gabe's cisnormative community. "John loves me for who I am, and that's a rare thing" (254), Gabe shares, before turning his attention to the Ugly Children Brigade: "And thank you, Ugly Children Brigade, for accepting me. I can never tell you how much it means" (255). Parental acceptance is decentered in Cronn-Mills's novel by the decision to begin the timeline after Gabe has come out to his mother and father, but acceptance still concludes the narrative arc and functions as the lesson to be learned during the narrative.

The Art of Being Normal offers a further example of peer acceptance serving as the problem-solving dénouement. After deciding to boycott the school's annual Christmas ball, Kate's best friends, Essie and Felix, along with Leo, organize the Alternative Eden Park Christmas Ball so that Kate can go as herself in her wig, makeup, and "the most beautiful dress" (Williamson 327). Kate expects to see the alternative event attended only by the "oddballs of Eden Park High" (336) but realizes "it's not just the goths and the emos and the nerds out there [. . .]. There are other kids out there too, kids I've always dismissed as normal, kids who I never dreamed would choose a ball in an abandoned swimming pool in Cloverdale over Harry Beaumont's snow machine extravaganza" (337). The group of people Kate is dancing with "slowly expands until [she is] dancing alongside kids [she has] never even spoken to before" (339), and the evening ends with Kate and Leo slow dancing together. According to Amy L. Best, "[P]rom is often heralded as one of the most important experiences in high school, perhaps even all of adolescence [. . .]. Images of the prom as a coming-of-age rite permeate our culture" (2). While a prom is more likely to feature in a US YA novel given its cultural importance in US high school life, it nevertheless provides *The Art of Being Normal* with a moment to demonstrate that Kate's identity has been embraced by a variety of her peers (albeit while invoking some problematic stereotypes about what constitutes "normal"). The scene concludes with Kate contemplating her future: "And even though I know that there's a ton of stuff ahead I'm so terrified about I can't breathe sometimes, tonight I can't help but feel like no matter how hard it gets, everything might just be OK in the end" (Williamson 345). C. Butler aptly suggests that the conclusion of Williamson's novel "combines optimism with realistic restraint" ("Portraying Trans People in Children's and Young Adult Literature" 9), and it is in this vein that Kate's implied transition exists in a future beyond the novel's timeline (as UK age regulations as well as long waiting times for medical appointments make this the most realistic scenario). The conventional solution of the problem novel is provided by the protagonist becoming Kate through the adolescent ritual of the prom, signaling that her cisgender peers—even the ones Kate has "dismissed as normal"—have grown from knowing Kate.

Clark's *Freakboy* is the only novel examined in this chapter to offer a messier and more disruptive narrative arc for its genderqueer protagonist. Not only does Brendan not come out to their family during the text's timeline, but they also experience "[n]o / mo- / ment / of *Aha!*. I'll just / go have / surgery and / that will make / it all better. And / definitely no *Aha!/* I'm in just the right / body, I'll leave it / as it is" (Clark, *Freakboy* 425). The future is unclear, reflecting a more neoteric way of characterizing trans adolescence than is otherwise available in *Freakboy*'s contemporary book market. Instead of certainty, the story concludes with a recognition that cisnormative social structures, as well as cisnormative narratives, do not accommodate nonbinary people: "There Is / No Tidy Ending / for Someone / Like Me" (425). Clark's use of tidiness as a concept to depict trans futures can be read to imply that the next steps are not immediately apparent for someone whose gender is nonbinary, but it can also function to problematize the neat endings of other transgender YA fiction titles that prioritize the protagonist's acceptance into cisnormative society.

Narrative arcs that foreground acceptance may ostensibly work to normalize transgender identity by co-opting it into cisgender structures and assumptions, but they nevertheless establish a causal relationship between trans-ness and social rejection and center cisgender characters and readers. For Thomas Crisp, the frequency with which intolerance is represented in children's and YA literature means that readers and producers are "conditioned" to accept discrimination—for Crisp's purposes, homophobia—as a "'normal' part of life" (339). Corinne Wickens speaks to similar concerns as Crisp, making the case that attempts to "problematize homophobia" (153) in YA literature instead lead to homophobia becoming the central problem and, thus, the entrenchment of discrimination in the fictional storyworlds. "Having to say that queers are normal," Epstein argues, "puts the question in readers' minds about whether these people actually are normal. It emphasises that they diverge from the norm and that they have lives that may be different, abnormal, and problematic" (*Are the Kids All Right?* 45). I pick up the conversation of discrimination and transphobia in chapter 3's discussion of how fantasy worlds are utilized to expose and challenge prejudiced perspectives, but here it is important to acknowledge the implications of portraying acceptance as a solution to the transgender problem. By repeatedly showing trans characters becoming accepted within the cisgender societies of the novels, the texts are collectively working to reinscribe transgender identity outside of what the novels define as normal, even as transgender identities were brought into the mainstream book market.

C. Butler notes that "[e]very trans book is a 'teaching moment'—and while this may be a valuable function, it does make it hard to move trans narratives on from the tropes of coming out, disclosure to cisgender characters, and so on" ("Portraying Trans People in Children's and Young Adult Literature" 17). Butler's analysis—published in 2020—perhaps does not take into account some of the transgender stories I explore in subsequent chapters of this book that have "moved on," such as C. B. Lee's Sidekick Squad series (2016–22), Anna-Marie McLemore's *When the Moon Was Ours* (2016), and Linsey Miller's The Mask of Shadows duology (2017–18), or the ways that my analysis shows recent novels are adapting and/or disrupting those tropes across different genres. Yet the pedagogical impulse to educate readers is a prevailing convention of queer and transgender issue books like those discussed in this chapter, even as the sociocultural context has changed for many LGBTQ+ people in the Western world.

Trans-ness and the Book Market

The reflections of trans-ness available offer revealing commentaries about what is acceptable, desirable, and considered marketable by mainstream publishers in the YA book market at the time of the texts' publications. Fitzsimmons and Wilson's introduction to *Beyond the Blockbusters: Themes and Trends in Contemporary Young Adult Fiction* (2020) suggests that the YA literature category "has undergone many transitions and transformations throughout its decades of existence [. . .] efficiently respond[ing] to the whims of reader demands" (xiii). It is that responsiveness and flexibility—the capacity to "respond nimbly"—Fitzsimmons and Wilson argue, that causes the ongoing popularity of YA literature in years when many other categories of book publishing are in decline (ix). Terri Suico similarly points out that, "[s]ince its inception, young adult literature has experienced a number of changes and growing pains, with some phases being especially conspicuous" (11). When trans-ness was first introduced into the YA book market, representing transgender identity as a social issue was deemed the most acceptable, desirable, and marketable reflection by publishers.

Not all books are guaranteed, or even expected, to be "blockbuster" titles (Fitzsimmons and Wilson ix) that sell in high volumes like *Harry Potter*, *The Hunger Games*, and *The Fault in Our Stars*. The market does, however, influence publishing decisions in telling ways. In 2015, the publication of an updated version of *Parrotfish* spoke to a commercial decision to capitalize on the unprecedented demand for transgender characters and issues in the mainstream book market for young readers that occurred in the mid-2010s (a demand that my next chapter interrogates) and to restate the importance of Wittlinger's ur-text. Wittlinger admits that "we [the publishing team] knew that if *Parrotfish* was to remain part of the discussion [. . .] the language had to be correct" ("Parrotfish Needed an Update" n.p.). The desire for a book to be popular and relevant implies that who reads matters and catering to those readers' wishes, wants, and interests matters most.

The differences between the original and republished editions of Wittlinger's *Parrotfish* can give insight into how the YA book market and the sociocultural environment for transgender people developed by the mid-2010s. In addition to the removal of offensive language, such as "tranny," that was included in the original publication, the novel's 2015 edition notably uses "transgender" in place of the 2007 edition's use of "transgendered." Wittlinger gives a rationale for the lexical amendment in her online article also published in 2015:

> If you say, for example, that paper has "yellowed," something has happened to the paper to make it yellow. But "yellow paper" has always been yellow, just as transgender people have always been who they are—nothing has acted upon them to make them transgender. ("Parrotfish Needed an Update" n.p.)

In this way, the revision of "transgendered" to "transgender" reflects an ideological shift in the mainstream understanding of trans-ness. Bittner and colleagues argue that, through this re-issue, Wittlinger "stresses the importance of correct terminology and models the behaviour of an ally" (955), though I question the extent of Wittlinger's success in doing so. Take, for example, the updates made to the blurb of the novel. The 2007 blurb of *Parrotfish* declares "Angela Katz-McNair never felt quite right as a girl. Her whole life has led up to the day she decides to become Grady, a guy," while, in contrast, the 2015 edition blurb reads: "Angela Katz-McNair has never felt quite right as a girl, so she decides to live as Grady, a guy." On one hand, the alteration in phrasing from Grady deciding to "become" male to deciding to "live as" male indicates an attempt, on the part of Wittlinger and the novel's publishing team, to exhibit what Bittner and colleagues term an increased "mindfulness" (955) regarding the language used to describe trans people. The 2007 edition's blurb implies one chooses to become transgender, while the 2015 edition takes steps to portray that the decision is, instead, to honor one's identity. The subtle shift functions in much the same way as "transgendered" versus "transgender," or "yellowed" versus "yellow" (to use Wittlinger's analogy).

On the other hand, Wittlinger's determination that the "language had to be correct" fails as both versions of the blurb accord agency and identity to Grady's deadname in ways that perpetuate the misunderstandings of trans-ness the republished edition is ostensibly intended to remedy. Both versions of the blurb link the protagonist to the female name he was given at birth and to his previously understood-to-be female identity. The name "Angela Katz-McNair" begins both blurbs, standing as Grady's true and original identity in ways that portray Grady as an alternative personality. Grady is not given a surname; he is positioned as secondary to Angela, and, ultimately, his existence remains a decision made by what is implied to be the female protagonist from whom Grady transitions. Crisp's critique of the performative nature of some LGBTQ+ YA novels can usefully be applied to Wittlinger's *Parrotfish*, and perhaps especially to the novel's republication. Crisp suggests that, while "it may be appealing [for publishers] to release books that look progressive and appeal to larger trends in popular media" because "publishers seek to reach the widest possible audience with the titles they publish," these novels often "ultimately reaffirm what is taken for granted (i.e. heterosexuality, hetero/homonormativity)" (345). The editorial decision to update *Parrotfish* for a 2015 edition reveals a desire on the part of Wittlinger and Simon & Schuster to maintain *Parrotfish*'s relevance—its readability and marketability—in a society and book market with shifting approaches to trans-ness, but the updated version has done little to challenge *Parrotfish*'s cisnormative understandings of gender and identity that disadvantage its transgender protagonist.

A similar attempt to maintain the relevance of an early trans YA novel can be inferred from the inclusion of an updated version of Cronn-Mills's author's note in a 2014 edition of *Beautiful Music for Ugly Children*, though the main narrative was not changed. The note explains that "[i]t's time for an update to this author's note" because "it's 2014, and times have changed" (Cronn-Mills, *Beautiful Music for Ugly Children* 263). Among the revisions, Cronn-Mills takes care to educate readers that, though "Gabe has a strong need to take testosterone and have surgery to alter his body so it's more like a man's body, which only make sense," Gabe's presentation of trans-ness is "not the only way to be transgender" (264). Cronn-Mills's decision to amend the author's note was probably driven, at least in part, by the research she conducted for her 2014 nonfiction title, *Transgender Lives: Complex Stories, Complex Voices* (a short collection of interviews with transgender adults and teens), but Bittner and colleagues have justifiably criticized the note for "clos[ing] Gabe's story off to any ambiguity that might allow non-surgery bound trans teens to see themselves in the novel" (957). For my purposes, it is especially interesting that an updated author's note was considered necessary only two years subsequent to the initial publication of *Beautiful Music for Ugly Children*, signaling the pace at which understandings of trans-ness have evolved in the twenty-first century.

Considering how trans-ness is reflected in the YA book market at various points in its recent history of inclusion usefully reveals patterns in authorship, publication, and readership that can offer insights into who was privileged in the editorial decisions. As Ambelin Kwaymullina points out, "[t]he fundamental disconnection between the world of literature and the real world springs from, and is maintained by, a set of structures and attitudes that consistently privilege one set of voices over another" (n.p.). In short, Kwaymullina argues, "a lack of diversity is not a 'diversity problem.' It is a privilege problem" (n.p.). The representation of trans-ness as a new problem for problem novels to explore signals a privileging of cisnormative concepts, as well as cisgender voices and readers, that was not disrupted in the mainstream market until the introduction of transauthored representation that I examine in the next chapter.

Conclusion

In this chapter, I have given an account of trans representation that spans the first decade or so of its explicit inclusion in the mainstream YA book market. Using Coats's concept of the distorted mirror, I have asked how transgender adolescence is portrayed, framed, and reflected in the YA novels published during these years. Building on previous work that has suggested queer novels position queer identities as social issues, my investigation evidenced the fact that trans-ness was similarly introduced into the YA book market as a problem to be overcome. Wrong-body discourse is central to these novels' representations of trans-ness as somehow fixable, perpetuating cisnormative ways of perceiving transgender identity. I have also shown, through consideration of the novels' narrative arcs, how the channeling of young adults to normative adulthood (in this case, with the acceptance narrative) ostensibly normalizes the protagonists while reinscribing their adolescent, transgender identity as something that needs accepting; something that is inherently outside of the norm. In doing so, the problem novels foreground the education of unknowing readers, signaling that the readerly needs of cisgender teenagers were most likely at the center of the decision-making processes behind the introduction of trans representation into the YA book market. Subsequent chapters aim to displace the expectation established by early trans YA fiction that texts should function to interrogate trans-ness, present transgender identity as intriguing subject matter for a cisgender market, and foreground the needs of cisgender readers. My next chapter, in particular, transforms the picture of the market that this chapter has created, showing how the publishing category has expanded to include more trans authorship, intersectionality, and variety and questioning how post-2015 texts are pitched to a broader range of target readers.

Chapter 2

THE PERITEXTUAL MATERIALS OF TRANSGENDER YOUNG ADULT FICTION

In *Are the Kids Alright?* (2013), B. J. Epstein analyzed how, and to what effect, LGBTQ literature for young people was shelved in the Norfolk and Norwich Millennium Library, UK. Epstein was interested in the ways the paratexts of the books—a term she employs to refer to peritextual material, any stickers placed on books, and where the books are shelved—provide keys to how texts are perceived and how they are intended to be used by readers (32–39). Epstein found that LGBTQ YA literature was located within its own section of the library with the problematic effect of "othering" the texts shelved within it. While this placement may make it easier to locate LGBTQ books, it also "implies LGBTQ topics are specialised and must be purposely sought out" while also keeping "LGBTQ people and subjects separate from more general ones" (34). To the same effect, the books themselves "encourage[d] the view that they are for a select group—usually those who belong to that minority but occasionally those who just want to learn more about that group" (36) by including discussion questions, names of LGBTQ organizations, and helpline numbers. The peritextual components of the books Epstein surveyed demarcate a niche audience of LGBTQ readers, or at least those who are reading with the purpose of understanding LGBTQ identities.

Epstein's study demonstrates the important role that the peritextual features play in situating a book within a field of literature. However, her conclusions can be revised in light of the subsequent developments in trans YA fiction that are the focus of this chapter. First, trans titles were subsumed into the category of LGBTQ YA fiction in Epstein's analysis, just as the books were shelved in the Norfolk and Norwich Millennium Library. My introduction showed that grouping trans titles in broader queer literature can preclude an accurate picture of their publication history. Moreover, there were only a small number of trans YA fiction titles published prior to Epstein's investigation, and it is not clear how many of those titles were included in her paratextual analysis or, indeed, in the library collection itself. The small number and range of texts available in the early years of trans YA fiction, as outlined in chapter 1, opens up Epstein's findings for further investigation.

In the first section of this chapter, I show there has been a significant increase in the quantity and variety of the trans YA titles being published since the mid-2010s. As such, it is necessary to consider the peritextual materials of a much more diverse selection of trans YA fiction published from 2015. This is important for the publishing industry and for critics because peritexts are designed to "capture potential readers' attention and compel them to engage with a book's content" (Matos, "The Undercover Life of Young Adult Novels" 85). As this chapter shows, a book's packaging provides information that can both factor into a potential reader's decision whether or not to purchase, borrow, or read the narrative, and can guide a reader's engagement with the text.

In spite of the peritext being recognized as "a key conduit through which negotiations take place between authors, the book trade and readers" (Matthews ix), peritextual features of trans YA fiction have often appeared as peripheral subjects of enquiry in critical work that considers the growing body of primary texts (aside from in work that encompasses transgender texts in the broader category of LGBTQ YA fiction). For example, Catherine Butler looks briefly at the endpapers of Louis Sacher's *Marvin Redpost* (1992) in her examination of the intersection of transgender discourse and feminism in books for younger readers ("Experimental Girls"); Barbara Pini and colleagues argue that the cover image of Brian Katcher's *Almost Perfect* (2009) is one example of the text's stereotypical portrayal of its transgender character that their article discusses at length; Megan E. Friddle mentions the author's note of Cris Beam's *I Am J* (2011) in a discussion about how recent YA novels that address nonnormative genders can be connected to the legacy of the tomboy in American books for girls; and Jennifer Putzi's investigation of wrong-body discourse in books featuring transgender girls briefly analyzes the ways the author's note of Meredith Russo's *If I Was Your*

Girl (2016) speaks to the compromises Russo made in the characterization of her protagonist. Collectively, these articles and chapters show interest in how tropes or features of the narratives are supported or problematized by the peritextual material. Each article provides valuable insights into transgender YA fiction; however, they also demonstrate that critics have largely favored the examination of the textual features of the corpus. In contrast, this chapter takes peritexts as its core primary material to show their evidential value in revealing the audience a book is targeting and the assumptions that the publishing industry makes about that audience.

The role the peritext plays as a method of communication between the publishing industry and potential readers means the peritextual materials in my research corpus are an important site for critical attention for two key reasons. First, understanding how transgender adolescent readers might be exposed to these narratives is vital for ensuring all teens are able to see their identities represented in the literature they read. Second, as Mike Cadden has suggested, the peritext "has so much to do with assumptions about the implied reader" ("Introduction" vii), so assessing how these texts are packaged helps us to understand the different types of trans representation that are available in the commercialized book market.

This chapter is a chronological sequel to chapter 1 and traces the transformation of the picture of transgender YA fiction that I extrapolated from early transgender problem novels. I show how the field has developed since 2015 to include more variety, intersectional diversity, and trans authorship and consider how the commercial packaging of various books might usefully signal the audience each book is intended to attract. My aim is not to provide an exhaustive list of texts, but rather to use case studies to investigate how the decisions regarding the peritextual features made by authors, illustrators, editors, and publishers offer important insights into the space different types of transgender narrative are intended to occupy within the growing market of twenty-first-century YA literature. I begin by setting out the key changes that have occurred in the field of transgender YA fiction since the mid-2010s in the context of both the We Need Diverse Books movement and the "transgender tipping point" (Steinmetz, "The Transgender Tipping Point" n.p.). Next, I analyze how a selection of trans YA titles are pitched to different potential readers using different sorts of signals that trans characters or themes are included in their narratives, in order to interrogate the type of audience these books are intended to attract. Then, I consider how peritextual features are used to construct an identity for the author which brings readers' attention to the author's knowledge, expertise, and relevant experience to write trans characters.[1] I argue that the choices made by authors, illustrators, editors, and publishers regarding books' peritextual features can be interpreted to determine the spaces the books are intended to occupy within their contemporary market, and my findings reveal that trans YA novels are still often marketed to cisgender readers at the expense of transgender adolescents who may encounter reflections of their lived experiences within the novels.

Recent Developments in Transgender Young Adult Fiction

Compared with the "woefully low" (948) number of titles that appeared in the early years of publication as discussed in a 2016 critical review by Robert Bittner and colleagues, the field of transgender YA fiction has seen exponential growth in both the quantity of titles published and in the variety of works available in the latter half of the decade. While my earlier analysis showed that trans characters have been included in YA fiction since the beginning of the century, two cultural moments occurred in the mid-2010s and fostered an environment in which fictional titles that include trans characters and that are written by trans authors became more desirable acquisitions for the children's and YA publishing industries. As I briefly outlined in the introduction, the increased visibility of transgender celebrities in popular culture coincided with a proliferation in online discourse about the lack of diverse representation and authorship in literature for young people.

The June 2014 issue of *Time* magazine claimed there had been a "transgender tipping point" (Steinmetz, "The Transgender Tipping Point" n.p.), a phrase that has itself fueled more public discourse about transgender identity. The assertion was not that transgender people were absent prior to the twenty-first century, but that trans celebrities were increasingly visible in the media. While the so-called tipping point is indicative of a changing public attitude towards transgender individuals, it is important to acknowledge the article by no means marked a definitive shift to universal acceptance for transgender people. As Susan Stryker has argued, "this 'tipping point' is more like the fulcrum of a teeter-totter, tipping backwards as well as forward, than like a summit where, after a long upward climb, progress toward legal and social equality starts rolling effortlessly downhill" (*Transgender History* 196). What is clear is that the trans characters and authors that became more present in the YA book market from the mid-2010s are part of, and catalyzed by, the "explosion of highly visible transgender presence in the mass media" (*Transgender History* 197).

Other critics have similarly noted how social changes result in a shift in the content of contemporary popular literature. For example, Ester Saxey acknowledges that "the [coming out] story sprang into print as soon as cultural changes allowed it to be spoken and heard (changes embodied by landmarks such as the decriminalisation of sex between men in 1967 in the UK, and the removal of homosexuality from the DSM [*Diagnostic and Statistical Manual of Mental Disorders*] in 1973 in the US)" (2). Kimberley Reynolds similarly argues for a link between the "the epoch of sexual liberation that occurred in the years after the contraceptive pill and before AIDS" and the rise of YA fiction in which "pubescent and adolescent readers could find books about people of their own age, with feelings they recognised doing things with their bodies that they wanted to do—or indeed were succeeding in doing" (115). To this discourse, I add that trans YA fiction is influenced by the sociohistorical context of its composition and publication, as well as contemporary trends in the book market to which I now turn my attention.

Campaigns such as We Need Diverse Books, alongside social media hashtags including #OwnVoices, were launched in the mid-2010s to call for increased diversity in the characters, authors, and publishers of children's and YA literature, with widespread attention and support. One article published in 2015 recommends that "if you haven't seen or heard this demanding motto ['we need diverse books'], it's time to get on board" because "the professional networks have been abuzz about this for the past year" (Killeen 52). While scholars including Ebony Elizabeth Thomas remind us of the long history of conversations about diversity in "a protest tradition launched decades ago by leaders in the multicultural children's movement" (*The Dark Fantastic* 4–5), the broad reach of digital conversations allowed calls for diversity to gain unparalleled traction in the mid-2010s. As Melanie Ramdarshan Bold has suggested, "contemporary YA trends are in constant evolution: they develop in accordance with influences such as current affairs, global discussions, and social media" (*Inclusive Young Adult Fiction* 33). In the case of transgender YA literature, widespread online demands for diversity coincided with the increased fame of transgender individuals, such as Caitlin Jenner, Laverne

Cox, and Janet Mock, heightening the marketability of transgender fiction from the mid-2010s onwards.

The influence of this cultural moment on the British and American YA publishing industries can be seen in the way publishing houses continue to actively seek a more diverse catalog. As we have seen, Ramdarshan Bold argued that "diversity" "has become a buzzword in the Anglo-American publishing industries" (*Inclusive Young Adult Fiction* 45), and this is evident from language used by publishing houses to seek new acquisitions. For example, the editorial director for children's fiction at Simon & Schuster, Jane Griffiths, is "especially keen to find new authors from different backgrounds and writing that reflects the multi-cultural and diverse world we live in" ("Corporate Information" n.p.). Whether or not publishing houses are delivering the diverse catalog they are seeking is, however, up for debate. In March 2014, the *New York Times* published an essay by author Christopher Myers that challenged the publishing industry for its false promises: "[T]he mission statements of major publishers are littered with intention, with their commitments to diversity, to imagination, to multiculturalism, ostensibly to create opportunities for children to learn about and understand their importance in their respective worlds [. . .] but there are numbers and truths that stand in stark contrast to the reassurances" (Myers n.p.). While the discussion that follows shows that the picture has improved somewhat for trans characters and, indeed, trans authors in the YA book market, there is still a disconnect between the intentions set out by mainstream publishing houses and major conglomerates and the experiences of authors trying to publish trans YA titles.

Ray Stoeve, author of the transgender YA novel *Between Perfect and Real* (2021), has written an online article that considers the barriers faced by transgender authors attempting to access mainstream, traditional publishing channels, including "structural oppression that exists outside of the industry; the pressure, real or perceived, to educate, within the book itself and with one's publishing team; and transphobic reviews from trade publications" ("Trans Representation in YA Fiction Is Changing, But How Much?" n.p.). Collating the experiences of several transgender authors of transgender YA fiction, Stoeve's work highlights some of the challenges in getting trans YA fiction published. For example, Aiden Thomas, author of *Cemetery Boys* (2020), had initially feared that the "marginalizations were so unmarketable that it would be impossible to successfully pitch" a title with a Cuban/Mexican gay transgender protagonist (qtd. in Stoeve, "Trans Representation in YA Fiction Is Changing, but How Much?" n.p.). Similarly, Mason Deaver, author of *I Wish You All the Best* (2019), recalls they "had two agents tell me they couldn't see a world where my little trans book was published because they didn't see a market for it" (qtd. in Stoeve, "Trans Representation in YA Fiction Is Changing, but How Much?" n.p.). Notwithstanding the difficulties faced by these authors, as well as their persistence through these difficulties, the publication of their books by mainstream publishing houses demonstrates that there is a market for transgender YA fiction.

Since the We Need Diverse Books campaign began, there has, in fact, been a significant increase in the mainstream book market in the proportion of novels with a transgender protagonist written by authors who are openly transgender. While transauthored trans YA has often been referred to as "Own Voices" fiction, including in my own earlier work, here I have chosen not to adopt the term by way of acknowledging its problematic nature for LGBTQ+ authors specifically, as well as marginalized authors in general. In June 2021, We Need Diverse Books released a statement in which it shared that it would no longer be using #OwnVoices and had removed the label from all previous posts. Noting that the hashtag had "become a 'catch all' marketing term," We Need Diverse Books highlighted "issues due to the vagueness of the term, which has then been used to place diverse creators in uncomfortable and potentially unsafe situations" (Lavoie n.p.). In August of the same year, a coming-out blog post by YA author Becky Albertalli titled "I know I'm late." drew further attention to the problematic nature of the Own Voices label in a specifically LGBTQ+ context. Albertalli shared: "I'm doing this because I've been scrutinized, subtweeted, mocked, lectured, and invalidated just about every single day for years, and I'm exhausted" (n.p.). Her post served as a catalyst for widespread recognition of the pressure that some authors experience to publicly identify whether or not their fiction includes Own Voices representation, thus forcing them to disclose their personal identity. I have therefore opted to use the term "trans-authored" to describe openly transgender[2] authors of trans YA, owing to the fact that some authors may identify as transgender without making that identity known, as was the case for Anna-Marie McLemore, many of whose novels were published before they publicly announced their nonbinary gender identity in 2019.

The first openly transgender author to have a trans YA fiction book published through traditional publishing channels was Rachel Gold with *Being*

Emily (2012). Four years later, Russo's *If I Was Your Girl* (2016) was the first transgender YA novel authored by a transgender person to be published by one of the major five publishing conglomerates (Macmillan). Since 2016, the number of trans-authored titles with transgender protagonists from both independent presses and the conglomerates has notably increased. Trans-authored trans YA novels published by independent presses include the following: April Daniels's *Nemesis* series, comprising *Dreadnought* (2017) and *Sovereign* (2017); Hal Schrieve's *Out of Salem* (2019); and Mia Siegert's *Somebody Told Me* (2020). While outside of my British and American scope, trans-authored trans YA titles have also been published by independent presses in Canada, including Bridget Liang's *What Makes You Beautiful* (2019), Tash McAdam's *Blood Sport* (2020), and Joshua Whitehead's Two-Spirit Indigequeer *Jonny Appleseed* (2018).

With regards to the five major conglomerates, Macmillan has published titles including Russo's *Birthday* (2019) and McLemore's *When the Moon Was Ours* (2016), as well as titles from them with secondary transgender characters, including *Blanca & Roja* (2018) and *Dark and Deepest Red* (2020). Macmillan has also published A. Thomas's *Cemetery Boys* (2020). HarperCollins's catalog includes Kacen Callender's *Felix Ever After* (2020). Penguin Random House has published titles including Akwaeke Emezi's *Pet* (2019); Amy Rose Capetta's *The Brilliant Death* (2018); and Isaac Fitzsimons's *The Passing Playbook* (2021). Hachette published Juno Dawson's *Wonderland* (2020). To my knowledge, at the time of writing, Simon & Schuster is yet to publish trans-authored novels with transgender protagonists, however Caroline Palmer's middle grade graphic novel *Camp Prodigy*, featuring two nonbinary protagonists, is forthcoming in 2024. The press has also published titles by trans authors with secondary transgender characters, such as Ashley Shuttleworth's *A Dark and Hollow Star* (2021), and two YA memoirs by transgender people in 2014: Katie Rain Hill's *Rethinking Normal* (with Ariel Schrag) and Arin Andrews's *Some Assembly Required* (with Joshua Lyon). With the number of titles published by the five major conglomerates in 2020 and 2021, these years were the first that they have published more trans-authored transgender YA fiction than independent publishers. It is important to note that these numbers may be distorted by the fact that independent presses may have been more severely impacted by the Covid-19 pandemic. However, whether or not the major conglomerates have out-published the independent presses, the increase in the number of titles from the conglomerates indicates that trans-authored transgender YA fiction is seen to be increasingly desirable in a market that was dominated by cisgender authors in 2015.

The field has also seen an increase in the intersectional diversity of the characters included in trans YA fiction since the mid-2010s by both openly transgender authors and authors who do not identify as transgender. In her investigation of LGBTQ characters in children's and YA books (2012), Epstein argued that "the lack of [intersectional] diversity implies that it may not be possible to be GLBTQ and something else. One aspect of diversity seems to be enough" ("We're Here, We're [Not?] Queer" 296). This was largely the case for the earlier works of transgender fiction; however, the picture changed somewhat in the latter half of the decade with the publication of more books featuring transgender characters who are part of at least one other marginalized group. Importantly, there are a growing number of adolescent protagonists who are both transgender and a person of color. To give a few examples: Sam, the transgender protagonist of McLemore's *When the Moon Was Ours* (2016), is of Italian-Pakistani heritage; the transgender protagonists of C. B. Lee's second novel in the Sidekick Squad series, *Not Your Villain* (2017), Emezi's *Pet* (2019), and Callender's *Felix Ever After* (2020) are Black; and the transgender protagonist of Sonia Patel's *Jaya and Rasa* (2017) is part of an Indian family originally from Gujarat.

A greater proportion of titles now also include trans character(s) who have a nonheterosexual sexual or romantic orientation or who engage in nonheterosexual relationships. For example, the transgender female protagonist of Daniels's Nemesis series is in a relationship with another female, the nonbinary protagonist of Deaver's *I Wish You All the Best* is exploring their bisexuality, and there are queer transgender characters in titles including Callender's *Felix Ever After*. It is important to note that there is still a paucity of characters who are both transgender and disabled and/or neurodivergent, though the field is growing: for example, McLemore's *Blanca & Roja* (2018) includes both a transgender character and a disabled character, and *Lakelore* (2022) features two neurodivergent, nonbinary teens; Alexandra Latos's *Under Shifting Stars* (2020) includes both a genderfluid character and a neurodivergent character; and the protagonist of Emezi's *Pet* is a transgender female with selective mutism. Notwithstanding the shortcomings of the intersectional diversity in the field of transgender YA fiction, it is clear that a corpus in which it seemed "it may not be possible to be GLBTQ and something else" (Epstein, "We're Here, We're [Not?] Queer" 296) only a few years ago now includes a greater proportion of characters who represent more than one marginalized identity, though there is much work still to be done by the publishing industry to present an inclusive catalog.

Changes in the field can also be seen in the gradual increase in the spectrum of transgender identities being represented in YA literature published by mainstream publishers. In 2016, Bittner and colleagues suggested "there is an empty space within publishing" for "gender nonconforming stories in which characters, like so many real youths, do not necessarily identify with a specific binary gender" (949). While there are a mix of male and female transgender characters in titles that were published prior to the study by Bittner and others, the characters typically identify with the gender normatively understood to be opposite to their assigned gender with only a very few titles depicting nonbinary identities (notably Kristin Elizabeth Clark's *Freakboy* [2013] and Robin Talley's *What We Left Behind* [2015]). More recently, books with trans protagonists and major secondary characters with an identity in the nonbinary spectrum have become more prominent. For example, McLemore's *Lakelore* (2022) includes two nonbinary teens, while *Blanca & Roja* includes a genderqueer character as the love interest of the protagonist; Linsey Miller's fantasy duology Mask of Shadows, comprising *Mask of Shadows* (2017) and *Ruin of Stars* (2018), features Sal, a genderfluid assassin, as its protagonist; Capetta's *The Lost Coast* (2019) includes a nonbinary character among its cast of queer witches; Deaver's *I Wish You All the Best* includes Ben, a protagonist who comes out to their parents as nonbinary and is forced to deal with the consequences of their parents' rejection; Schrieve's *Out of Salem* has a genderqueer protagonist who has to adjust to being a zombie after a car crash that killed members of their family; and Callender's *Felix Ever After* features a protagonist who identifies as a demiboy whose catfish[3] revenge plot leads to a quasi-love triangle. Since the mid-2010s, a transgender reader has been able to access an increasingly broad spectrum of transgender characters and has, therefore, more opportunities to see parts of their own identify reflected in the available literature.

Together, these key developments demonstrate a growing publishing appetite for trans YA literature. While it is possible that the increased publication of transgender characters stems from the success of previous titles, it also likely follows the widespread calls for diversity that influenced the acquisition and marketing strategies of publishing houses from the mid-2010s. For Malinda Lo, the discourse on diversity in YA publishing has "had a measurable impact on the number of LGBTQ YA books being published" as she can find no other explanation for the recent spike in publishing ("LGBTQ YA by the Numbers" n.p.). The increase of quantity, variety, intersectional diversity, and trans authorship in transgender YA fiction that the aforementioned titles evidence is undoubtedly tied to this discourse, but it is also indicative of the increased awareness of transgender identity in contemporary society and a greater freedom for transgender authors to write from their own lived experiences. The next section turns its attention to the peritextual features of a selection of those titles published during or after the mid-2010s to consider how packaging is designed to "entice consumers" (Yampbell 349) in the YA book market.

Appealing Peritexts for Different Audiences

Whether scanning the catalogs of online retailers, shopping in a book shop, or perusing the shelves of a library, a potential reader's engagement with a book as they decide whether to select it usually begins with, and is often limited to, the peritextual materials. These materials, according to Gérard Genette's definition, are "a 'vestibule' that offers the world at large the possibility of either stepping inside or turning back" (2) and consequently bear the responsibility of ensuring the book effectively appeals to its intended audience. The peritext provides an essential site for interrogation because the various elements used to frame a book indicate which audience(s) the book is intended to attract.

Peritexts are used in various ways by authors, editors, and publishers to signal the inclusion of transgender characters. Some describe or code transness in subtle ways that perhaps speak more directly to a transgender reader seeking a complex, or safely ambiguous, mirror; others signal the character's transgender identity in ways that imply its problematic nature within the narrative. Considering how these peritexts present the trans character(s) is useful when inferring the type of reader the book is intended to attract and, by association, where the book sits in relation to the YA literature market. My research corpus demonstrates four broad approaches taken by YA novels to signal or conceal the trans identity of the character(s) and engage the interest of potential readers, with a limited number of books utilizing multiple approaches in the various elements of their peritexts: describing one or more experiences relating to trans-ness; labeling the character's trans identity; revealing a character is trans; and providing no explicit reference to trans-ness.

In the first method, the peritextual materials disclose the transgender identity of a character by describing lived experiences that relate to them being transgender, speaking more directly to a transgender potential reader. For example, the blurb of Lee's *Not Your Villain* informs potential readers that, for the protagonist, "being a shapeshifter is awesome. He can change his hair whenever he wants and, if putting on a binder for the day is too much, he's got it covered." The protagonist's binder is the only indication of trans identity included in the outer packaging of the novel, seemingly addressing a knowing potential reader with preexisting awareness of trans-centered terminology and experiences. To a similar effect, the front cover illustration of Callender's *Felix Ever After* shows Felix with visible scarring from top surgery.[4] While the blurb included in the inside cover flap spells out Felix's identity in a way that aligns with the second approach that I discuss shortly, a potential reader's first encounter with the novel's trans-ness is likely through the lived experience represented in the illustration. Both examples disclose the transgender identities of their protagonists by sharing their experiences to attract a reader who is already familiar with transgender issues, indicating each book's nuanced approach to the portrayal of trans-ness.

The second and most common method used to signal a book's inclusion of transgender characters is to name the character's identity in the peritextual materials. This method is perhaps the most effective way of ensuring transgender characters are locatable within the extensive catalog of YA fiction published each year because it provides potential readers with an easily recognizable (and often searchable) signal that transgender identity is represented in the book. As Christine A. Jenkins and Michael Cart have recently argued, "YA literature, like other media for teens, still does not represent the full range and diversity of the lived experiences of young adults in the twenty-first century" (*Representing the Rainbow* xii). Peritexts that give a clear indication of a book's trans-ness are a useful means for connecting adolescent readers with opportunities to see trans identities reflected in fiction. For example, the paperback edition of Russo's *If I Was Your Girl* uses symbolism within its cover image to signify its trans focus. The colors of the transgender flag—pink, blue, and white—are used, in conjunction with transgender-themed graphics. That is, the masculine and feminine circles of a Venn diagram overlap with an image of the transgender flag occupying the space they create. Russo's cover announces the books' trans-ness with overt symbolism, which, while more immediately obvious to a potential reader than Felix's scars, offers a less nuanced approach to the representation of transgender identity (though it does not necessarily follow that the narrative will be less nuanced).

Notwithstanding the above example, most books that label transgender characters and themes do so in the written elements of their peritexts, especially their blurbs: as Mark Davis argues, "the blurb has the ability to provide a framing narrative for the books it represents [. . .], serving as both invitation and introduction" (251). For example, the blurb of Patel's *Jaya and Rasa: A Love Story* informs a potential reader of the book that "Jaya is a transgender outsider with depressive tendencies and the stunningly beautiful Rasa thinks sex is her only power until a violent pimp takes over her life"; Amber Smith's *Something like Gravity* (2019) is pitched as "a romantic and sweet novel about a transgender boy who falls in love for the first time" in the blurb; and the inside flap of L. Miller's fantasy novel *Mask of Shadows* explains protagonist "Sallot Leon is a thief, and a good one at that. But gender fluid Sal wants nothing more than to escape the drudgery of life as a highway robber." Though far from a comprehensive list, these few examples illustrate the prevalent trend whereby the trans identities of characters are made explicit in the peritextual materials, whether or not that identity is incidental to the narrative. In doing so, books announce their inclusion of transgender characters and themes to direct potential readers to the representation the books offer, or perhaps introduce a transgender character to a reader by linking the character to a potential reader's preferred genre.

Contrastingly, some peritextual materials take a third approach whereby the trans identity of a character is positioned as a hook or dramatic revelation which functions most effectively to capitalize on the intrigue of cisgender consumers. Revelationary signaling occurs most frequently, though not universally, in the peritexts of narratives that are written by cisgender authors who depict their transgender character(s) through the lens of a cisgender protagonist's perspective and are thus likely intended to attract and/or assume a cisgender audience. For example, from the potential reader's first engagement with the title and cover images of both the hardback and paperback editions of John Boyne's *My Brother's Name Is Jessica* (2019), Jessica's transgender identity is employed as an enticing reveal. The juxtaposition of the traditionally masculine word "brother" and traditionally feminine word "Jessica," in conjunction with male and female sex symbols being embedded in the lettering of "brother" and "Jessica" in both versions of the front cover makes a transphobic spectacle of Jessica's identity. Furthermore, the blurb repeats the dialogue used when Jessica shares her identity with her brother, Sam, the cisgender protagonist, to create a scandalous hook for a potential reader: "'You're the best brother in the world, Jason [Jessica's male name], you know that.' 'But that's just it Sam. I don't think I'm your brother at all. In fact, I'm pretty sure I'm your sister.'" With a similar effect, the blurb of Brie Spangler's *Beast* (2016) explains: "[T]here is something Dylan [the cisgender protagonist] doesn't know about Jamie, something she shared with the [therapy] group the day he was wallowing in self-pity and not listening. Something that shouldn't change a thing. [. . .] She is who she's always been—[. . .] a devoted friend who is also transgender." *Beast*'s peritextual treatment of Jamie is certainly more sensitive and empathetic than *My Brother's Name Is Jessica*'s treatment of Jessica. Nevertheless, in both instances, the transgender identity of the character is revealed as an intriguing plot twist that attempts to capture and sensationalize the coming-out process, positioning the potential reader alongside the surprised cisgender character. An exception is to be found in the blurb of Russo's *If I Was Your Girl*, which, though a trans-authored novel told from the perspective of a trans protagonist, includes the centralized and emboldened statement: "Amanda has a secret." The trans identity of the protagonist, Amanda, is deployed as an exciting reveal to "lure readers in" (Yampbell 348) as they learn that "at her old school, she used to be called Andrew" (*If I Was Your Girl* blurb). As I will show by reading Russo's author's note in the section that follows, *If I Was Your Girl* targets a cisgender readership, so this revelatory element of its peritext is likely designed to entice cisgender consumers by dramatizing transgender issues.

The final approach taken by authors, editors, and publishers is to not disclose the transgender identity of the text's characters or themes in the blurb (or anywhere in the peritexts). For some, signaling is simply absent where a transgender character has a minor secondary role that does not warrant inclusion in the peritext, a space that is dedicated to the main characters, themes, and events of the narrative. For example, the trans representation in novels, including Libba Bray's *Beauty Queens* (2011), Dawson's *Clean* (2018), and McLemore's *Dark and Deepest Red*, is not indicated in their peritexts. In these instances, neither the character nor the the character's identity is featured in the peritextual materials. However, there are two more significant examples to which I want to draw attention: Simon Packham's *Only We Know* (2015) and Akwaeke Emezi's *Pet*. *Only We Know*, like *If I Was Your Girl*, uses the written elements of the peritext to entice readers with the promise of a secret to be discovered—the transgender identity of its protagonist. However, unlike *If I Was Your Girl*, the secret is not revealed until late in the narrative itself. The blurb poses a question: "[W]hat is the secret of Lauren's past?" A potential reader learns that the protagonist is "determined to reinvent herself" when she moves to a new school and that when she receives a message alluding to a hidden past, "she has to admit that someone knows her secret" (blurb). Phillipe Lejeune refers to the paratext as "the fringe of the printed text which, in reality, controls the whole reading" (qtd in. Genette 45), and, in the case of *Only We Know*, the decision not to reveal Lauren's transgender identity in the peritext is made to advertise and preserve a plot twist for the reader to encounter as the climax of the reading experience. In this way, Packman's reveal is reminiscent of books such as Gene Kemp's 1977 UK children's title *The Turbulent Term of Tyke Tiler* in which the gender identity of the protagonist is concealed to "tease readers and keep them in suspense" (Khuman and Ghosal 280). While trans-ness is not used explicitly in *Only We Know*'s peritextual material as a hook to capitalize on the intrigue of cisgender readers, the inclusion of transgender identity as a mysterious secret is demonstrative of the cisgender gaze[5] through which the protagonist is framed in the text.

In contrast, nonbinary author Emezi's novel, *Pet*, provides no hint of the protagonist's transgender identity in its peritextual materials, nor is trans-ness dramatized or sensationalized. If a potential reader does decide to open *Pet*, they do not learn the protagonist is trans until a flashback explains that the protagonist shouted "Girl! Girl! Girl!" in response to being called "such a handsome little boy" (Emezi, *Pet* 16) when she was three years old (I analyze this unusual flashback further in the following two chapters). *Pet* offers a nuanced example of the incidental diversity which Ramdarshan Bold and Leah Phillips find to be "key to fully inclusive representation" (3). While the decision not to signal the protagonist's transgender identity in *Pet*'s packaging has the potential to make the representation the book offers harder for a reader to seek out,[6] it also offers all readers—both transgender and cisgender alike—an opportunity to encounter a trans protagonist who is fully integrated into the YA book market.

The differences between the aforementioned descriptive and revelationary approaches taken by authors, editors, and publishers hint at the various ideological attitudes the books adopt when portraying the lived experiences of transgender people and the intended audience they imagine. As Jane Wangari Wakarindi has suggested, a book's packaging "act[s] as a window through which a reader is aided to a better understanding of the book, at a glance, even before delving into the core text" (95). Where the approach is descriptive, a potential reader can expect the trans character to appear as a subject in their own story (albeit with varying levels of sensitivity across the corpus). Where the disclosure has been revelationary, the trans character is portrayed as an object of cisgender scrutiny who, in the same way as Tom Sandercock has argued is the case for trans characters in a selection of mainstream television for young adults, provides a "knowable and legible curiosity, shoring up boundaries of self/other and cis/trans" ("Transing the Small Screen" 441). The peritextual materials of these revelationary examples are indicative of the fact that, to be considered marketable and financially viable by publishers, trans YA fiction is often pitched at the cisgender readers who constitute the majority of consumers in the YA book market. Such commercial decisions that follow the precedents of cisgender-focused trans representation established in the "genre world" (Fletcher et al. 997) by texts examined in chapter 1 are often to the detriment of the transgender adolescents seeking complex, authentic, and nuanced mirrors from the YA book market. I now examine how peritextual features are used to construct authorial identities that bring readers' attention to the authors' various knowledge, expertise, and relevant experience to write transgender characters.

Constructing Authenticity

With the emphasis on diverse literature and the #OwnVoices label from the mid-2010s, ideas of cultural authenticity (or lack thereof) have attracted significant attention from readers and critics. For example, cisgender author Boyne temporarily withdrew from Twitter as a result of the large-scale negative reaction he received in response to his problematic portrayal of a transgender character (O'Connor n.p.). As the reception of *My Brother's Name Is Jessica* exemplifies, authenticity is a key concern for both readers and critics of diverse literature, though there is no consensus on what authentic depictions look like or how authors may create them. According to Kathy G. Short and Dana L. Fox, literature that is "authentic" includes "cultural facts and values and what is considered 'truth' about a particular cultural experience" (20). For Rudine Sims Bishop, such authenticity is more likely achieved when narratives about marginalized identities are written by those who belong to the cultural group they represent: "[T]here is a certain arrogance in assuming that one can incorporate into a work a cultural perspective that is only superficially familiar, and [...] writers who attempt to do so should understand the difficulties and risks inherent in trying" ("Reframing the Debate about Cultural Authenticity" 32). Bishop's belief speaks to what is arguably the biggest question in ongoing debates about diverse literature: Should an author tell stories about an experience they have not had, a culture of which they are not part, and an identity they do not share?

This question is "complex and perhaps irresolvable" (Sivashankar et al. n.p.). In contrast to the cisgender-dominated market examined in chapter 1, the Own Voices label brings with it "the unspoken understanding that this personal connection will lead to more authentic depictions of identities and experiences represented" (Booth and Narayan, "'The Expectations That We Be Educators'" 2). However, as Laura B. Smolkin and Joseph H. Suina point out, "no culture is monolithic," and therefore no single person "can be seen as able to issue a final assessment of the cultural authenticity of a text" (222).[7] While authenticity is certainly an important consideration in relation to trans YA fiction at a time when transphobic narratives in and around the publishing industry are especially prominent,[8] here my intention is not to argue the extent to which various authors are successful in creating authentic and accurate depictions of transgender identity. Rather, I am investigating how peritextual materials such as author notes, acknowledgments, and afterwords construct an author persona which is designed to attract certain readers more than others and affect potential readers' engagement with the narratives. In particular, these elements are used to imply that the fictional transgender characters provide authentic representation of transgender identity. They demonstrate that authenticity is itself a market force by variously bringing readers' attention to the author's knowledge, expertise, and relevant experience to write such characters.

It is necessary to acknowledge that, as the visibility of trans narratives, representation, and authorship grows, so does the economic incentive for publishers to publish them. In "Capital T Trans Visibility, Corporate Capitalism, and Commodity Culture" (2017), Emmanuel David suggests that "trans visibility has the potential to produce social, political, and economic value" because "[t]rans inclusion, it turns out, can be highly profitable, a source of yet untapped value" (30). By presenting trans novels as offering authentic representation, publishers and marketers can amplify the perceived value of these narratives and attract readers (and, importantly, buyers) seeking genuine and, often, relatable experiences. The various claims to authenticity that I explore in this section could therefore be seen as a commercial strategy that reinforces the idea that identities, including transgender ones, can be commodified, packaged, and sold as marketable products, sometimes overshadowing the actual impact and lived experiences of trans individuals. In such a context, it is crucial to keep in mind how these neoliberal and capitalist dynamics shape the production, marketing, and consumption of trans-authored YA, ultimately influencing both societal perceptions of trans identities and literary landscapes.

Critics have already noted where peritextual elements are used to underpin authenticity for texts that portray other kinds of marginalized experiences. For example, Elwyn Jenkins's study of South African children's books found that the peritexts often "added credentials that emphasised (for adults?) how well-equipped the author was to write a story set in South Africa" (117). Jenkins talks about examples of books including "prefaces containing exaggerated boasts" to "persuade readers [. . .] their stories came from personal experience" (117). Similarly, Megan Brown argues that the peritextual elements of YA disability fiction build a narrative of authenticity using the authors' experiences with disability to mark "the text[s] for the reader, both disabled and able-bodied, as having the capacity for accuracy that affords a factual reality in the ways that the information is being presented" (141). Brown uses her analysis to argue for the importance of authors having personal experiences with disability when portraying the lived experiences of disabled adolescents, saying that "with increased experience, there is increased potential of the reality of disability being presented within the pages of the book" (141). I add that the peritexts of a selection of trans YA novels, written by openly transgender authors as well as authors who do not identify as trans, are used to entice various teenage readers and heighten the marketability of the books in the context of the We Need Diverse Books movement by framing the fictional narratives with the authors' experiences or researched knowledge of being transgender. As I will demonstrate, the suggestion of an intimate understanding of transgender identity offered by authors who have a close personal connection with a transgender person, and even more so by authors who are transgender themselves, perhaps speak to transgender readers who are seeking complex mirrors of their own identities, while the research-focused approach described in the peritextual materials of titles written by other authors might better appeal to cisgender readers looking for opportunities to read about trans-ness as a curious or sensationalized subject.

For authors who have a close personal relationship with one or more transgender people, the packaging is often used to emphasize that their knowledge comes from outside of their book research. For example, Kristin Elizabeth Clark's author's note for *Jess, Chunk, and the Road Trip to Infinity* (2016) shares information about Clark's daughter. Clark explains to potential readers: "[M]y daughter was held up at birth and erroneously pronounced male. Many years later, when she was a young adult, she let me know her truth—an act of bravery that changed us both for the good." The peritext of *Jess, Chunk, and the Road Trip to Infinity* is unusual because it is placed immediately before (as opposed to after) the narrative. According to Jonathon Gray, paratextual elements "guide our entry to texts, setting up all sorts of meanings and strategies of interpretation, and proposing ways to make sense of what we will find 'inside' the text" (*Show Sold Separately* 38). In this way, the atypical arrangement of *Jess, Chunk, and the Road Trip to Infinity*'s peritextual materials implies that Clark's experiences with her daughter are an important framing device for the narrative by increasing the probability that a reader will encounter Clark's experiences prior to engaging with the story. The author's note for McLemore's *When the Moon Was Ours* (published in 2016; prior to them coming out as nonbinary) focuses on the book's transgender character, issues, and themes in the context of McLemore's husband's transgender identity, as well as McLemore's researched knowledge of the specific cultural tradition of "bacha posh,"[9] in which their protagonist participates prior to coming out as transgender. As Clark's and McLemore's notes demonstrate, a number of the peritextual materials of novels by authors who have a personal relationship with a transgender person offer information regarding those relationships that can validate and authenticate the novels' fictional transgender representation by implying the characters have been written through the lens of the authors' personal experiences with their loved ones. In doing so, these peritexts are designed to appeal most to a transgender potential reader who is seeking nuanced and sensitive portrayals of trans identities.

When the novels are written by openly transgender authors, the peritexts have an even greater capacity to authenticate the books' fictional portrayals of transgender identity for transgender potential readers. In these cases, peritexts frequently use autobiographical elements to frame the fictional narratives with the author's own lived experiences of being transgender in order to "compliment the story in the text, while also promoting [the story's] authenticity" (50), as Brown puts it. For Sivashankar and colleagues, the peritext is a space "where book creators (including authors, illustrators, and publishers) work to establish cultural authenticity and power relationships by highlighting their connections to the represented culture" (n.p.). Most commonly, the peritexts do this by drawing connections between the book and the author's memories of exploring their own gender identity. For example, the author's note of *Felix Ever After* focuses on the role that fictional representations of transgender identities played in Callender's self-discovery: "Adam [from Canadian television series *Degrassi: The Next Generation*] was the first transgender character I'd ever seen who explained what his identity meant to him. [. . .] I'm so lucky that I discovered Adam—so lucky that he helped me understand myself and helped me realize that I could transition." With a similar effect, Deaver's author's note for *I Wish You All the Best* begins: "I started writing *I Wish You All the Best* when I decided I wanted to tell the story that I needed when I was younger." Drawing on their experiences, Callender and Deaver both use the author's note to point out the importance of transgender young people having access to complex fictional mirrors. Callender's hope is that "Felix can do for even just one reader what Adam did for me" (Author's Note), and Deaver wants *I Wish You All the Best* to "help people feel less alone" by "see[ing] a piece of themselves in these words" (Author's Note). In doing so, the peritexts of both *Felix Ever After* and *I Wish You All the Best* position transgender teens as the primary audience for their works, signifying that the culture I traced in chapter 1 in which trans characters were mostly aimed at a cisgender readership has changed.

Russo's *If I Was Your Girl* (2016) provides a notable exception to the convention exemplified by Callender and Deaver because the peritext dissociates the novel's portrayal of its transgender character from the lived experiences of its transgender author and explicitly signals cisgender people, as well as transgender people, within its target readership. Though my focus in this section thus far has been on transgender readers, it must be acknowledged that if YA trans novels are to achieve commercial success, then they should also appeal to cisgender readers: readers who are in the majority and also who have traditionally been centered in the decision making of the cisgender-authored narratives that predate trans-authored trans representation. With two separate reader addresses—one to transgender readers and another to cisgender readers—Russo challenges the idea that *If I Was Your Girl* offers readers authenticity because it has been written by a transgender author. Russo assures transgender readers that "it's ok if you're different from Amanda [the protagonist]. She isn't real, and you are [. . .]. Trust me when I say that my life story is radically different from Amanda's" (*If I Was Your Girl* "To my trans readers"). To the novel's cisgender readers, Russo sets out her concern that they might interpret her fictional portrayal as truth:

> I'm worried that you might take Amanda's story as gospel, especially since it comes from a trans woman [. . .]. I am a storyteller, not an educator. I have taken liberties with what I know reality to be. I have fictionalised things to make them work in my story. I have, in some ways, cleaved to stereotypes and even bent rules to make Amanda's [the protagonist's] trans-ness as unchallenging to normative assumptions as possible. (*If I Was Your Girl* "To my cisgender readers")

Russo's address acknowledges and undermines the notion that trans-authored stories necessarily offer more authentic portrayals of marginalized identities by pointing out that she has favored storytelling over accuracy.

As the first trans-authored trans YA fiction title to be published by one of the five major conglomerates, Russo's dual author's note offers interesting insights into the demands on authors of trans YA fiction to cater for both transgender readers and the cisgender readers who account for the majority of consumers in the YA market. According to Markus Appel and Barbara Malečkar, "paratextual cues can inform recipients about norms and conventions that guided the production of a text" (462). In the case of *If I Was Your Girl*, the author's note points to how the novel's portrayal of transgender identity is shaped around the publisher's understanding of the expectations of the majority cisgender consumers, with the aim to increase the mainstream appeal of the book: Russo offers "want[ing] you [cisgender readers] to have no possible barrier to understanding Amanda as a teenage girl" (*If I Was Your Girl* "To my cisgender readers") as her reason for constructing a binary transgender character who is heterosexual, easily passes as female, and has had gender affirming surgery. For Putzi, "Russo's admission of the narrative compromises that she had to make as an author in order to make Amanda understandable to her readers is a fascinating commentary on what is currently acceptable within the young adult market" (439). As such, Russo's author's note also usefully signals what the publishing industry considers to be desirable trans representation for cisgender readers in the YA book market.

For transgender YA titles written by authors who have no personal experience or connection with transgender identity, the target reader signaled in the peritext is most often cisgender. The peritext provides a space where authors, editors, and publishers can show a potential reader that the portrayal of transgender identity is well-researched, as well as justify the author's reason for writing a transgender character because, as Friddle has pointed out, "the politics of representation" is an issue that "plagues" transgender books written by cisgender authors (127). For example, Boyne's afterword for *My Brother's Name Is Jessica* assures the reader that he was "talking to young transgender people while writing this novel." Similarly, Eric Devine's acknowledgments in *Look Past* (2016) refer to his "hours of reading through blog posts and message boards, mining the everyday battles as well as the heart of the struggle through words left on the Internet," which he credits as "some of the most enlightening moments." The approaches that Boyne and Devine describe in these materials target cisgender readers by presenting the narratives as opportunities to learn about transgender people from a position outside of the transgender community. For Boyne:

> The worst piece of advice anyone can give a writer is to write about what they know. Who wants to do something so limiting? One of the reasons I write is because I want to explore the lives of other people. I find it both interesting and challenging to write about what I don't know and to use my writing to learn about a subject, to understand it and to represent it as authentically as possible in order to help others make sense of it too. (Afterword)

The emphasis on learning and understanding in the afterword of *My Brother's Name Is Jessica* positions the novel's transgender character as a well-researched depiction of an unfamiliar subject. With a similar effect, the acknowledgments of *Look Past* justify Devine's interest in trans-ness with the following pseudoanthropological explanation: "I have boundless interest in humanity. I am intrigued by all facets of life, especially for contemporary teens, who live in a world that would shock and amaze Darwin" (Acknowledgments). The language in both Boyne's and Devine's peritexts frames the transgender subject matter of the novel through the cisgender gaze. Framing their transgender characters as objects of interest, the peritextual materials of recent transgender novels by authors without lived experiences of being trans often (mis)use trans-ness to attract an inquisitive cisgender readership by seemingly offering the opportunity to read about a marginalized culture of which they are not part.

Over the last nine or so years, the increased public interest in trans topics around the so-called transgender tipping point has contributed to a YA book market in which the peritexts of transgender titles do not necessarily "encourage the view that they are for a select group—usually those who belong to that minority," as Epstein found to be the case in 2013 (*Are the Kids All Right?* 36). As we have seen, both transgender and cisgender readers are in fact addressed in the peritextual materials—whether implicitly or explicitly—as the target market of a number of transgender YA titles.

Conclusion

As this chapter has demonstrated, the packaging of various trans YA novels "create[s] an identity for the book and author, which helps the reader place it within a field of literature" (Ramdarshan Bold, *Inclusive Young Adult Fiction* 24). While alerting potential readers to the growing quantity and variety of transgender representation in a field dominated by cisgender characters, various peritextual elements, including covers, blurbs, afterwords, author notes, and acknowledgments, offer clues about how transgender experiences will be portrayed that implicitly demarcate the book's intended readership and signal its position in the YA book market. This chapter has also shown that, counter to Epstein's findings in her investigation of LGBTQ literature in the Norfolk and Norwich Millennium Library, transgender readers are not always the audience most catered for in the peritextual materials of recent transgender titles. Transgender subjects are also often marketed to cisgender readers through the use of pseudoanthropological language, curiosity, and sensationalism, to the detriment of the transgender adolescents who are seeking "the community on the page" (Jenkins and Cart, *Representing the Rainbow* xiii) that these books may provide with increasingly nuanced portrayals of trans adolescence. The books considered in this chapter are only a sample of the field of trans YA fiction, which is slowly remedying what Ramdarshan Bold and Phillips have deemed the "implicit refus[al] to acknowledge difference through the sheer weight of omission" (1). Though there is still much to be done to promote inclusivity in the publishing industry, readers have access to a greater proportion of intersectional diversity, trans authorship, and variety in books which portray the lived experiences of transgender adolescence with sensitivity and nuance, starting from their packaging. In the next chapter, I trace a parallel increase in the genres of YA fiction that include transgender representation from the mid-2010s, asking how speculative novels function in the transgender YA book market.

Chapter 3

CAN TRANSGENDER REPRESENTATION GET MORE FANTASTIC?
Speculative Young Adult Fiction

In *Fantasy and Mimesis: Responses to Reality in Western Literature* (1984), Kathryn Hume makes the case that "it is an astonishing tribute to the eloquence and rigor of Plato and Aristotle as originators of western critical theory that most subsequent critics have assumed mimetic representation to be the essential relationship between text and the real world" (5). Ever since this relationship was conceptualized, she argues, "our critical perceptions have been marred by this blind spot, and our views of literature curiously distorted" (Hume 6). Realistic fiction is often viewed as more adept at reflecting our everyday lives, to the detriment of speculative fiction—a category I use to encompass genre texts that portray alternatives to consensus reality—which is frequently perceived as a supposedly frivolous form of escapism. As such, YA fiction has traditionally been dominated by these "superior" realist narratives. Realism is the genre that "founded" the field (Cart, *Young Adult Literature* 126) and was, or perhaps is (dependent on who you ask), believed to be best placed to guide and nurture teenagers through the liminal phase of adolescence.

As Ursula K. Le Guin contests, however, "the fantasist [. . .] may be talking as seriously as any sociologist—and a great deal more directly—about human life as it is lived, and as it might be lived, and as it ought to be lived" (*The Language of the Night* 58). Le Guin's statement concerning the sociocultural relevance of fantasy narratives speaks to the belief that fantasy can, in fact, offer meaningful commentary on the reality of the past, present, and future. While it is frequently considered the case that "the real and the not-real (or fantastic) have been mutually exclusive terms" (Sullivan 98) in Western thought, the phrase "fantasy is not the opposite of reality" appears across different academic disciplines. Literary critic and theorist Terry Eagleton, for example, argues that "fantasy is not the opposite of reality: it is what plugs the void in our being so that the set of fictions we call reality is able to emerge" (41), while in his examination of spirituality and religion through superhero fiction, Ben Saunders notes that "fantasy is not the opposite of reality but is rather another way of making sense of that reality" (5). Sociologist Parisa Dashtipour similarly makes the case that "fantasy is not exactly opposite to reality, because it works to *structure* social reality" (79). Judith Butler draws a comparable connection between fantasy and reality to examine the challenges to normative gender politics leveled by the existence of transgender people, stating that "fantasy is not the opposite of reality; it is what reality forecloses" and, as such, "the critical promise of fantasy [. . .] is to challenge the contingent limits of what will and will not be called reality" (29). According to Butler, fantasy and trans-ness are aligned by their shared articulation of an alternative to what is often considered possible within a normative understanding of reality. Together, these voices create a cross-discipline discourse which seeks to show the function of fantasy as an interpretive tool for understanding and shaping our everyday lives.

It is in this vein that fantastic and realistic texts can be understood as complimentary subsets of YA fiction, sharing a relationship of "continuum and not opposition" (*Myth [Un]Making* 58), as Leah Phillips puts it. Speculative trans YA fiction and realist trans YA fiction are not opposites either. Indeed, chapter 2 showed how the same marketing strategies operate across some of the different genre texts that were published in recent years. This chapter turns its attention to speculative fiction to consider the specific contribution it makes to the "genre world" (Fletcher et al. 997). Although realistic transgender fiction has already been noticed for its ability to "model a way of being in the world" (Putzi 425) for trans teens, speculative narratives have thus far received no extensive critical attention. As the first section of this chapter will demonstrate, trans adolescents have become more frequent characters within the field of speculative YA fiction. Since the publication of the earliest example of speculative trans YA fiction I have identified, Pat Schmatz's *Lizard Radio* (2015), readers have gained a greater amount of choice regarding the types of transgender YA texts they want to enjoy and in the imaginary worlds in which they can encounter transgender teenage representation. Coinciding with the developments in authorship and representation that chapter 2 brought to the fore, the emergence of speculative fiction at this time suggests an attempt within publishing houses to increase the diversity of their catalogs. While the previous chapter focused on the intended, frequently cisgender, audience of different sorts of peritextual materials, in this chapter, I shift my attention to implied trans readers to ask whether recent speculative fiction has offered empowering reflections of trans adolescent identities.

For some readers, these speculative texts may offer relief from what Robert Bittner has identified as a sense of "reader fatigue" ("[Im]Possibility and [in]visibility" 200) with the proportion of LGBTQ+ narratives that are coming-out stories. Bittner suggests such fatigue results in readers' "desire for people to 'just happen to be' [LGBTQ+] within literature" (200). This is, for Bittner, "unfortunately a very reactionary desire that leaves little room for the nuance necessary for fully developed characters to be created" (200). Bittner finds "it is difficult accepting that, with the vast majority of people being heterosexual, it is possible to truly just happen to be gay in fiction without the characters also happening to live in a world where the norms are shifted to suit the narrative" (211). Pointing to the impossibility of incidental queerness in contemporary, realist fiction, Bittner's argument invites more careful consideration of how the imaginary worlds of speculative texts change the representation of trans-ness and expand the "horizons of expectation" (Todorov 18) that chapter 1 showed were established by early, cis-dominated, realist texts.

Responding, in part, to Bittner's perspective, this chapter asks how far the increased distance between the imaginary worlds of speculative transgender YA texts and consensus reality, or what Peter Hunt calls the "known world" (7),[1] is used to draw attention to, and critique, the normative structures—such as cisnormativity, heteronormativity, and aetonormativity (age-based norms that assign authority to the adult)—that inflect the textual lives of trans teen characters. I begin by offering an overview of the development of the subfield that demarcates a new tradition of transgender speculative fiction and situates the texts in their contemporary publishing context. Then I interrogate how the "honest" (Mendlesohn 59) and overt world-building strategies of several of the speculative texts in my corpus can be read in relation to the known world, with the aim of considering the potential sociocultural function of speculative narratives in the context of better understanding the realities of transgender teens' lives. Finally, I turn my attention to two post-2015 superhero narratives, C. B. Lee's Sidekick Squad series (2016–2022) and April Daniels's Nemesis series (2017–). For reasons I discuss later, Lee's and Daniels's narrative serve as excellent case studies to analyze how extraordinary adolescent characters can offer ordinary readers opportunities to explore two key issues of relevance to trans teenagers—identity and empowerment—through allegory and metaphor. Not all speculative texts utilize imaginary spaces and fantastic characters to challenge the status quo, just as not all contemporary realist texts maintain it by replicating harmful ideologies in their pages. My contention is that a number of speculative trans YA texts have been employed to disrupt aspects of the known world for transgender teenagers, at the same time as offering escapism into fantastical spaces and expanding the imaginative mirrors available to them.

Publishing Trends in Speculative Transgender Young Adult Fiction

The first decade or so of transgender YA fiction produced a horizon of expectation for readers of a category that foregrounded contemporary realist novels written by cisgender authors and that principally depicted white, middle-class teenagers overcoming the "transgender problem" by gaining acceptance from those around them. Compared with these early novels where the "action centres on the practical and mental challenges involved in being trans [. . .] in the context of a life otherwise presented as relatively mundane" ("Portraying Trans People in Children's and Young Adult Literature" 9), as Catherine Butler puts it, the previous chapter demonstrated how texts published since 2015 have begun to expand the horizon with more intersectional diversity, trans authorship, and variety in their plots and narrative arcs. While contemporary realist stories and problem novels that depict a teenager coming out as transgender and dealing with the aftermath have continued to be published in earnest, with Meredith Russo's *Birthday* (2019), Mason Deaver's *I Wish You All the Best* (2019), and Ray Stoeve's *Between Perfect and Real* (2021) offering three recent examples, the generic distribution of trans YA fiction has begun to shift. As we will see shortly, adolescent transgender characters have been included in speculative YA fiction with increasing regularity.

In addition to being part of the exponentially growing demand for inclusive representation and the increasing public visibility of trans celebrities in the mid-2010s that the previous chapter brought to the fore, the fantastic turn in trans YA fiction that began with the publication of Schmatz' *Lizard Radio* in 2015 can be situated within a broader increase in the publication of fantastic trans fiction in other markets. In "Tipping the Fantastic: How the Transgender Tipping Point Has Influenced Speculative Fiction" (2017), Cheryl Morgan introduces and reviews several adult and two YA speculative texts that have included transgender characters in major or minor roles, noting a marked increase in recent years. Around the time *Lizard Radio* was published, a significant increase can also be seen in the number of nontrans YA fantasy and science fiction texts entering the market from both independent and conglomerate publishers. Michael Cart's 2016 observation that "times change, and fantasy has, for the past decade, been in the ascendent" (*Young Adult Literature* 98) can be bolstered by quantitative analysis from scholars such as Kim Wilkins, who notes that fantasy became the biggest-selling juvenile category in the US in 2016 after increasing its market share by 38 percent in 2014, leveling out in 2015, then rising a further 17 percent in 2016 (*Young Adult Fantasy Fiction* 1).

When LGBTQ+ YA fiction is distinguished from the broader field of YA literature, speculative texts are a smaller part of the market than contemporary realism, owing to a pervasive and ongoing proclivity for realistic coming-out stories. For instance, of the fourteen publications included in Laura M. Jiménez' survey of the Lambda- and Stonewall-winning YA novels from 2000 through 2013, only two titles were identified as "neither realistic fiction nor coming out stories" (417), one of which was a fantasy novel, and the other, a work of historical fiction. Nevertheless, a sharp rise in the publication of speculative titles can also be observed for LGBTQ+ YA fiction since the mid-2010s. With a bibliography of LGBTQ+ YA texts published between 1969 and 2016, Christine A. Jenkins and Cart note that "historically LGBTQ+ titles have been almost exclusively novels of contemporary realism" (*Representing the Rainbow* 128) but at least 55 LGBTQ+ speculative novels published since 2010 (per Jenkins and Cart's count) are starting to redress the balance. Malinda Lo, a prominent LGBTQ+ YA author, draws a similar conclusion ("A Decade of LGBTQ YA Since Ash" n.p.). Lo has documented a huge shift between 2013 and 2018 (the end point of her data collection) based upon statistical analysis of the number of LGBTQ+ YA titles published over nearly two decades. Lo observes that between 2003 and 2013, contemporary realist novels constituted 80 percent of all LGBTQ+ YA fiction, while the combined categories of fantasy and science fiction made up only 10 percent. By 2018, contemporary novels accounted for only 47 percent of the total number of LGBTQ+ YA publications, with the number of fantasy and science fiction texts published growing to 34 percent of the market share. What is more, the relative increase in LGBTQ+ speculative fiction is even more substantial when contextualized within the overall growth of the LGBTQ+ YA book market in that time, where the number of titles published by mainstream publishers increased by more than 300 percent between 2013 and 2018.[2]

Transgender YA titles are included in both Jenkins and Cart's and Lo's analyses and therefore contribute to the trends and patterns they have identified. Their conclusions, however, do not offer detailed insights into the specific publishing developments of trans YA fiction as a standalone category. As I have already argued in the introduction, the investigation of trans titles only among the other strands of LGBTQ+ literature obscures an accurate picture of the development of trans YA fiction. As such, I want to supplement existing analysis with a closer look at the generic trends within trans YA fiction. I have identified that at least sixty YA speculative titles with an explicitly trans adolescent character included as the protagonist or in a major secondary role have been published by either UK or US publishing houses since 2015 (including series novels). This is likely to be a conservative estimate due to the exponential growth in the publication of LGBTQ+ YA fiction, in conjunction with the frequency with which transgender young adults are appearing as secondary characters in speculative novels without explicit reference in the peritextual materials. For example, Holly Black's *The Coldest Girl in Coldtown* (2013),[3] Amy Rose Capetta's *The Lost Coast* (2019), and Shaun David Hutchinson's *The Past and Other Things That Should Stay Buried* (2019) each include transgender characters who are not advertised in the books' packaging.

At least forty of the trans speculative fiction titles I have identified are written by trans authors. A large number of these titles have been published by small, independent, and/or queer presses, speaking to the fact that LGBTQ+ fantasy has historically been regarded as a niche and indie category of publishing. For example, NineStar Press has published Sara Codair's *Power Surge* (2018) and three of the novels in Tash McAdam's *The Psionics* series (2019),[4] and Month9Books has published J. R. Lenk's *The Missing* (2017) and

Nikki Z. Richard's *Demon in the Whitelands* (2019). The five major publishing conglomerates have, however, also made a significant contribution to the market. Penguin Random House has published Akwaeke Emezi's *Pet* (2019), Capetta's *The Brilliant Death* (2018), *The Storm of Life* (2020), and Gabe Cole Nova's *The Wicked Bargain* (2022). HarperCollins's catalog includes M. K. England's *The Disasters* (2018) and *Spellhacker* (2020). Hachette has published Juno Dawson's *Wonderland* (2020), and Simon & Schuster has published Ashley Shuttleworth's *A Dark and Hollow Star* (2021). Macmillan has brought the biggest share of trans-authored speculative transgender YA fiction to the market, including Anna-Marie McLemore's *When the Moon Was Ours* (2016), *Blanca & Roja* (2018), *Dark and Deepest Red* (2020), and *Lakelore* (2022); Charlotte Nicole Davis's *Sisters of Reckoning* (2021); Aiden Thomas's *Cemetery Boys* (2020); and Charlie Jane Anders's *Victories Greater than Death* (2021). Though outside the scope of this investigation, I have also identified trans-authored middle-grade titles, including Lisa Bunker's *Felix YZ* from Penguin Random House in 2018 and L. D. Lapinski's *The Strangeworlds Travel Agency* from Hachette in 2020. The number of speculative trans YA titles published by the Big Five pales in comparison to their output of speculative YA books with cisgender protagonists. Nevertheless, the fact that the last few years has seen each of the major conglomerate houses publish at least one work of trans-authored speculative fiction featuring one or more transgender character demonstrates that the publishing of these stories is gaining traction in the mainstream book market, and the importance and marketability of the books is being recognized.

Following the "boom in mass-market series fiction" (Fitzsimmons and Wilson xiii), brought about by a select number of blockbuster titles with cisgender leads, the introduction of speculative texts into the market of trans YA fiction has also brought about several works of series fiction written by both transgender and cisgender authors: Linsey Miller's Mask of Shadows duology (2017–2018) by Sourcebooks, C. B. Lee's Sidekick Squad series (2016–2022) by Duet, April Daniels's Nemesis series (2017–) by Diversion, Capetta's The Brilliant Death duology (2018–2020) by Penguin Random House, Rick Riordan's Magnus Chase and the Gods of Asgard series (2015–2017) by Disney-Hyperion Books,[5] and McAdam's The Psionics series (2014–2019) by NineStar Press, alongside Molly Landgraff's self-published Fatebane series (2017–2018) and S. J. Whitby's self-published graphic novel series Cute Mutants (2020–). This chapter's investigation of fantastic genre tropes and representation reads series fiction alongside standalone titles, but future research could usefully question how series fiction, specifically, offers readers the opportunity for prolonged engagement with a range of transgender characters—as both protagonists and major secondary characters—across multiple texts.

With these recent fantastic publications, the horizons of expectation set out in the first chapter of this book have been transformed and expanded as the field of literature now intersects with a range of different genres. Rebekah Fitzsimmons and Casey Alane Wilson have commended YA literature for its role as "a publishing category that encompasses *multiple* genres, therefore allowing the market to more efficiently respond to the whims of reader demands" (xiii), and transgender YA fiction is beginning to catch up with the variety of cisgender fiction available. Though my focus is speculative fiction, it is notable too that adolescent transgender characters have started to be included in other genres (Eric Devine's murder mystery *Look Past* [2016] and Marie Nijkamp's thriller novel *Even If We Break* [2020] offer two examples). The fiction I am investigating in this chapter challenges the expectation that trans YA fiction exclusively deals in contemporary realist problem novels and, as such, offers a remedy to the fact that LGBTQ+ people and subjects have typically been kept "separate from more general ones" (Epstein, *Are the Kids All Right?* 34). Individual texts do not belong to one genre according to Jacques Derrida's definition, but instead, they "participate in one or several genres" (230), and some of the texts I am placing in the recent strand of trans speculative fiction can simultaneously be situated among more established literary traditions.

Schmatz's novel offers a clear illustration of this participation. As a science fiction novel, *Lizard Radio* transports readers to a near-future, dystopian society where adolescents are forced to become conforming adults by a powerful government with a restrictive regime. *Lizard Radio* contributes to the corpus of trans YA fiction because its protagonist, Kivali, is genderqueer: a "bender" (39) who has a "boy-girl human-lizard bender-comrade soul" (204). The novel can also be located within an established tradition of speculative fiction, which subverts the contemporary binary and cisnormative gender systems of the Western world. For instance, the portrayal of the Saurian race, who challenge the normative gender binary of *Lizard Radio*'s human world, also has similarities with Le Guin's *The Left Hand of Darkness* (1969), where the inhabitants of the imaginary world, Gethen, are ambisexual (meaning they have no fixed sex). In addition, a small number of the texts in my primary corpus can also be situated among cross-dressing YA fantasy. Teodora DiSangro, the demigirl protagonist of Capetta's The Brilliant Death series (which also includes gender-fluid shapeshifter Cielo as a love interest), shares many similarities with the female protagonist of Tamora Pierce's The Song of the Lioness series (1983–1988), for example, as each protagonist intentionally uses a male-coded appearance as a disguise.[6] Gender transgression or "gender disguise" (*Into the Closet* 19), to use Victoria Flanagan's term, has a longer history in children's and YA fiction in which, in most cases, female protagonists cross-dress to benefit from the privileges afforded to males in their societies. For Flanagan, Pierce's The Song of the Lioness series is an example of a "female cross-dressing narrative [that] question[s] socially assumed understandings in relation to gender by playfully exposing the redundancies of two polarized gender identities and ridiculing the limitations that such a system imposes on supposedly autonomous individuals" (*Into the Closet* 23), and the same claim can be made of Capetta's series.

Trans-ness has a history of being grouped with cross-dressing as a form of subversive behavior. Earlier, I drew attention to how Judith Butler's connection between transgender people and fantasy situates transgender identity as a challenge to the status quo, and it is through the lens of subversion that representations of gender nonconforming characteristics are frequently interpreted. In *The Routledge Companion to Feminism and Postfeminism* (2001), for example, Sarah Gamble's binary definition of cross-dressing includes "a range of behaviour which involves adopting the uniform of the opposite sex: although their motivations may differ widely, drag queens, female impersonators, transsexuals, transvestites and butch lesbians are all cross-dressers" (209). Similarly, Flanagan's analysis of cross-dressing in children's and YA literature in *Into the Closet* posits three categories of cross-dressing behavior she has identified, the third of which describes trans characters in YA fiction. The association of cross-dressing with trans-ness in these critics' analyses problematically implies that transgender people are aligned with the sex they were assigned at birth, rather than the gender with which they identify. Flanagan argues that cross-dressing children's and YA texts "strive to elevate the notion of gender to a level where the fact of biology becomes less significant, or temporarily irrelevant, in relation to the cross-dresser's ability to subvert gender stereotypes" (*Into the Closet* 108), while Rosemary Jackson argues that many of the themes in fantasy are "concerned with erasing the rigid demarcations of gender and of genre" (49). In contrast, speculative trans YA fiction recognizes and represents transgender people as a diverse identity group in its own right, not merely as a means or method of subversion. I argue that these texts open the imaginative possibilities for transgender teens who are looking for fiction to mirror their lived experiences.

Many of the speculative trans YA texts discussed in this chapter (as well as those I have not had space to discuss) can be read as an attempt to create alternative ways of tackling the issues perceived to impact transgender teens in the books' contemporary society. As Karen Coats suggests with her concept of the literary mirror, texts "have an important function in that they frame experiences and situations and offer them back to us for analysis and contemplation; they reflect in their ways so that we can reflect in ours" (*The Bloomsbury Introduction* 2). Speculative trans texts often blend the generic conventions of the transgender problem novel—such as the focus on "wrong-body" discourse and the acceptance resolution—with the generic conventions of fantasy and science fiction, in much the same way as Cart argues that "much of contemporary imaginative fiction has become an interesting mélange, an exercise in bending and blending, in shape-shifting and morphing" (*Young Adult Literature* 97). For example, A. Thomas's *Cemetery Boys* depicts a transgender protagonist attempting to gain acceptance for his gender identity from his traditional Latinx family by summoning a ghost—an ability that is limited to the male members of the Brujx community; Daniels's Nemesis series, comprising *Dreadnought* (2017) and *Sovereign* (2017), depicts its superhero protagonist undergoing a fantastical gender transition and struggling to be herself in an abusive family who do not accept her trans-ness. I return to both of these examples in chapter 4, building on this analysis to offer detailed discussion of parental relationships across my primary corpus. For now, what is relevant is that these novels use speculative storytelling modes to stage and resolve challenges faced by marginalized transgender youth. They offer implied transgender readers a space for "analysis and contemplation" of familiar lived experiences that both contains and escapes reality.

Not all speculative YA fiction that includes trans representation works in this way. Lo has argued that "genre fiction often allows LGBTQ characters to have stories other than coming-out narratives, which still predominate in contemporary fiction. [. . .] We can be heroes, too" ("A Decade of LGBTQ YA Since Ash" n.p.), and this is indeed the case for a select few novels. Novels in which the transgender character is a secondary character are less likely to offer an in-depth exploration of trans-ness as a central theme: examples include McLemore's *Dark and Deepest Red* and *Blanca & Roja*, England's *Spellhacker*, and Capetta's *The Lost Coast*. In addition, novels such as L. Miller's high fantasy Mask of Shadows duology offers more incidental trans representation, depicting Sallot Leon, a genderfluid protagonist whose gender identity is merely an aspect of their characterization, while the basis of the plot is their attempt to survive a potentially deadly audition to become part of the queen's team of assassins. Notwithstanding these examples, the majority of available speculative trans YA titles explore many of the same core concerns as contemporary realist trans fiction—cisnormativity, parental rejection, transphobic harassment including physical assault, ostracization from friendship groups, ignorance, discrimination, and marginalization—through a fantastic lens. As Maria Pallotta-Chiarolli has argued, it is important that the representation of marginalized people and their experiences in fiction allows marginalized readers to "locate themselves as having experienced some form of marginality and prejudice" without the "fears and questions inherent in challenging social, familial, institutional prescriptions and ascriptions" (35) that they may experience in their known world. Using an implied transgender reader as my critical vantage point, I now want to interrogate how fantastic worldbuilding strategies create mirrors of transgender adolescents' experiences by "select[ing] particular moments, highlight[ing] them, and put[ting] a frame around them" (Coats, *The Bloomsbury Introduction* 1) in order to explore and disrupt issues particularly pertinent to contemporary transgender teenagers: discrimination and prejudice.

The Imaginary Worlds of Young Adult Fiction

Thomas Crisp suggests that "careful consideration must be given to the possibilities imagined and offered within [imaginary] worlds" because "every 'reality' constructed in YA literature relies upon ideological assumptions about how the world looks and operates" (339). This chapter takes up Crisp's call by considering how, and to what end, those imaginary worlds can be seen to function in speculative trans YA fiction. Imaginary worlds, also referred to as "subcreated worlds," "secondary worlds," "diegetic worlds," and "constructed worlds" (M. J. P. Wolf 13–14), are fictional realms that can afford readers (viewers, listeners, etc) a sense of transcendence from their own realities. Every title in my primary corpus may be considered to possess an imaginary world in that, as Farah Mendlesohn suggests, "all literature builds worlds, but some genres are more honest about it than others" (59). However, speculative fiction makes visible the world-building mechanisms of the texts by offering readers explicit and overt alternatives to the known world. Such imaginary worlds abound in the YA market of past and present owing, in part, to the popularity of hugely successful fantasy works, including J. R. R. Tolkein's *The Lord of the Rings* (1954) and George R. R. Martin's A Song of Ice and Fire series (1996–).

The dystopian worlds of blockbuster YA trilogies, such as The Hunger Games, Divergent, and Chaos Walking, have dominated the best seller lists of the last decade (Fitzsimmons 16). The magical world of the Harry Potter series has become so prolific in contemporary popular culture that Harry Potter Worlds have been built in Orlando and London. The "transmedia imaginary worlds" (L. Phillips, "Mythopoeic YA" 135) of popular fantasy texts, including the "Grishaverse" of Leigh Bardugo's Shadow and Bone series and "Orïsha" of Tomi Adeyemi's Legacy of Orïsha series, have offered, and continue to offer, readers significant opportunities for in-depth engagement with fantastic places. The epic worlds of series including Sarah J. Maas's Throne of Glass and Cassandra Clare's Mortal Instruments have gained global popularity, with the former translated into thirty-five different languages, and the latter having more than 50 million copies in print worldwide (Wilkins, *Young Adult Fantasy Fiction* 1). Together, these texts stand as the "blockbuster trees" of speculative YA fiction beyond which a "vast forest of YA texts exist" (Fitzsimmons and Wilson xxi). Imagined spaces including the near-future, utopian city of Lucille in Emezi's *Pet*; the fantastic version of Salem, Oregon, that is inhabited by werewolves and zombies in Hal Schrieve's *Out of Salem* (2019); and the superhero-filled cities of Andover and New Port in Lee's Sidekick Squad series and Daniels's Nemesis series respectively have received less critical attention than the above examples, owing both to their relative newness and their nonblockbuster status. Yet these texts open up arenas for implied transgender readers to explore their known world, and their experiences of that world, in creative and figurative ways.

The imaginary spaces of many speculative trans YA texts can be read as commentaries on what it is to be a trans adolescent in a society that inscribes cis-ness into its everyday practices. Jackson's theory of fantasy privileges the relationship between the fantastic text and the social context of the text's production in the interpretation of the narrative: "[A] literary fantasy is produced within, and determined by, its social context. Though it might struggle against the limits of this context, often being articulated upon that very struggle, it cannot be understood in isolation from it" (3). Fantasy traces "the unsaid and the unseen of culture: that which has been silenced, made invisible" (Jackson 4) and, in the case of speculative trans YA fiction, imaginary worlds open up a range of ways of exposing, challenging, and undermining cisnormativity and transphobia and creating engaging stories that speak critically to the experiences of transgender teenagers.

Imaginary worlds offer some titles a means of heightening the manifestations of transphobia (and other types of discrimination) in order to critique its underlying ideology. Daniels's Nemesis series (a series I also return to in the final section of this chapter) offers an example of this sort of imaginary-world story telling. *Dreadnought*, the first novel of the series, incorporates superheroes into an imaginary world that otherwise strongly resembles contemporary US society. When transgender protagonist Danielle Tozer unexpectedly gains superpowers from the most powerful superhero in the fictional society, she is inducted into the Legion Pacifica—the league of superheroes. Daniels explores a spectrum of responses to trans-ness through the different characters in the league. One, in particular, represents an especially antitransgender stance that is explored, challenged, and criticized in the novels. Myra Graywytch—a character whom Danielle identifies as a Trans Exclusionary Radical Feminist (TERF)—claims that transgender women "cannot possibly understand what it means to be a woman" and likens bodily transition to "rape" and "the holocaust of gender" (Daniels, *Dreadnought* 223). These beliefs culminate in Graywytch carrying out the "worst supervillain attack in history" (Daniels, *Sovereign* 302) in the second novel with a magical spell that targets the Y chromosome as a means of killing every person that she defines as male. Through its association of transphobia with the villain character, Daniels's series draws on preestablished conventions regarding the dichotomies of right and wrong in the superhero genre. In contrast to the series' transgender hero, the supervillain "symbolise[s] evil," with traits that include "an affinity for destruction, cruelty, [and] unscrupulousness" (Kokorski 148; 147). The convention provides an avenue for the Nemesis series to deplore transphobia via its alignment with the role.

Despite significant differences in genre and narrative style, Devin Harnois's *The Rainbow Islands* (2017) shares Nemesis's approach, interrogating discrimination by fantastically amplifying its manifestations. Harnois's novel is set in an extremely religious dystopian imaginary world where homophobia and transphobia fuel the narrative drama: the premise of the novel is a conflict between the mainland Republicans and the LGBTQ+ people of the Rainbow Islands, who have chosen to accept exile over the Republic's cruel conversion camp. Fitzsimmons makes the case that "dystopian fiction magnifies unjust, repressive elements and pushes them to the extreme, building a fictional world devoted to critiquing aspects of society that seem fundamental and unchangeable" (4). In this light, Harnois's novel can be understood to use the dystopian genre as a space from which to challenge and undermine the discriminatory beliefs that are emphasized in the characters of the Republicans. The drama of speculative narratives such as the Nemesis series and *The Rainbow Islands* hinges upon acts of discrimination against the transgender adolescent protagonist, with the fantastic conventions opening up sensationalized ways of confronting and overcoming prejudice.

In other examples, imaginary worlds offer a means of explicitly exploring the acceptance of trans identity, an issue on which contemporary realist novels also "focus heavily" (Bittner et al. 955), by creating space for the narrative to challenge and rectify transphobia through a fantastic lens. As Deborah O'Keefe has argued, the speculative genres give authors opportunities to "work through serious issues in truthful and imaginative ways" (16). The narratives within my primary corpus that use their imaginary worlds to examine and dismantle misunderstandings about transgender people offer readers alternative stories through which to see transgender identities gain recognition. A. Thomas's *Cemetery Boys*, for example, invites readers into an imaginary world inspired by Latinx myth in which the most traditional elements of the culture are employed to affirm the protagonist's gender identity. Set around Día de los Muertos, *Cemetery Boys* uses the protagonist's "quinces" ceremony (12)—a ceremony in which Lady Death's blessing is given for the adolescent to become a brujo (a male with the ability to transition lingering spirits into the afterlife) or a bruja (a female with healing abilities)—to bring about acceptance from the family who believe that Yadriel's transgender identity precludes him from the traditionally male elements of their culture. While "being transgender and gay had earned Yadriel the title of Head Black Sheep amongst the Brujx" (13), the quinces ceremony becomes an opportunity for Yadriel to "show his family what he was, *who* he was" (10). The imaginary world is conventional and steeped in binary assumptions, but as the events of the narrative progress, and Yadriel successfully becomes a brujo, the novel reveals a family who loves Yadriel and are willing to adapt their traditional beliefs and values to accommodate his identity.

The imaginary world of Emezi's *Pet* offers an even greater opportunity to rectify the transphobia of the book's contemporary society by transporting readers to a place in which trans-ness is universally accepted. Lucille, the novel's futuristic, Black society is absent of transphobia and homophobia, with queer characters positively represented across multiple generations of *Pet*'s Black cast. In addition to Jam, the adolescent transgender protagonist, Malachite, Beloved, and Whisper—the mother, father, and parent, respectively of Jam's best friend—are in a polyamorous relationship, and Whisper uses gender neutral pronouns (Emezi, *Pet* 82). As an alternative to most of the trans YA titles available whereby trans-ness represents a significant personal and/or social problem for the transgender teenager to overcome, *Pet* reveals the transgender identity of its protagonist in a short and positive recollection of an event from her childhood. At three years old, Jam shouted "Girl! Girl! Girl!" in response to being called "such a handsome little boy" (16). While *Pet*'s imaginary world mimics the cisnormativity of the book's contemporary society—Jam is assumed to be a "boy"—the characters exhibit a more forward thinking, liberal approach to addressing an incongruence between gender identity and assigned sex. "It wasn't like how it used to be," the novel tells us, "back when the world was different for girls like [Jam]" (17).[7] The imaginary world offers children and teenagers a sense of autonomy over their bodies that is not afforded to readers in the known world, overtly critiquing the restrictions placed on care for trans young people.

Counter to the "just happen to be" trope in contemporary fiction that Bittner fervently critiques, the inclusive social system of Lucille is justified via a revolution described in the novel's opening chapter: "There shouldn't be any monsters left in Lucille" because the angels (a metaphor for the revolutionaries) "took apart the prisons and the police," "banned firearms," "took the laws and changed them," and "tore down those horrible statues of rich men who'd owned people and fought to keep owning people" (Emezi, *Pet* 1–2). With this fantastic revolution, Emezi explicitly dislocates *Pet*'s imaginary world from the book's contemporary society. The postrevolution possibilities of the imaginary world are utilized to lambast the known world for Black people, a world with quotidian experiences of discrimination, injustice, and "persistent and totalizing oppression" (E. E. Thomas, "Young Adult Literature for Black Lives" 2). As a matter of fact, Emezi has drawn a connection between the desire for change and the activist potential of fiction:

> Some people might have difficulty imagining a world where black trans kids are safe, where there are no police, where there are no prisons. So books kind of help you. Or Pet, in this case, can help create that window of possibility. If you can imagine it, that's the first step in making it happen. ("Akwaeke Emezi on 'Pet'" n.p.)

It is not surprising, then, that Emezi shows a Black, neurodivergent, transgender teenager thriving in an imaginary world where discrimination is not part of the everyday fabric of her reality.

Emezi's novel undoubtedly goes the furthest in creating a utopian space for transgender teens with its imaginary world building, but other speculative trans YA novels also use the fantastic to guide characters (and readers) towards an acceptance of transgender identity. The metaphorical possibilities of imaginary worlds function, for a number of books, as a toolkit with which to examine the mechanisms of normativity and discrimination away from, or in conjunction with, identities or issues that directly apply in the known world. As Ebony Elizabeth Thomas has recently observed of YA fiction, "vampires and werewolves, witches and wizards, and seers and shifters often function as recognisable stand-ins for majorities and minorities and the inevitable conflicts that emerge between identity groups" (*The Dark Fantastic* 30). In trans YA titles, these "stand-ins" operate in place of transness as the issue around which the narrative drama revolves. The alternative set of assumptions can create space to examine normativity and discrimination in creative and metaphorical ways. For example, it is broadly accepted that Western ideology privileges being straight, cisgender, able-bodied, thin, and middle class, but the inclusive imaginary world of Lee's Sidekick Squad series, comprising *Not Your Sidekick* (2016), *Not Your Villain* (2017), *Not Your Backup* (2019), and *Not Your Hero* (2022),[8] instead privileges being an "A-Class Metahuman." I offer extended analysis of the series in the next section of the chapter, but here I want to draw attention to its metaphorical critique of social norms. Set out in the novel's "North American Collective Meta-Human Registration" document (Lee, *Not Your Sidekick* 12), individuals are ranked from A to D according to their superpowers, and these categories offer insights into the privileges and marginalizations that underpin the relationships between different identity groups in the known world.

With similar effect, Hal Schrieve's novel *Out of Salem* (2019) provides an imaginary world where the narrative drama is based around the "undead" (31) identity of the genderqueer protagonist, Z, who has recently transitioned to become undead after surviving a car crash that killed their parents because of a protective spell that was cast over them. The undead, along with other minorities including werewolves and fairies, are marginalized within *Out of Salem*'s magical imaginary world and can be read as "stand ins" for the LGBTQ+ community, experiencing discrimination and social injustice as the events of the narrative unfold, though the novel also includes several LGBTQ+ characters alongside the protagonist. Upon first attending school following their transition, for instance, Z is met with hostility from the principal, who "turned to Z and glared at them. 'Other schools have had undead students in the past and they have been less that completely in control of their own actions, and I have no desire to repeat those incidents. The last thing I need on my record is an outbreak of necromancy" (31). This fantastical scene is reminiscent of scenes included in several realistic transgender problem novels whereby the transgender adolescent attempts to explain their gender to an authoritative and ignorant adult. For example, in Wittlinger's *Parrotfish*, Grady's request to the principal to be referred to with he/him pronouns is met with the insinuation that Grady is causing unnecessary problems for himself and the school (according to Dr Ridgeway, "[T]eenagers rarely know what's good for them, I'm sorry to say. Take my advice now, Angela, and don't tell anybody else about this. [. . .] I don't want to see my school get turned upside for nothing" [55]). Mr Brentwood's concern with how Z's undead identity might disrupt the school's community offers a fantastical exploration of the same problems addressed in *Parrotfish*'s more realistic take. Both scenes explore the powerlessness of marginalized teens against adults who represent institutional power, yet *Out of Salem* translates it into a darkly humorous scene with the tropes of its urban fantasy genre. The use of metaphor to show how cisnormative structures impact transgender teenagers offers an alternative strategy to realistic representations, employing fantasy to delve playfully into complex social issues in the known world.

The explorations of discrimination in these fantastic narratives might be considered to offer less quotidian insights into the known world than can be found in works of realism, which, according to Alison Waller, "create structures of commonality" that can expose "shared worlds of routine and sometimes boring lives" ("The Art of Being Ordinary" 3), but they nevertheless invite readers to consider how cisnormativity and transphobia inflect the lives of transgender teens. Now I turn my attention to how transgender teen characters inhabit and function in speculative spaces through the case study of two particularly fantastic examples: the superhero protagonists of Lee's Sidekick Squad series and Daniels's Nemesis series. These series are of particular interest owing to the generic emphasis on power and empowerment in superhero fiction. Comparing how these two authors use the tropes of the superhero genre to portray trans-ness and adolescence as overlapping subject positions allows us to consider how their kick-ass transgender protagonists might function as positively distortive mirrors for young transgender readers.

Fantastic Teenagers

Critics have already noted how fantastic characters manifest the potential of teenagers through allegory and metaphor. According to Waller, "fantastic tropes (such as magic powers and gifts) might represent allegories for the material and psychological opportunities available to teenagers" while also "portray[ing] teenagers as empowered and dynamic" (*Constructing Adolescence in Fantastic Realism* 91, 95). For Katharine Kittredge, such tropes grant teenage readers "possibilities beyond the limits of contemporary reality; they get a glimpse of what it would be like to have true autonomy and wield real power" (671). The possibility of transcending the so-called "limits of contemporary reality" and vicariously experiencing such power through YA fantasy fiction has, however, typically been created with certain readers in mind.

In *The Dark Fantastic*, E. E. Thomas makes the case that "readers and hearers of fantastic tales who have been endarkened and Othered by dominant culture can never be plausible conquering heroes" (23), while readers who are white, middle class, cisgender, heterosexual, and able-bodied are perpetually empowered in fantasy narratives. Thomas's argument hinges upon an implicit message to people of color in fantasy fiction that says "you are the alien Other. You are the Orc. You are the fell beast" (24). *The Dark Fantastic* speaks directly to the reading experiences of people of color, but Thomas's assertions can usefully be extended to other marginalized identity groups. Taking a similar stance in her provocative monologue to Victor Frankenstein, Susan Stryker draws connections between herself and Frankenstein's monster—"like the monster, I am too often perceived as less that fully human" ("My Words to Victor Frankenstein" 245)—by way of exposing the dehumanization transgender people experience in popular culture. The growing market of YA fiction that places transgender young adults—as well as those with other marginalized identities—as the heroes of their stories is beginning to provide a counter-narrative to the depiction of nonnormative characters as monstrous that recent scholarship is exposing and critiquing (E. E. Thomas's *The Dark Fantastic*; Colleen Elaine Donnelly's "Re-visioning Negative Archetypes of Disability and Deformity"; and L. Phillips's *Female Heroes in Young Adult Fantasy Fiction: Reframing Myths of Adolescent Girlhood* offer examples of where this work is taking place). Heroes who are characters of color, LGBTQ+, disabled, and/or neurodivergent, for example, are opening the transcendental possibilities of fantasy to a marginalized readership.

With the market shift towards the more inclusive, positive representation of nonnormative identities that I traced in the previous chapter has come a plethora of trans authors for whom the empowerment of trans readers is a primary concern. Daniels has highlighted her aim of "making scared trans girls feel powerful" ("An Interview with Author April Daniels" n.p.). Similarly, A. Thomas has revealed how important it was for them that marginalized readers of *Cemetery Boys* would encounter a Latinx, gay, transgender protagonist who is "loved," "supported," and "powerful" ("Our Friend Is Here!" n.p.). For transgender teens, fantasy might be understood to offer an even greater (and, perhaps, vital) opportunity for transcendence than realism owing to the harsh, challenging, and transphobic social environments many transgender teens face as part of their everyday lives. Though few speculative trans YA texts step away from the realities of discrimination, several offer readers escapism into fantasy worlds in which transgender teenagers are empowered to triumph over discrimination. To further explain my argument, this final section focuses on two teenage transgender characters who manifest power and potential in a particularly fantastic way: transgender superheroes.

The superhero genre is becoming an increasingly common feature of YA literature. For example, Penguin Random House's recent DC Icons series comprises YA novels each focused on teenage versions of superheroes, including Leigh Bardugo's *Wonder Woman: Warbringer* (2017), Sarah J. Maas's *Catwoman: Soulstealer* (2019), and Matt de la Peña's *Superman:*

Dawnbreaker (2020). For young adult readers, the protagonists of superhero fiction have been predominantly portrayed as heterosexual. When LGBTQ+ characters have been included, they have been mostly portrayed as gay and male, including in Perry Moore's *Hero* (2007), Hayden Thorne's *Rise of Heroes* (2008), and J. K. Pendragon's *Junior Hero Blues* (2016). Transgender teenagers with superpowers offer an example of what Jes Battis has named "perverse structuralism," meaning the narrative act of "encod[ing] both liberatory and marginal codes of representation by switching the switch of fantasy" (2), with examples including a teenage character who is both psychically gifted and physically disabled. Chameleon/Bells Broussard and Dreadnought/Danielle Tozer, the transgender superhero characters of Lee's Sidekick Squad series and Daniels's Nemesis series respectively, combine marginalized identity features—adolescence and trans-ness (and Blackness in Bells/Chameleon's case)—with being the most powerful superhero in their respective imaginary worlds. In both series, being a superhero is balanced with the more ordinary and realistic demands of adolescence. For example, Danielle gets "swamped with homework," so Dreadnought's "campaign to find and capture Utopia [the supervillain] has to be put on hold until the weekend" (Daniels, *Dreadnought* 140), while Bells distributes his time between "homework for his classes, and writing articles, and doing layout for the yearbook holo [hologram] and going on [superhero] assignments" (Lee, *Not Your Villain* 72). At the same time, Danielle/Dreadnought and Bells/Chameleon each possess extraordinary abilities, which make them far from ordinary teenagers: Dreadnought has superstrength, the ability to withstand vast physical trauma with little injury, and can manipulate the laws of physics, while Chameleon is a skilled shapeshifter. With irreplicable abilities, Danielle/Dreadnought and Bells/Chameleon are both creations of fantasy, and the fact raises questions about how such extraordinary adolescent characters can speak to the needs of the texts' trans implied readers who are perhaps seeking "self-affirmation," "characters with which to identify," and to "decrease the feeling of alienation" (2–3), as Sandra Hughes-Hassell and colleagues put it. If superhero narratives, or fantastic narratives more broadly, cannot offer attainable versions of transgender adolescence, then what—if anything—can they offer their adolescent readership?

The answer, I suggest, lies in the superhero's function as a metaphorical device for exploring the more everyday concerns of young people. According to Robin S. Rosenberg and Peter MacFarland Coogan, the superhero genre serves as a way of "discussing immigration, Americanization, urbanization, American identity, changing conceptions of race and gender, individualism, capitalism, modernism, and so many other central concerns" (xvii–xviii). To that I add, adolescent transgender superheroes offer useful metaphorical means for texts to explore identity and empowerment because the characters' "perverse structuralism" enables the narratives to reflect the lived experiences of transgender teenagers in fantastic ways. As we will see, the hero's superpowers might be understood to bring adolescent readers' fantasies of power and liberation from adult authority to life. First, I want to consider how Dreadnought's and Chameleon's superhero personas can be read as metaphors for identity construction.

The shift from civilian to superhero functions as a framework through which teenage readers can explore issues, such as maturation, transition, and liminality, that resonate with their everyday lives. Chapter 1 pointed to Jennifer Putzi's assertion that "the experience of determining one's gender identity and receiving medical treatment is often figured [. . .] as a type of adolescence (or second adolescence)" (429) by way of solidifying the importance of trans YA fiction for trans studies and YA studies alike. Robyn McCallum claims that "modern adolescence—that transition stage between childhood and adulthood—is usually thought of as a period during which notions of selfhood undergo rapid and radical transformation" (3). It is clear that YA novels that grapple with identity formation through new and interesting plots are thus particularly useful to transgender teenagers who are often navigating both types of adolescence at the same time.

The Nemesis and Sidekick Squad series' narrative arcs are based upon the protagonists exploring their selfhood and maturing into adulthood, and the authors draw upon conventions of the superhero genre to communicate such development. Costume, the means with which a superhero "constructs one of his two identities" (Brownie and Graydon 1–2), offers the Nemesis series a playful way of illustrating the protagonist's maturation. In the series, costumes—colloquially referred to as "colors"—are used to differentiate between superhero identities, as well as to communicate a character's intentions. In the imaginary world, nondescript camouflage colors symbolize the wearer's desire to remain anonymous as a protection against conflict. Danielle is too young and inexperienced to identify herself with the Dreadnought persona when she first gains her superpowers, so she is given a super suit of these nondescript "throwaway colors" (Daniels, *Dreadnought* 53) by the league of superheroes. Throwaway colors are heavily associated with young and provisional members of superhero leagues precisely because they "won't signify a cape persona but will protect [their] identity from anyone who sees [them]" (53). Mendlesohn suggests that a popular tactic for fantasy writers when putting together imaginary worlds is "the creation of a vocabulary" (83), and superhero costume becomes a language, of sorts. Danielle's first costume indicates passivity and inexperience to other characters in the imaginary world, and to readers this costume reveals a protagonist who is childlike, callow, and vulnerable.

"Claim[ing] your colors" (Daniels, *Dreadnought* 112), the process whereby young superheroes of the Nemesis series begin to wear the super suit that signifies their recognizable superhero persona, then offers a way for readers to visualize the adolescent protagonist's coming of age moment that is considered a rite of passage in many YA titles (Trites, *Disturbing the Universe* 3). When Danielle is trying to save the city from the villain's human-powered robots at the climax of the first novel, she realizes that "the cops need help. [...] They don't need some kid nobody's heard of or has any reason to trust. Right now, I'm just some loser in throwaway colors" (Daniels, *Dreadnought* 236). Danielle then presses a button on her suit that transforms its colors from camouflage to the "dark blue and clean, glittering white" (236) of Dreadnought's recognizable costume. Danielle's development as a superhero parallels her development as an adolescent, and we can read this process as an imaginative version of the more realistic tropes that signal a character's coming of age in YA fiction, such as those identified by Waller: "first experience of death; first sexual encounter; first relationship; movement between school or into work; cultural signifiers such as alcohol, drugs, music, film or computer games; and general markers of identity achievement or maturation and empowerment" (*Constructing Adolescence in Fantastic Realism* 16). The claiming-the-colors process works on the level of metaphor, parodying the serious approach that realistic transgender YA problem novels usually take to the subject of coming of age. The extraordinariness of Nemesis's protagonist creates space for the series to approach maturation through a different lens that acknowledges readers' desires for entertaining and imaginative stories.

In Lee's Sidekick Squad series, the protagonist's shapeshifting power opens even greater fantastic possibilities for readers to explore themes of identity and selfhood from the perspective of a Black, transgender teenager. The superhero's body is often a site of "fantasy, aspiration, codified desire, and identification" (MacFarlane et al. 2), and Bells's ability to change his physical appearance offers just that for many of the teenage readers experiencing gender dysphoria as part of their everyday realities. The series includes scenes in which Bells makes sensational and exciting shifts: "[H]e cycles through several different looks, lightening quick," impersonating four other people in the room before returning to "Chameleon in his green, metallic, shimmering bodysuit" (Lee, *Not Your Villain* 264). It is notable, too, that Bells's powers also facilitate more quiet, subdued moments of transition that speak to his transgender identity.

According to Jeph Loeb and Tom Morris, it is the superheros' ability to embody the feelings of their readers (or viewers) that is key to their enduring popularity: "[S]tories of these characters [superheroes] embody our deepest hopes and fears, as well as our highest aspirations, and they can help us deal with our worst nightmares" (11). For transgender adolescents who are unable (for a variety of reasons) to transition, while also enduring a period of life defined by involuntary and highly socialized (and gendered) changes in their bodies, an escape into the fantastic body of Bells offers a transcendence that relates specifically to trans-ness. Shapeshifting also offers Bells a means of reducing his breasts, for example, as he practices his super ability by lasting increasing amounts of the school day without having to wear a binder (Lee, *Not Your Villain* 37). The previous chapter argued that the Sidekick Squad series's peritextual materials signal a nuanced approach to the representation of trans identity and, while shapeshifting offers the series a playful way of examining liminality and transition, Lee also creates space for a more serious, didactic moment with the aim of encouraging transgender teenagers to feel comfortable in their own bodies. When the supervillain of the series threatens to take away Bells's powers and leave him "stuck in that body forever" (*Not Your Villain* 213), a body that has normatively feminine characteristics, Bells's response is underpinned by a message of self-acceptance: "I knew I was trans before I knew I had abilities. My body is just one aspect of who I am, and if you take my powers away, I'm still me" (214). The response steers readers towards an understanding of gender identity that privileges self-definition over a person's conformance to society's normative and narrow definitions of gender. It functions in two capacities simultaneously: to educate readers about the complexities of gender and to empower transgender teenagers with the insight that their genders are not limited by their assigned sex.

In contrast to Bells's flexible physical appearance, superpowers bring about a change for Danielle that is permanent but that nevertheless functions to guide readers to interrogate the importance of physical appearance against ideas of selfhood. Daniels, who is a transgender woman herself, brings the fantasy of an ideal female body (a contentious idea that I will discuss shortly) to life on the page when Danielle's superpowers cause her to morph in extraordinary ways that far exceed more realistic gender affirming treatment options. Daniels depicts Danielle's transcendental experience in a fragmented, poetic passage that I quote in full:

—a billion, trillion suns roaring silently in the night
—becoming light, scalding everywhere
—spilling out inside of me as
—a lattice of light and heat, blinding glare against the black
—but *more* than that
—twisted up out of potential and into *being*
—the pain is everywhere, filling me
—Everything. I see everything. From the biggest galaxy to the smallest atom.
  I understand it all. And I can *change*—
—the part of the Universe that is me
—wrap it around
—folds in on itself
—unravels, reweaves
—tightens up into a new
—bones melting, my ligaments melted
—begins to fade
—What was clear it
—no! No, please!
—I'm not done yet!
—grab and heave
—shove back the darkness
—fight
—almost, *pull*—
(*Dreadnought* 10–11)

Extraordinary images—"a billion, trillion suns roaring silently in the night," "blinding glare[s]," galaxies, and atoms, among others—in conjunction with distinctively positioned poetic text function to underscore the significance of this transition in the protagonist's story. The pauses created by the em dashes at the beginning of each line elongate the passage. The dashes also emphasize the fragmented and disorientating nature of Danielle's experience, possibly evoking the fragmented and frequently overwhelming medical and legal processes of transition that transgender people often endure.

In serving as a dynamic interlude in the prose of the novel, these poetic lines underscore a momentous moment of transition for Danielle. Shelly Chappell argues that "the metamorphosis motif metaphorically conveys powerful, often naturalised ideologies about childhood and adolescence, the processes of maturation, and other significant aspects of youth experience" (1), and it is worth observing how the extraordinary is brought into dialogue with the pervasive wrong-body discourse that we see in transgender problem novels in these lines. Jay Prosser has pointed out how "the figure of being trapped in a wrong body, of being wrongly encased, continues to be evoked" as an explanation of "transsexuality" (69), and Daniels brings a level of sensationalism to this age-old discourse through this fantastic scene. Secondary sex characteristics are not changed in isolation from the remainder of Danielle's body in her transition: it is also her ligaments, bones, and the other "parts of the universe" that constitute Danielle that are made new, exaggerating the extent to which her former body can be read as somehow "wrong."

Danielle's body morphs in fantastic ways that exceed the possibilities available with gender affirming medical treatment in the known world, but Danielle's transition is also unusual in regard to the scene's narrative placement. Occurring at the beginning of the story, Danielle's transition scene subverts the conventional narrative arc of the transgender problem novel in which transgender adolescents are driven towards gender transition. According to Daniels, the decision to position Danielle's gender transition unusually early in the first novel of the series was made to use the transition scene as an exciting and dramatic hook for readers: "[Y]our goal on page 1 is to get the reader to want to reach page 5. By the end of page 5, they should want to finish the chapter [. . .]. That's literally the only reason why the book is so heavily front loaded" ("An Interview with Author April Daniels" n.p.). In doing so, however, Daniels greets new readers with an expectation that Danielle's physical transition is integral to understanding her as a character. As the narrative progresses, the importance of Danielle's physical appearance is emphasized. It is the changes to Danielle's body that constitute the most impressive aspect of gaining superpowers for Danielle, as she reveals that "the flying and the strength, that's cool and all, but being able to look the way I'm supposed to, that's the important part. That's the best thing anyone has done for me" (Daniels, *Dreadnought* 123). In linking her normatively female aesthetic with the idea of how she is "supposed" to look, Danielle's feelings manifest a particularly body-orientated approach to gender identity, but it is an approach that is widely shared in Western society. Danielle's fantastic transition opens space for readers to examine how and why gender identity and physical appearance are entangled.

For Flanagan, the process of coming to terms with a body that may not conform to social expectations in fact constitutes "a vital aspect of maturation within representations of adolescent femininity in young adult fiction" ("Girl Parts" 40) and encouraging readers to identify the role that the body performs in the production of identity is a frequent objective of YA fiction. Accepting a body that falls short by society's unattainable standards is not something that Daniels's super protagonist has to do, though Danielle, too, is aware of the expectations placed on her female body: for example, Danielle muses how "nobody cares if a boy is a little chubby, but that's not true for girls" (Daniels, *Dreadnought* 80). Instead, Danielle's extraordinary body, brought about by her fantastic transition, is a bricolage of the airbrushed, unrealistically "perfect" bodies she has seen in the media.

In a moment of introspection, Danielle realizes that "this 'ideal' new body—the magazine cover perfection, the shampoo commercial hair, even the fashionable shape of [her] thighs—it's more than a different look. It's a window inside of [her] head" (Daniels, *Dreadnought* 51). Danielle's fantastic body offers readers an illustration of how young people's body images are shaped by advertising (and other forms of visual media), while her self-reflective commentary encourages readers to understand that bodies like Danielle's are a fantasy. Lisa Brocklebank makes the case that literature for young people is used by authors "not only as a vehicle for the instillment of normative social codes of conduct, but also as a means of voicing an implicit and often social critique" (127), and Daniels's story can be read in both lights. On one hand, Danielle's view that having a normatively feminine body aligns with how she is "supposed" to look remains uncontested throughout the series and Danielle never reaches the same explicit conclusion that Bells does about appearance being only one aspect of identity. On the other hand, Danielle's impossibly fantastic appearance sheds light on how the body, and perhaps especially the female body, is enculturated with normative ideals that shape how young people see themselves.

The extraordinariness of the transgender superhero protagonists of both Daniels's Nemesis series and Lee's Sidekick Squad series opens up metaphorical and allegorical possibilities for examining the norms, desires, and everyday experiences of transgender teenagers and guides readers to an understanding of how identity and selfhood are shaped by social environments. All readers may find enjoyment and comfort in the physical escape and transformation in these series. Yet the expanded generic possibilities offered by this new strand of trans YA fiction might allow trans readers, in particular, to indulge in fantasy and to escape into an imaginary world in which trans teenagers can shape their bodies to look how they choose, while concurrently being powerful superheroes that save the world from evil.

Stories featuring teenage superheroes can be read as a means of bringing adolescent readers' fantasies of power to life on the page. That is, after all, how Daniels sees it when she reveals her aim to "make trans girls feel powerful" ("An Interview with Author April Daniels" n.p.) by creating a strong and mighty transgender superhero. By showing adolescent protagonists struggling to identify and claim their power in relation to adults and inviting readers to consider whether teenagers can, in fact, "disturb the universe" (Trites, *Disturbing the Universe* 2), these super teens offer an important opportunity to continue Trites's discussion.[9] Extraordinariness can offer transgender teenage characters a type of strength that is not available to young people in the known world who are perhaps, as Anneke Meyer suggests, "physically vulnerable (e.g. their bodies are smaller and weaker), socially vulnerable (e.g. they lack certain social skills) and structurally vulnerable (e.g. there are asymmetrical power relations between children and adults)" (90). In much the same way as Waller characterizes the construction of adolescence in the known world—"[A]dolescence is always 'other' to the more mature stage of adulthood, often perceived as liminal, in transition, and in constant growth towards the ultimate goal of maturity" (*Constructing Adolescence in Fantastic Realism* 1)—the two super protagonists' statuses as adolescents repeatedly informs how they are perceived and treated by the fictional adults in their imaginary worlds.

Both protagonists are, for example, rhetorically infantilized by way of challenging their might. The soon-to-be-former Dreadnought exclaims, "Christ, you're just a boy" (Daniels, *Dreadnought* 10) to signify his doubt over Danielle's suitability for the super role (Danielle's gender transition does not occur until after this scene, so her gender identity is interpreted as male by the former Dreadnought), while Bells's age makes him seem incompatible with Chameleon's reputation: "Chameleon? [. . .] The League said he was the most powerful meta-human [. . .]. You're just some kid with cool hair" (Lee, *Not Your Villain* 264). Maria Nikolajeva's attention to the "imbalance, inequality, [and] asymmetry between children and adults" (*Power, Voice and Subjectivity in Literature for Young Readers* 8) depicted in books for young people through the theory of aetonormativity has shed light on the marginalization experienced by adolescents and children. When responding to Nikolajeva's theory, however, Clémentine Beauvais has usefully opened up the question of what type(s) of power young people are specifically deemed to lack in relation to their adult companions: "[P]ower can mean authority, ability, domination, strength, impact, influence, potential, importance, prominence, superiority, energy, and much more" (*The Mighty Child* 79). Power—and empowerment—for extraordinary protagonists has a more physical, visible, and immediately apparent manifestation than for the teenage characters of more realistic narratives. The next chapter carries on this discussion by considering a more ordinary, subtle form of empowerment at work across fantastic and realist texts.

Conclusion

Fantasy is not the opposite of reality, nor is the fantastic the opposite of the realistic in trans YA fiction: fantasy can be read to gain insights into the known world for transgender teens while offering (at times) vital opportunities for escape into alternative imaginary places. The titles that have been given attention in this chapter are only a sample of the sixty-or-so speculative YA books with transgender characters that have been written by transgender and cisgender authors since the mid-2010s, but they represent a range of realities for transgender teens to explore away from their known worlds. By blending the generic conventions of the trans problem novel with the tropes and possibilities of fantasy, many of the novels I have included in this analysis demonstrate a pattern of socioculturally engaged stories that are underpinned by a desire to challenge discrimination and show transgender young people navigating their various worlds in ways that are perhaps entertaining, enlightening, and/or informative, depending on the lived experiences of individual readers. As I have argued, speculative transgender YA fiction is offering a significant and timely contribution to the field by expanding the generic variety of fiction through which transgender teenagers can see reflections of their own identities. These novels do not necessarily always offer relief from the "reader fatigue" (Bittner, "[Im]Possibility and [in]visibility" 200) with coming-out stories (though they sometimes do), but instead offer alternative and imaginative ways of engaging with the same core issues that can be found both in realist texts and the known world for many transgender teens. To expand further, I bring realist and speculative texts from my corpus together in the following chapter and examine how parent-adolescent conflict, a seemingly "ordinary" issue for transgender teenagers, operates across trans YA fiction.

Chapter 4

THERE'S NO PLACE LIKE HOME
Parent-Adolescent Relationships in
Transgender Young Adult Fiction

The known world has changed significantly since 2020, with the mental distress caused by the global Covid-19 pandemic being felt acutely by many young transgender people who were forced to quarantine with families that are unsupportive of their gender identities and, in more severe cases, with family members who attempted or succeeded in forcing them to present as the gender they were assigned at birth (Fowers and Wan n.p.). The lockdown measures implemented around the world exacerbated the already significant impact of familial rejection and disapproval faced by many transgender adolescents. An investigation into the lives of British LGBTQ+ young people, published by the Stonewall charity and BritainThinks in February 2020, revealed that many have "experienced significant problems at home" (Bradlow et al. 13). Several of the LGBTQ+ young people surveyed were "rejected or bullied" by one or more family members, and some were "forced to leave home," experiences that "often profoundly impacted their mental health and self-esteem" (Bradlow et al. 13). Transgender young people are particularly likely to face discrimination or rejection from their families. Only 26 percent of transgender people surveyed for Stonewall's "LGBT in Britain—Trans Report" (2018) felt they were supported by their whole family and 11 percent were not supported by any family members (Bachmann and Gooch 14). Stonewall's pre-Covid findings reveal that many transgender teenagers were already living in difficult circumstances, and Lisa D. Hawke and colleagues note that the situation has only worsened for transgender youths who are facing "particular challenges with self-isolation in the family home, potentially including high levels of familial conflict, invalidation of gender identity, and possibly even abuse" (2) during the pandemic. The "genre world" (Fletcher et al. 997) will likely continue to reflect the specific difficulties brought about by Covid-19 over the coming years.[1] According to Utsa Mukherjee, "emergency [lockdown] measures have reassembled children's everyday geographies—reshaping the social institutions, processes, and relationships in which their daily lives are embedded" (24), suggesting that even realist pre-Covid texts offer a sort of fantasy to teenagers whose lives were restricted by lockdown measures. Yet, examining pre-Covid texts provides a way of interrogating how YA literature has reflected transgender teenagers' relationships with their parents and their experiences of home.

Home—as "not merely a physical structure or a geographical location but always an emotional space" (Rubenstein 1)—is or has been a focal point in most young people's lives and is a concept to which they readily relate. This situation forces many trans young adults to ask: How can I tell my family that I am transgender? How will my family react? What will happen next? Is my home a safe place for me? Will I be forced to leave my home? Where do I belong? These are just some of the questions that many novels in my primary corpus allow transgender readers to consider. After all, the YA books comprising my primary corpus are full of teenagers disclosing their transgender identities and navigating the fallout. For instance, Luna, the titular trans character of Julie Anne Peters's *Luna* (2004), leaves her home to begin a new life, fleeing from parents who have proven they will never support her choice to honor her female identity. April Daniels's Nemesis series (2017–) explores the breakdown of the relationship between its transgender protagonist, Danielle, and her parents, culminating in her legal emancipation from them. When Jessica comes out to her family in John Boyne's *My Brother's Name Is Jessica* (2019), her parents forbid her from ever mentioning it again and suggest different types of conversion therapy as "medical help" for her "personal crisis" (38). As these examples begin to demonstrate, conflicts between transgender young people and their parent(s) are a recurring trope within trans YA fiction, functioning among the events of the YA narratives to create friction and drama. Heeding Maria Nikolajeva's warning that a mimetic approach to character analysis risks treating literary characters as if they are real people and "easily ascrib[ing] to them features that the author had no intention of providing" (*The Rhetoric of Character* 15), Vanessa Joosen argues that "considering genre, plot and context needs to be an integral part of the analysis of adulthood in children's books if one does not want to fall into the mimetic trap" (18). Bringing together the genres or subgenres discussed in my previous chapters, I want to examine both realistic and fantastic literary representations to ask how authors use the generic and narrative tools at their disposal to construct the "complicated social and political environment [for LGBTQ+ teens] that is mirrored (and sometimes distorted) in YA literature" (Jenkins and Cart, *Representing the Rainbow* xiii).

Chapter 1 showed that the reflections are frequently distorted, applying Karen Coats's argument that fiction "doesn't fully reflect or represent reality in a transparent and unproblematic way" (*The Bloomsbury Introduction* 1) to the sort of mirrors that Rudine Sims Bishop talked about when she asked whether fiction reflects the lived experiences of marginalized young people. This chapter questions what images of parent-adolescent relationships and domestic spaces are reflected in a range of trans YA novels and considers how these reflections might encourage change. We will see that the parent-adolescent relationships in my primary corpus are frequently, though not always, shown to be tumultuous. In much the same way as Lydia Kokkola points out that the "covert messages" of many LGBTQ+ novels are that queer adolescents "will probably suffer from immense angst and may well be rejected by those who are dear to them" (109), the precedents set by trans YA fiction suggest transgender teens are more likely to be rejected (at least initially) than supported by at least one of their parents. I will also show that conflict paves the way for transgender teenagers to show their authority, creating more empowering mirrors for transgender readers than might be assumed to exist at first glance.

Trans YA fiction offers a useful, newly politicized space to update and transform Nikolajeva's insights into power in adult-child relationships. Chapter 3 introduced Nikolajeva's concept of aetonormativity (age-based norms that favor the adult) and Clémentine Beauvais's further examination of the different sorts of power that operate in the adult-child relationship ("authority, ability, domination, strength, impact, influence, potential, importance, prominence, superiority, energy, and much more" [Beauvais, "The Problem of 'Power'" 79]) into my interrogation of transgender adolescence. I offered a brief suggestion that being fantastic and, more specifically, possessing superpowers has opened up possibilities for empowering transgender teenagers in fiction through physical power that supersedes adult power. In this chapter, I expand on the new and provocative insights that trans texts can bring to aetonormative readings of YA fiction. Trites has already laid the foundations for this work: while age stands as the most significant or disenfranchising marginalization in both Nikolajeva's and Beauvais's readings of power, Trites suggests that "taken together, intersectionality and aetonormativity help us to consider the unique forms of oppression that occur in the matrix of age and other forms of difference" (*Twenty-First-Century Feminisms* 32). This chapter further develops the debate by showing how an intersectional approach to aetonormativity reveals a much more complex configuration of power, as well as oppression, within these novels' reflections of home.

The often-conflicting relationships between cisgender parents (because the parents of transgender teenagers in my corpus are always cisgender)[2] and transgender teens in YA fiction can subvert the quasi-naturalized idea that the adult has all of the authority (even as the child has the power of potential or what Beauvais calls "might"). Several of the novels build scenes and narrative arcs that reflect the trans teenagers' authority on trans-ness. In other words, these novels depict transgender young people knowing and understanding their genders (even when they are challenged by cisgender adults). I argue that YA literature's portrayal of trans teenagers' authority reflects (and contributes to) the contemporary cultural zeitgeist's recognition of marginalized people's authority on their identities, experiences, and stories. This change is driving the demand for trans-authored literature in the YA book market that chapters 2 and 3 have reflected.

Asking how transgender teenagers are given authority on the page offers another way of examining the shift towards trans people as authors and readers that this book is tracing. Authority is, after all, a "first cousin of 'authorship'" (Beauvais, "The Problem of 'Power'" 81). I begin by considering some of the different sorts of parent-adolescent conflicts in my primary corpus using examples from a number of realist and fantastic novels. Then I explore how parent-adolescent conflicts play out in domestic settings with "reality effects" (Barthes, "The Reality Effect" 141) that frequently yoke angst and rejection to the ordinary and everyday lives of the fictional teens. Finally, I push back against the ostensible powerlessness of transgender teenagers reflected in these mostly negative fictional parent-adolescent relationships. Coats's concept of the literary mirror suggests that readers "almost always judge what we see against what we expected to see" (*The Bloomsbury Introduction* 1). A reader might expect relationships in which transgender teenagers are oppressed by their cisgender parents, because both aetonormativity and cisnormativity suggest this is the likely finding. Foregrounding an implied trans adolescent reader in my analysis, I want to propose an alternative interpretation that shows how trans teenagers are empowered by these novels.

Parental-Adolescent Conflict

In *The Fantasy of the Family: Nineteenth-Century Children's Literature and the Myth of the Domestic Ideal*, Elizabeth Thiel argues that the myth of the ideal family was "replicated through popular children's literature to create a template for a world in which father and mother, devoted to the moral and/or spiritual well-being of their offspring, were ever-present and ever-mindful of their duties" (5). More recent fiction often works to destabilize this idealized myth and represent the broad spectrum of children's experiences.[3] The parent-adolescent relationships depicted in trans YA fiction, as in YA fiction more broadly, are often unstable, turbulent, and rife with tension. For Trites, "parents of teenagers constitute a more problematic presence in the adolescent novel [compared with the children's novel] because parent figures in YA novels usually serve more as sources of conflict than as sources of support" (*Disturbing the Universe* 56). Parent-adolescent conflicts regularly appear among the drama of YA novels, providing opportunities for the narratives to portray teenage protagonists as angry, rebellious, and defiant towards adult authority. The "conflict with parent-as-authority-figure" seems to Trites to be "one of the most pervasive patterns in adolescent literature" (*Disturbing the Universe* 54). In addition to the fact that the parental home is where the majority of teenagers are most likely to live their lives, the frequency with which YA fiction depicts parent-adolescent conflict can be attributed, in part, to the ongoing cultural influence of early psychologies of adolescence. Notably, Granville Stanley Hall's *Adolescence* (1904) conceptualizes adolescence as a period of "storm and stress" (73), with mood disruption, risk-taking behavior, and conflict with parents forming the characteristic behaviors of the transition from childhood to adulthood.

With the depiction of adolescent development forming the core subject matter of YA fiction and, within contemporary Western culture at least, the pervasive notion that adolescents rebel against adult authority figures in order to come of age, YA fiction and its criticism frequently depict conflict with parents as a rite of passage. Take, for example, Trites's analysis of parent-adolescent conflict in a selection of nineteenth- and twentieth-century novels. Trites makes the case that "since Anglophone cultures, by and large, usually accept as a given the premise that adolescents must separate from their parents in order to grow, the literatures of these cultures reflect the same bias" (*Disturbing the Universe* 55). As such, YA fiction "serve[s] both to reflect and to perpetuate the cultural mandate that teenagers rebel against their parents" (Trites, *Disturbing the Universe* 69). Underpinning Trites's argument is the assumption that YA fiction is influenced by contemporary cultural understandings of adolescence but also has an influential role in creating and perpetuating those understandings. Parent-adolescent conflict is deemed inevitable in many examples of YA fiction because it is generally considered inevitable in the real world of its teenage readers.

In conjunction with this adolescent angst, the earlier finding from Stonewall—that only 26 percent of British transgender people felt supported by all of their family—suggests that parent-adolescent conflict is conceivably more inevitable for transgender teenagers. What, then, does parent-adolescent conflict look like in the context of trans YA fiction, specifically? As I will show, it is overwhelmingly related to the trans-ness of the adolescent characters. In terms of their relationships with each other, trans adolescents are often shown to be rebellious, strong-willed, and unreasonable, while cisgender parents are frequently portrayed as ignorant and, at times, abusive: failing to recognize or acknowledge the transgender adolescents' genders and, in more severe examples, violating the adolescents' right to define their own identities. The related conflicts offer tension and drama, reflecting new and alternative versions of the clash between the adolescent and "parent-as-authority-figure" in Trites's cisnormative corpus.

As Barthes suggests, works of "creation or reflection are [. . .] a fabrication of a world which resembles the first [original] one, not in order to copy but to render it intelligible" ("The Structuralist Activity" 159). Readers can read to "imagine real lives to help them understand the possibilities of their own" (Appleyard 104) by exploring their own social realities through textual relationships. Though our primary material is very different, my approach to reading transgender texts resonates with Jonathan Todres and Sarah Higinbotham's analysis of adult characters in children's texts who "convey powerful messages [. . .] about the ways in which grown-ups can both protect and exploit children, and how children might navigate their relationships with the adults in their world" (171). As my previous chapter argued, fictional depictions can and do, to an extent, endeavor to reflect the real world for trans teenagers, and we can also see that from personal testimonies given by trans authors of trans fiction. For example, Daniels reveals that some of the transphobic dialogue in the Nemesis series is based upon "real things that real people had said" ("An Interview with Author April Daniels" n.p.), while Deaver said of their novel, *I Wish You All the Best*, that "a lot of it came from my own experiences dealing with my gender and first loves. [. . .] a lot of it comes from real life" ("Interview with Mason Deaver" n.p.). The following examples are by no means a comprehensive account of the transgender YA book market, but they do offer further illustration of some of the sorts of parent-adolescent frictions reflected to readers of transgender YA fiction.

In some titles, scenes of conflict portray the complexities of parent-adolescent relationships that involve love and affection, as well as conflict and misrecognition. This is a reality that plays out for protagonist Grady of Wittlinger's realist problem novel *Parrotfish* in a scene featuring Grady's mother: "Ange . . . honey . . . this new name . . . I don't know if I can get used to it. [. . .]. I feel like you're asking me to speak a foreign language. It's so strange. You're my *daughter*! I can't just think of you as my . . . " (36). As far as conflict goes, the scene is a particularly gentle example: Grady's mother "poked a finger into the corner of her eye rather than say 'son,'" though "the tear escaped anyway," and Grady only asks, "Not ever?" in a voice that "came out in a whisper," to which his mother responds "I don't know" (36). In addition to patently misgendering Grady by using "Ange" and "my daughter," two gendered terms Grady has rejected, trans-ness is constructed as an unfamiliar, challenging, and incomprehensible concept for Grady's mother, who is unable to become accustomed to the so-called "strange" and "foreign" rhetoric she is asked to use and so chooses not to try. What is more, the pauses, silences, and omissions created by numerous ellipses in the mother's dialogue show that Grady's trans-ness is incomprehensible and unspeakable to her, and thus deny him recognition of his male identity. The scene speaks to how transgender identity is construed as a burden on cisgender, normative families. As Kerry Mallan points out, in fiction for young people, "the complication of a queer child living in a heterosexual family is often a site of contention and struggle, particularly when the family structure conforms to normative models of parenting" (6). Christine A. Jenkins and Michael Cart similarly suggest that "even well-intentioned and loving parents can also be obstacles when their priorities are in direct conflict with those of their children" (*Representing the Rainbow* 199). The novel invites readers to consider how the idealistic image of selfless parental love can be destabilized by the parent's struggle to accommodate their transgender child's identity when their perspective is tinted by their own complicity in cisnormativity.

Aiden Thomas constructs another complex relationship between transgender protagonist Yadriel and his father in their recent fantasy novel, *Cemetery Boys* (2020). The traditional Latinx family of Thomas's narrative is not forthcoming with their acceptance of Yadriel. His mother, to whom I return later, was a supportive ally to Yadriel before she died a year prior to the novel's timeline, but Yadriel's father has trouble accepting, understanding, and legitimizing Yadriel's identity as a teenage boy—and as a Brujo.[4] This difficulty becomes all the more apparent in times of stress. When Yadriel's father, who is also the leader of the East LA Brujx community, is organizing the men to search for a missing Brujo, he gives the following order to Yadriel: "You stay here with the rest of the women!" (A. Thomas, *Cemetery Boys* 28). Thomas conveys the hurt this misrecognition causes to Yadriel with descriptions of "hot shame flood[ing] his cheeks" and his "eyes burn[ing] and his hands quak[ing]" (28). At the same time, physical gestures are used to convey a nuanced spectrum of emotions for Yadriel's father. He "spit the words out as if they were poisonous," but his anger soon "flick[ed] to confusion" and then remorse as "his shoulders sank; his expression went slack," and he "sighed," physically "reaching out" to Yadriel while also using his name (28). Thomas sensitively navigates this tense scene, creating a complex and empathetic picture of Yadriel's father while also reflecting the burden on trans teenagers of being misgendered by their parents.

The refusal to recognize trans teenagers' gender has been shown by critics, like sj Miller, to be one of the most destabilizing encounters for them. This is a reality that plays out for both Grady and Yadriel, in spite of the novels' differences in genre, authorship, and publication date, suggestive of its ubiquity in trans YA novels. In the introduction to *Teaching, Affirming, and Recognizing Trans and Gender Creative Youth* (2016), Miller suggests that "the struggle for recognition is at the core of human identity," and transgender and/or non-conforming people are often "misrecognized and misunderstood" (4). Such people, Miller argues, can suffer from a "recognition gap" that "subverts the possibility to be made credible, legible, or to be read and/or truly understood" (4). Kristin Elizabeth Clark's realist road trip novel, *Jess, Chunk and the Road Trip to Infinity* (2016), offers another example of this recognition gap for its transgender protagonist. Misrecognition occurs between Jess and her estranged father, who is surprised to see Jess unexpectedly arrive at his wedding and even more surprised to see how much she has transitioned since they last met. Though Jess's father was already aware of Jess's identity, their exchange comprises him struggling to process her gender presentation. Jess explains that it is "hormones" but is hurt by her father's lack of understanding and recognition and his attempts to justify his uncomfortable reaction with the fact that he is "not used to it" (Clark, *Jess, Chunk, and the Road Trip to Infinity* 250, 251). Jess realizes that her father just does not comprehend her identity, even more hurt by the fact that "he's had plenty of time to educate himself, and clearly he hasn't" (251). The scene escalates to conflict with a series of progressively hostile exchanges that reflect a common narrative pattern in trans YA fiction: the representation of cisgender parents as well-intentioned but misinformed and/or disconnected. Jess's father "raises his voice" to insist Jess "help [him] understand" and, when she refuses on the grounds that "it is not [her] job to educate [him], he chastises Jess with ignorant, condescending, and misgendering rhetoric: "Listen, *mister*! You don't get to have it both ways. You can't just show up here, tell me I don't understand, refuse to help me understand, and then bitch that I don't get you" (my emphasis 251). Much like with Yadriel's father in the earlier example, Jess's father's previously cautious word choices are undermined by his frustration, and he reverts to outwardly treating Jess as male. It represents a microaggression commonly experienced by transgender people, perhaps especially adolescents (owing to the inflection of aetonormativity). Julia Serano has coined the term "gender entitlement" to describe "the arrogant conviction that one's own beliefs, perceptions, and assumptions regarding gender and sexuality are more valid than those of other people" (89). Though Jess's father is ostensibly seeking a better understanding of Jess's gender identity in this scene, his return to male-coded language speaks to his belief that Jess's transness is "just a phase" (Clark, *Jess, Chunk, and the Road Trip to Infinity* 251), and she will revert back to what he understands to be her true male identity.

Jess, Chunk and the Road Trip to Infinity is one of several examples where a previously estranged father is employed to represent and emphasize the recognition gaps experienced by transgender teenagers whose cisnormative parents default to the identity the teens were assigned at birth. The single-parent trend follows other twenty-first-century literature in recognizing "the fragility of the nuclear family" (Alston 59). There are absent mothers represented in my primary corpus, such as Felix's mother in Kacen Callender's *Felix Ever After* (2020) and the deceased mothers in A. Thomas's *Cemetery Boys* and Russo's *Birthday* (2019). There are also novels in my primary corpus where both parents are absent, including Hal Schrieve's *Out of Salem* (2019) and Linsey Miller's Mask of Shadows duology (2017–2018). The recurrence of the absent father trope as a means of creating conflict, though, perhaps signals that stereotypical ideas about parental gender roles are at work in these novels, even as the authors attempt to subvert other norms with their transgender protagonists. In Russo's realist novel, *If I Was Your Girl*, protagonist Amanda had "rehearsed this moment over and over in [her] head" (10). That is, the moment she would see her father for the first time in six years. The scene in her imagination—"I would run up and hug him, and he would kiss the top of my head, and for the first time in a long time, I would feel safe" (10)—could not be further from the reality: "That you?" he asks, as Amanda steps off the bus and into the "sickly humid afternoon heat" (10). A strained conversation occurs between the two characters in the car on the way to the diner. Amanda asks her father: "Have you come to terms with it [her identity] now that you've seen me?" to which he responds, "give me time, kiddo [. . .] I guess I'm just old-fashioned" (12). The affectionate "kiddo" signals Amanda's father's love for his child (though his "lips puckered" [12] at the word) and, given time, he does become increasingly supportive, accepting, and accommodating of her gender (an arc I return to in the final section of this chapter). The deflating disconnect between Amanda's imagined scene and the scene that actually occurs works similarly to the examples taken from *Parrotfish* and *Cemetery Boys* in that it disrupts the idealized notion of parental love with a gritty example of how love can be strained by absence, disconnect, and misrecognition.

Overtly transphobic conflicts between cisgender parents and trans teenagers are explored in other novels, though. In Beam's *I Am J* and Boyne's *My Brother's Name Is Jessica* (both realist problem novels written by cisgender authors), for example, tense and uncomfortable scenes are underpinned by a specific form of antitrans ideology that transgender people frequently encounter. Susan Stryker states that the construction of "transgender phenomena as symptoms of mental illness or physical malady" (*Transgender*

History 35) has been, and continues to be, a prerequisite for transgender people accessing the medical care that they require. A significant sociocultural effect of the historic, as well as legislative, pathologization of transgender identity is the pervasive inclination to figure trans-ness as a "birth defect" (Putzi 429) or a disease in need of a cure. The transphobic viewpoints portrayed by cisgender parents in transgender novels frequently derive from this discourse, manifesting in the equation of transgender identity with a derogatory picture of mental illness. Beam's *I Am J* offers an early example. In J's coming out scene, J's father condemns his transgender identity: "Jesus, J. That's disgusting. [...] You're sick. You need help," while suggesting J's gender dysphoria is equal to "major problems in the head" (Beam, *I Am J* 315, 316). A more recent example occurs in Boyne's *My Brother's Name Is Jessica*, specifically in a scene during which Jessica's mother offers outdated and harmful suggestions designed to "cure" Jessica's gender identity: "Pills, perhaps. Or hypnosis. Electric shock therapy" (39). The latter treatment is explained to Jessica as a process of "strapping lots of wires to you, and whenever you think something—something you shouldn't—then you get a shock. [...] And eventually, you become too terrified to think it any more" (39). The use of such types of conversion therapy as "treatment" for nonnormative genders and sexualities comes with a long history of abuse (see Reay's "Transgender Orgasms" for historical case studies of conversion, such as the "torturous regime" (154) endured by a patient of Banstead Hospital in the 1960s). The scenes in *I Am J* and *My Brother's Name Is Jessica* reflect a specific way of perceiving and responding to trans-ness—as deviant, undesirable, and in need of "fixing." As such, these novels construct reflections of cisgender parents as ignorant, misinformed, and transphobic, hinting at an intergenerational divide that ostracizes both parent and teen.

Jenkins and Cart's reminder of the often-distorted reflections of reality in YA fiction should not be overlooked. Yet the extent to which cisgender parents are shown—intentionally or unintentionally—to harm transgender teenagers in trans YA fiction is more than a significant literary phenomenon: it functions as a document of a much broader cultural crisis in the care for transgender teens. Given the frequency with which parental microaggressions appear in transgender YA fiction, it is possible that young readers might come to expect such behaviors from real-world adults. As Kokkola's investigation of "coming out" stereotypes in YA fiction demonstrates, placing individual texts within their book market context is an important element of analyzing fiction that portrays different elements of the lived experiences of marginalized people. For her, "although it [negative experience] is perfectly reasonable in any one novel, when *all* the images presented to young readers are so negative, adolescent fiction can fairly be accused of continuing the current state of affairs rather than acting as a source of change" (Kokkola 119). The examples discussed in this section work to show how parent-adolescent relationships are inflected by misunderstanding, ignorance, normativity, and transphobia, creating mirrors and windows for readers to cogitate on the complex realities of what home can mean for nonnormative teenagers. I now consider the interplay between parent-adolescent relationships and domestic spaces, suggesting that the "reality effects" (Barthes, "The Reality Effect" 141) in several novels yoke transphobia to the ordinary, everyday experiences of transgender teenagers in YA fiction.

Domestic Tension and The Myth of the "Ideal Home"

Ann Alston suggests that "the home, like the family, is central to children's literature" (69). The two concepts are "almost inseparable," she argues, "for home *is* essentially family" (69). Children's and YA books are progressively representing diverse family structures and households, and they are also reflecting the less-than-saccharine reality of many children: "[S]ometimes the wild things are in the child's real home where there is no warm dinner waiting" (4), as Melissa B. Wilson and Kathy G. Short put it. Yet the myth is still pervasive. Children's literature is "rife with the idea of home" (Wilson and Short 2); it "celebrates home and affirms belief in the myth of home" (V. L. Wolf 54); and the home-away-home narrative pattern—stories beginning and ending with the child in the safety of their home—is among its most common storylines. Home is occasionally a place of safety for the adolescent protagonists of trans YA fiction to return to at the end of the novel. British transgender author Juno Dawson's dark, *Alice-in-Wonderland*-inspired *Wonderland* (2020), for example, concludes with the transgender protagonist, Alice, returning to the arms of her mother after venturing into Wonderland (a drug-filled London party) in search of her troubled friend, Bunny. In this instance, the narrative structure can perhaps be accredited to the novel's children's literature muse, as Alice of Lewis Carroll's *Alice's Adventures in Wonderland* (1865) returns home to her maternally minded sister. More frequently in YA narratives, home is the place from which teenagers depart. In contrast to the circular journeys of children's fiction, "the adolescent no longer has the option to return home to the safety of comforting familiarity" because YA narratives conventionally move teenage protagonists "away from childhood and towards adulthood" (Waller, *Constructing Adolescence in Fantastic Realism* 29). Home and family in my primary corpus are not always, or even usually, sources of "comforting familiarity," though.

The construct of home is often used to explore the frequently unpleasant and occasionally abusive domestic realities of transgender teenagers that are portrayed in YA fiction. The dynamics of parent-adolescent relationships are underscored by the "reality effects," to use Roland Barthes's term, of the domestic settings in which scenes of conflict take place. Reality effects are the narrative details that offer a "pure and simple 'representation' of the 'real'" (Barthes, "The Reality Effect" 146) such as the cups of tea and bus journeys that Waller finds to be of particular interest in British YA fiction. Waller makes the case that reality effects ground contemporary YA novels "in a world that is recognisable as occurring here and now," functioning as "pertinent touchstones for contemporary adolescent lives" ("The Art of Being Ordinary" 4). In my primary corpus, "reality effects" function across realist and speculative novels to create distinctly ordinary backdrops for parent-adolescent conflict that serve to stress the quotidian reality of abuse for many transgender teenagers. Not all novels work in this way: domestic scenes and reality effects can work to create comfort, rather than angst, in the lives of trans adolescents. For example, after coming out as transgender to her parents, Kate, the protagonist of Lisa Williamson's *The Art of Being Normal* (2015), sits with her parents "having a sort of picnic, sitting in a triangle" eating "cheese and pickle sandwiches," "biscuits," and drinking "massive mugs of tea" (316). The novel offers moments of narrative relief from what Victoria Flanagan considers to be inescapable cruelty of LGBTQ+ YA fiction: cruelty that "presents an omnipresent threat in narrative fictions for adolescent readers that focus on the formation of non-heteronormative identities" ("Kindness in a Cruel World" 257). The reality effects in the scene—tea, biscuits, and cheese and pickle sandwiches—offer a comforting environment. Williamson's scene is, in fact, referenced in Waller's analysis as an example of the depiction of "ordinary things" that allow us to consider more quotidian ways of being in the world in scenes that more frequently "revolve around sensational revelation, family tensions, and adolescent angst" ("The Art of

Being Ordinary" 1, 3). In enveloping Kate's trans-ness in quiet and ordinary domesticity, Williamson creates a scene that is far from a quotidian event for the teenage transgender characters in transgender YA novels: a coming-out moment that depicts love, warmth, and care from cisgender parents.

Coming out is more likely to be an uncomfortable, if not traumatic, event in trans YA novels. This follows a trend identified by scholars such as B. J. Epstein that queer YA novels "tend to offer the message that coming out is a dramatic, stressful experience that may involve rejection, verbal and even physical abuse" (*Are the Kids All Right?* 92). For example, the relationship between Danielle and her father in Daniels's *Nemesis* superhero series is replete with abuse, rage, and transphobia, and conflicts between the two characters recur throughout the series. I want to focus on one instance of conflict, in particular, as a defining moment in their parent-adolescent relationship: the scene in which Danielle's father realizes Danielle is transgender. Chapter 3 showed that Danielle's transition is rather unlike that of most teenagers, owing to the fact that she inherits superpowers from a prolific hero at the beginning of the first novel that feminize her body. When Danielle's father realizes that Danielle is ecstatic with the changes that have occurred—that she is transgender, rather than as worried about reversing the changes as he is—he is outraged:

> He sits back in his chair, and looks at me like he's never seen me before. The deep flush starts low on his neck and moves upward. His eyes go hard, and I brace for another Vesuvian detonation of Mount Screamer. His words are lost in the sheer noise of it. He gets up and paces around as he bellows, as if his rage is too wild for him to be still. [. . .] He's letting loose with everything now.
> *Freak. Tranny. Faggot.*
> He goes down the list.
> *Worthless. Disgusting. Failure.*
> There's no end to it.
> *Abomination. Sinful. Unnatural.*
> I'm fighting to become safely dead inside.
> *Queer. Homo. Shemale.*
> But he knows how to dig in under my guard. (Daniels, *Dreadnought* 163)

The metaphorical expression that shows Danielle brace for a "Vesuvian detonation of Mount Screamer," as if her father is a volcano and an explosive device, conveys both his volatility and the impossibility of containing his reaction. His anger manifests verbally and physically in his rising flush, hardening expression, and pacing. The transphobic and homophobic language comprising Danielle's father's speech exemplifies the contempt with which transgender people, and LGBTQ+ people more broadly, are often treated. Moving through slurs, demeaning adjectives, and religious condemnation, Danielle's father's speech also implies a greater level of preexisting awareness of transgender identity than the previous section showed many other cisgender parents are portrayed to have. The poetic alternation between four trios of hateful rhetoric and Danielle's attempt to escape emotionally or protect herself from her father's unending abuse heightens the emotional impact of the passage. While the earlier poetic extract from *Dreadnought* serves as a dynamic break in prose to emphasize the magnitude of Danielle's physical transition (as I argued in chapter 3), the poetic form in this scene functions to interlace the father's abuse and Danielle's own thoughts: it both underpins the sense that Danielle's father's words "dig in" to her inner self and weaves abuse into the ordinary fabric of her life.

This abusive outburst takes place in the kitchen, during breakfast, and the drama is interwoven with ordinary details of the scene. When Danielle's father enters the kitchen, she narrates: "[M]y gaze drops to my cereal, and I try to eat quickly without being obvious about it" (Daniels, *Dreadnought* 161). Narrative tension builds as her father "fills the coffee pot with water" and "pulls out a chair" (162), and when his attack is over, Danielle escapes from the table to the relative safety of her bedroom: "with my eyes on the floor and my heart slamming in my chest, I leave my bowl where it is and walk-run out of the room and up the stairs" (164). The reality effects in this scene destabilize the comfortable and safe idealized home by showing that the trans protagonist does not have unimpeded access to what is considered ordinary—such as breakfast—because it is interrupted by the transphobia and homophobia that also become a normal part of Danielle's relationship with her father. There is a gathering sense of urgency in this scene. Danielle's unwillingness to look at her father as her "gaze drops to [her] cereal," her eagerness to finish her breakfast quickly but without drawing attention to herself, and her "walk-run" to escape from her father all signal that he is a danger from which Danielle is trying to flee. Home is, according to Mavis Reimer's study of children's literature, an "auratic term" (xiii). In other words, "home" brings with it certain expectations and feelings. "Because home normally is the site of the satisfaction of the most basic human needs for shelter and food," Reimer argues, "the depiction of stable and safe housing in narratives for children can be read as the adult promise, or hope, that the world is a place in which children can not only survive, but also thrive" (xiii). What promise, then, is made to readers of Daniels's series? The answer is not that Danielle will thrive in her family home.

It is a promise of instability, turmoil, danger, and abuse that is also familiar to readers of Julie Anne Peters's realist novel *Luna*. Luna's coming-out scene, also set at the breakfast table, includes a verbally abusive and physically violent response from her father. Narrated by Luna's cisgender sister, Regan, the parent-adolescent conflict in this scene is accompanied by the consumption of Krispy Kreme Doughnuts—"the traditional O'Neill birthday breakfast" (Peters 219) served in honor of Luna's birthday. Luna enters the kitchen in a feminine outfit and a long, brunette wig and selects "a lemon-filled doughnut" (221) from the tray. She is presenting as female in the presence of her parents for the first time. Her father thinks that Luna's appearance is a joke, "some kind of senior prank" (221), but Luna reveals that she is, in fact, "a transsexual" (221). Awaiting her parents' reaction, Luna "picked up the doughnut and raised it to her mouth. Her hands trembled as she bit into it. She chewed and chewed and chewed. A tiny glob of lemon stuck to her upper lip" (222). As in Daniels's novel, transphobia impedes Luna's access to more ordinary moments. Peters's descriptive details disrupt what Barthes calls "the vertigo of notation" ("The Reality Effect" 145). Put simply, the description of Luna's doughnut eating creates a pause in dialogue between Luna's revelation and her parents' reaction that allows readers to assimilate the dramatic moment while also building narrative tension. Even chewing takes on a role in this abusive scene, constituting a manifestation of the trepidation and voicelessness that Luna is portrayed with in this moment by obviating her need to talk.

The awaited response from Luna's father is aggressive and visceral. There is an interesting similarity in the depictions of Danielle's father's and Luna's father's reactions: both parents are, themselves, vulnerable to shocking and unpleasant transitions as they process their children's gender transitions. While Danielle's father metaphorically takes on the form of an "explosive device" and a "volcano" to convey his anger in the scene, Luna's father "morphed. [. . .] His face, his body, they seemed to grow, contort [. . .] Dad's lips receded over his teeth like a snarling dog. 'You're sick,' he hissed. 'You are sick'" (Peters 222). The animalistic and monstrous language used to describe his body—contorting, morphing, snarling, and hissing—contrasts with Luna's quiet and measured demeanor as she asks Regan to pass the napkins and then "set down her doughnut and wiped her fingertips [. . .] scooted back her chair and replied calmly, 'I'm going out now'" (222). The interplay between Luna's retreat into the ordinary elements of the scene and her father's abuse serves to examine the way that transphobia can obstruct transgender teenagers' access to a safe home. The effect is only heightened when Luna's father "shot to his feet and thundered past Luna" (223) to prevent her from leaving. He insists that Luna will not *be* Luna in "[his] house," "not if [he] can help it" (223). In doing so, her father uses the domestic environment to lean on a particular type of authority in most parents' war chest: the "parent-as-homemaker" and, thus, rule maker.

Another example of conflict with the parent-as-homemaker occurs in Mason Deaver's novel *I Wish You All the Best* (2019), when protagonist Ben comes out to their parents as nonbinary. Ben and their parents begin the novel's opening scene at the dinner table. It is business as usual apart from the fact that Ben had "taken maybe one or two bites before it fell into [their] stomach like a rock and what little appetite [they] had to begin with was gone" (Deaver, *I Wish You All the Best* 1). Ben's interactions with the scene— leaving most of their dinner untouched, "sip[ping] water to give [themselves] something to do" (2) (much like Luna's chewing), and "drap[ing] over the sink, bracing [themselves] in case [their] dinner comes up" (2)—work to communicate the nervousness and trepidation they are feeling while they prepare to share their identity with their parents for the first time. After dinner, Ben keeps telling themselves that "*now* is the right moment. Over and over again as the movie keeps playing and commercial breaks keep coming" (5). When the time is eventually right, Ben tells their parents that they need to share something with them and "Dad reaches for the remote and turns the volume on the TV down" (6). This scene is replete with seemingly insignificant reality effects that contribute to a sense of verisimilitude readers can expect from realist fiction. Yet these ordinary details also work to create a feeling of a familiar, quotidian routine for Ben and their family that makes the following realization that Ben's nonbinary gender is intolerable within their cisnormative home all the more destabilizing.

When the novel cuts to the following scene, Ben is outside calling their older sister for refuge because they have been forced to leave that familiar home the novel's previous chapter created. "The door closed" (11) on Ben. Cold, alone, and with no shoes on, they "tried the knob but it was locked, even the spare key [their parents] hid under this fake rock didn't work because they'd locked the deadbolt too" (11). Gabrielle Owen suggests that "adolescent children are expected to move directly from an obedient childhood into a dutiful adulthood without questioning the authority or beliefs of their parents" (*A Queer History of Adolescence* 21), and when trans adolescents are believed to pose a threat to the cisnormative (and heteronormative) values of their parents in YA fiction, they are often removed. The same fate similarly awaits both Peters's Luna and Daniels's Danielle. Catherine Butler describes Luna's exit as a "symbolic death" (though it might more accurately be described as a rebirth): she is "forced from the family home to start a new life with a new identity in a different city" ("Portraying Trans People in Children's and Young Adult Literature" 8). Danielle is also made to leave her home when her father "walks over to the front door and rips it open [. . .]. From way at the back of my skull, I watch my body turn and leave the house I grew up in. The door slams behind me" (Daniels, *Dreadnought* 227). The doors and locks depicted in these scenes from *I Wish You All the Best* and *Dreadnought* form barriers between the transgender adolescent and the cisnormative family structure in which they are not accepted. The reality effects construct familiar domestic spaces that are disrupted and disturbed by tension, hostility, and the teens' eventual removal from what is ideally understood as, though clearly it is not, "stable and safe" (Reimer xiii).

As I have already suggested, in a time following "emergency [lockdown] measures [which] have reassembled children's everyday geographies—reshaping the social institutions, processes, and relationships in which their daily lives are embedded" (Mukherjee 24), it is especially important to unpick the layers of oppression and power that are shown to exist in the home. It is, after all, the place where young people have spent the most time. As Thomas Crisp suggests, YA texts "rely upon a representation and interpretation of reality" (238), so it can be reasonably assumed that teenagers read, at least in part, to explore their reality. Transgender adolescents live a shared reality of conflict in almost all of the examples I have discussed to this point. Given the frequency with which transphobia appears in the characterizations of cisgender parents in these books, young readers might come to expect (and perhaps accept) such behavior from adults in their real world. As I said earlier, Kokkola suggests that negative images are not in themselves problematic, but "when *all* the images presented to young readers are so negative, adolescent fiction can fairly be accused of continuing the current state of affairs rather than acting as a source of change" (109). In the introduction, I asked whether transgender representation in YA books creates, as well as documents, the changing sociocultural environment for transgender teens. Through examining positive and redemptive encounters between transgender teenagers and their parents in the following section, I want to push back on readings of parent-adolescent relationships that assign authority to the adult to reveal how some trans YA books are redefining what authority can mean for young people.

The Hidden Authority in Transgender Young Adult Fiction

In *Power, Voice and Subjectivity for Young Readers*, Nikolajeva is reconciled with the inevitability of aetonormativity as a disenfranchising marginalization in the adult-child relationship and its reflection in literature written for young people. She acknowledges that "naturally, there are other factors [. . .] which may both enhance and diminish the effect of the power imbalance" (Nikolajeva, *Power, Voice and Subjectivity in Literature for Young Readers* 8) such as the difference between "masculine and feminine plots" (105), where masculine is understood as "normative and empowered" and feminine "equals disempowered, oppressed, deviant, and silenced" (105). Nikolajeva considers how masculine and feminine plots interact with aetonormative assumptions, but she does not take into account compounding marginalizations like those in the relationships between cisgender (adult) parents and transgender (child) adolescents on the pages of my primary corpus (or, in fact, the relationships between cisgender adult authors and transgender teenage characters). Power only changes hands, Nikolajeva argues, when "yesterday's children grow up and become oppressors themselves" (9). Beauvais has nuanced this critical understanding of child-adult relationships with acknowledgment of the different sorts of power that coexist between them. For Beauvais, "authority is [. . .] the most relevant aspect of the vague concept of 'power' that we might attribute [. . .] to the physical and symbolic adult in the children's text," while "children are mighty because their specific form of 'power' is dependent on the existence of a future for them in which to act" ("The Problem of 'Power'" 81, 82). In other words, "to be mighty is to have more time left; to be authoritative is to have more time past" (Beauvais 82). What Nikolajeva's and Beauvais's accounts of cisnormative children's literature inevitably do not consider is that transgender young people do not (on the whole) "grow up and become" cisgender adults. The relationships between cisgender adults and transgender young people are a disruption to aetonormativity's underpinning developmental logic.

In *Twenty-First-Century Feminisms*, Trites recognizes that "all children's literature that involves multiculturalism, diversity, ability, or difference demonstrates how aetonormativity interacts with other forms of oppression" (32). For her purposes, Trites suggests using "intersectionality to think about the intersections of oppression that occur when characters are black girls—or differently-abled girls or lesbian adolescents or when their subject positions involve any form of alterity that interacts with age to create multiple sites of oppression" (32). The debate can be further developed, though, by considering the power as well as oppression at play. YA fiction's portrayal of trans teenagers with authority (knowledge, expertise, and understanding) regarding their trans-ness serves as an intervention in mainstream, cisnormative conceptions of parent-adolescent relationships. This trend is indicative of broader cultural recognition of lived experience as a form of authority, for which the increase of trans authorship can be considered another manifestation (though, of course, the attribution of "the perceived authenticity of a book to an author's real-life experiences is a far more established practice" [Booth and Narayan, "Identifying Inclusion" 3] than this most recent surge).

In Beam's novel, for example, J is portrayed as more authoritative about his gender identity than his cisgender mother, whose desire for a normative child remains unmet. On the surface, exchanges between J and his mother reflect the "imbalance, inequality [and] asymmetry between children and adults" (*Power, Voice and Subjectivity in Literature for Young Readers* 8) that Nikolajeva's analysis brings to the fore. J's request to transition with hormone therapy is presented as an alarming caricature of, or aberration from, the teenage rebellion that Trites has noted is a "cultural mandate" (*Disturbing the Universe* 69) in YA fiction: "'[O]ther girls your age want piercings, want tattoos. You—you want *testosterone*? What am I supposed to think?'" (Beam, *I Am J* 158), his mother says. Her rhetoric is constructed from assumptions about the stability of adulthood, used to undermine both J's trans-ness and his agency: "J, you're only seventeen. I thought I knew everything when I was seventeen, too. But things change as you get older. You realize certain things in life are good for you, others are not" (166). Ostensibly unwavering, J's mother's authority is substantiated by what Beauvais would describe as "a longer time past with its accumulated baggage of experience" (*The Mighty Child* 19). However, reading J's mother's claim that "things change as you get older" against *I Am J*'s narrative arc reveals an attempt to challenge the cisgender adult authority of J's mother. Beam depicts J continuing to present as male and even beginning his medical transition within the novel's timeline: for instance, the final line of the novel—"his new, deep voice didn't crack" (326)—serves to affirm the progression of his transition journey. In spite of J's mother's "authority," her demands for a normative, cisgender child remain unmet. J's knowledge and lived experiences as a transgender person represent a different sort of "baggage of experience" than merely time passed.

Acceptance dénouements like those I explored in chapter 1, as well as in more recent publications, work like *I Am J* to legitimize trans teenagers' perspectives on their gender identities. Waller points out that "discourses that are related to powerful or privileged voices are more likely to appear as 'truthful,'" but "these apparent hierarchies of discourse are, however, unfixed and temporary, contingent on shifting public perceptions" (*Constructing Adolescence in Fantastic Realism* 7). The discourses to which Waller refers—scientific, academic, and legal—offer legislative legitimacy, but the parent in the parent-child relationship is, too, most often afforded the power of authority. In the same vein as Waller's observations, it might be assumed that parental authority is incontestable. Yet these "unfixed and temporary" hierarchies are similarly open to disruption. I am not going to revisit any more of the acceptance arcs we have already seen in chapter 1's analysis, though the ideas I discuss here can equally be applied to them. Instead, I want to add to my earlier discussion with examples from a few more recent publications. Take Clark's *Jess, Chunk and the Road Trip to Infinity*, for example. In the final chapter, Jess's father introduces Jess to the "crowd" of guests at his wedding: "'[T]his is my kid,' my dad says to everyone. 'Jess.' And hearing him speak my chosen name keeps me smiling the entire time the three of us [Jess, her father, and stepmother] pose for pictures" (Clark, *Jess, Chunk, and the Road Trip to Infinity* 256). The scene shows Jess's father come to realize that Jess is his daughter, rescinding his previous position that Jess's transness is a "phase" and conceding to Jess's authority on her identity. Russo's *If I Was Your Girl* includes a comparable, albeit less public, recognition scene. Inviting Amanda to live with him again, her father suggests he would "be real happy to have [his] daughter back," before finally saying goodbye to Amanda's previous identity: "'Bye, Andrew,' I said softly. 'Bye, son,' Dad agreed, as we went inside" (Russo, *If I Was Your Girl* 278). Amanda's authority permeates the scene: her father yields to her knowledge of her gender identity, and he is rhetorically depicted following Amanda's lead through "agree[ing]" with her and echoing her speech. In both Clark's and Russo's novels, a disruption to the "incontestable" nature of the parent's perspective paves the way for the trans teenagers to hold authority within their intersectional relationships with their cisgender parents.

As in the above examples, the authority of the cisgender adult is dislocated in A. Thomas's *Cemetery Boys*, this time with an acceptance arc that portrays one of the parent characters criticizing his own ignorance. Yadriel's father—a doubly powerful figure because he is both a parent and a community leader—comes to understand that he can learn from his transgender son, a realization that culminates in a public declaration to that effect. Leading the *aquelarre* ceremony (an ancient ritual to induct new brujos), Yadriel's father gives public validation to Yadriel's identity that earlier discussion showed he previously denied: "'[T]his is a special aquelarre for me because my son—' Yadriel's heart leaped into his throat [. . .] 'joins me as a brujo.' *My son. A brujo*" (A. Thomas, *Cemetery Boys* 337–38). Serving as a more overt disruption to aetonormative discourse than Clark's and Russo's novels, Thomas depicts Yadriel's father delivering a speech to the community where he explains: "'I failed my son, Yadriel, as both a father and a leader [. . .]. He tried to tell me who he was, but I didn't listen, I didn't understand. [. . .] But now I am listening, and I will learn to do better'" (339). In its embrace of Yadriel's father's epiphany that he should have respected his son's authority on his identity, *Cemetery Boys* shows a parent engaging in self-reflection that challenges the myth of a "stable and coherent adult identity" (Waller, *Constructing Adolescence in Fantastic Realism* 54) that aetonormative power is based upon. Wickens's suggestion that "authors of contemporary LGBTQ novels appear to be [. . .] aware of the potential impact of their books on their audiences" (162) can almost certainly be applied to Thomas. The novel's narrative arc functions to empower transgender teenagers with an acknowledgment that their voices should be listened to, respected, and understood.

A more radical disruption of the aetonormative parent-adolescent relationship, and an explicitly legal one, appears in the second book of Daniels's Nemesis series, *Sovereign* (2017). Unlike earlier examples, the protagonist and her parents do not reconcile (at least, they do not reconcile in the first two books; the third novel is yet to be published, and analysis of the complete trilogy may yield a different argument). Danielle formally disputes, and ultimately rejects, parental authority by achieving legal emancipation from her mother and father: "[T]here's this thing called an emancipated minor" which is "not *technically* a divorce, but it's basically a divorce," where "my parents go one way. I go the other" (Daniels, *Sovereign* 78), she explains. The emancipation storyline allows readers to examine more subtle forms of parental abuse than physical and sexual violence through Danielle's eyes: "He [Danielle's father] thinks that because he never laid a hand on me, what he was doing wasn't abuse. Like it's normal for a kid to invent reasons to stay away from home. [. . .] And Mom just let it happen" (78). Readers follow along as Danielle challenges the legal right her parents have to control her as a minor and, before the end of the second novel, Danielle's mother and father have "dropped their objection" to Danielle's emancipation papers, and Danielle is "free" (311). In addition to confronting the "parent-as-authority-figure" (Trites, *Disturbing the Universe* 54) archetype for dramatic effect, Daniels's depiction of the legal process serves a didactic function. That is, the novels equip teenage readers with an awareness of emancipation as an option for "navigating their relationships with the adults in their world" (Todres and Higinbotham 171), should that world resemble the abusive domestic reality that plays out for Nemesis's transgender protagonist. As Belinda Y. Louie and Douglas H. Louie suggest, adolescent characters in YA fiction "can be so trapped by their situations that they convey a helpless, gloomy message," but when those characters are "responsible for solving their problems," readers are "likely to be empowered to develop confidence in overcoming similar problems of their own" (53). In stripping Danielle's parents of their authority, the series empowers teenage readers to push back against any harm they may also be experiencing in their lives.

 For Reynolds, the radical potential of young people's literature comes from its contribution to "the social and aesthetic transformations of culture by, for instance, encouraging readers to approach ideas, issues, and objects from new perspectives and so prepare the way for change" (1). Perhaps most radical of all, then, are the depictions of transgender adolescents sharing parent-adolescent relationships with cisgender parents who fully embrace their trans-ness and function to empower, rather than "repress" (Trites, *Disturbing the Universe* 56), them. As we have seen, there are several examples in trans YA fiction of parent characters who come to accept the gender of their trans adolescents after a period of misrecognition. There are also parent characters whose acceptance stems from other factors, such as the teenagers' unsuccessful suicide attempts in Russo's two novels: Amanda's mother expresses that "anything, anyone, is better than a dead son" (17) in *If I Was Your Girl*, while protagonist Morgan in *Birthday* (2019) explains that her father is "still uncomfortable at times, but glad I'm alive" (259). Yet the final two examples I discuss in this chapter are parents who do not only learn to accept but also actively empower their transgender teens.

The depiction of uplifting parent-adolescent relationships treats readers to images of teenage authority that do not depend upon conflict. That is, to representations of teenage authority that are already acknowledged and respected by cisgender adults. The second parent character of *Cemetery Boys*, Yadriel's deceased mother, functions in this way. In the memories of her, A. Thomas disrupts the aetonormative, repressive parent-as-authority-figure by exploring how a cisgender parent might act as an ally for their transgender child. It took Yadriel's mother "time to relearn old habits, but she'd caught on surprisingly fast" (Thomas, *Cemetery Boys* 16), despite trans-ness being a deviation from the community's traditional values. In stark contrast to the incidences of misrecognition and misgendering that earlier discussion has revealed to be prevalent in transgender YA fiction, Yadriel's mother had "taken on the task of gently correcting people so he [Yadriel] didn't have to. It was a heavy burden, small instances piling up, but his mom helped him shoulder some of the weight" (16). She had also "championed" for Yadriel to be allowed to become a brujo and "be welcomed into the community as he was—a boy" (32). In killing off Yadriel's mother, Thomas leaves Yadriel with "no one to stick up for him" (32), creating the conditions necessary for Yadriel to endure the dangers, and ultimate pay offs, of becoming a Brujx behind his father's back.

To explain some of his authorial choices as a writer of LGBTQ+ YA fiction, David Levithan suggests that "you don't have to write a book in order to reflect reality. You can also write a book to create reality" ("Boy Meets Boy, Ten Years Later" n.p.). We can see this activist approach to authorship no more overtly reflected in trans YA fiction than in Akwaeke Emezi's *Pet* (2019). Emezi explicitly disrupts aetonormativity with a teenage protagonist whose transgender identity was recognized, validated, and respected by her parents from a very early age. Chapter 3 showed that the radical work of Emezi's novel to criticize the contemporary world for trans people takes place in a futuristic, postrevolution, utopian world that is accepting of trans-ness.

We already saw that Jam did not come out to her parents as a teenager (a convention that is pervasive across my primary corpus). As a further contrast from earlier scenes from novels such as *I Am J*, there is also no hierarchical, aetonormative assumption—implicit or otherwise—that Jam's parents have more knowledge or authority than their young child. Instead, a flashback scene reveals Jam as a young child shouting "Girl! Girl! Girl!" after being called "such a handsome little boy" (Emezi, *Pet* 16). Recognizing their mistake for assuming Jam was a boy based on how she was assigned at birth, Jam's mother responds "all right, sweetness," before "thinking back on several arguments they'd had about Jam's clothes when Jam would sign refusal over and over" and realizing that "that explains that'" (16). Jam's father simply said "[S]orry, sorry [. . .]. We didn't know" as he "patted her head until she calmed down" (16). In contrast to the relationships between cisgender parents and transgender young people in fiction that the previous sections have represented, Jam's relationship with her parents is loving, supportive, and unchanged by her trans-ness.

Pet also contributes a particularly unusual scene to transgender YA fiction in its inclusion of coming out as a preteen moment.[5] Emezi uses the moment to explicitly critique the treatment of transgender children in the contemporary, nontextual world. Following Jam's outburst, her father begins researching medical options for Jam, and she is able to access gender affirming treatment while she is still a child. In a pushback against the lack of agency Emezi perceives children and young people to have in reality, Jam experiences a wholly joyful female puberty during her adolescence that is inaccessible to transgender young people in the nontextual world:

> When she was ten, Jam got an implant with the blockers [. . .] before she swapped it out at thirteen for a hormone implant, a tiny cylinder nestled in her upper arm, administering oestrogen to her body. Jam watched her body change with delight [. . .]. Jam was fifteen when she told Aloe [Jam's father] she wanted surgery, and her father sat and wrapped his arms around her. (16–17)

Opposed to a prerevolution time "back when the world was different" for transgender people, Jam "didn't have to wait to be considered an adult for her wants around her body to be acted on" (17). The parent-child and then parent-adolescent relationships Jam shares with her mother and father are in stark contrast with Trites's account of the field that I mentioned earlier, which suggests "parent-figures in YA novels usually serve more as sources of conflict than as sources of support. They are more likely to repress than empower" (*Disturbing the Universe* 56). Jam's mother and father respect Jam's insights into her own identity and respond accordingly. The parental relationships Emezi has created within *Pet*'s futuristic, utopian storyworld redistribute authority to Jam by way of advocating for an alternative way of treating (transgender) young people.

The possibility of being listened to and believed by cisgender adults constitutes an empowering, subversive alternative to the misrecognition, transphobia, and conflict that is more frequently experienced by the trans teenagers of YA fiction. Owen suggests that "the view of adolescence as a time of instability and transition justifies perceptions that young people are rebellious, hormonal, or confused, depictions which imply that they are not agents of their own actions, desires, or identities" ("Adolescence, Trans Phenomena" 563). Several transgender novels are disrupting such perceptions. Their teenage characters are not "rebellious, hormonal, or confused" but are, instead, shown (through characterization and/or narrative structure) to speak with an authoritative knowledge of their transgender identities that has been accumulated through their lived experiences as doubly marginalized trans teenagers. Angel Daniel Matos suggests that "YA literature and culture is a barometer, of sorts, for the limits of social acceptability, and the extent to which these limits can be transgressed" (qtd. in Corbett and Phillips 2). It is thus no coincidence that the most nuanced, disruptive, and boundary-pushing examples of parent-adolescent relationships occur in texts that are both recently published and written by transgender authors. Marginalized authors including A. Thomas, Daniels, and Emezi are working to redistribute authority to transgender teens. Such work is expanding the horizons for transgender YA literature and transforming the "patterns" (Trites, *Disturbing the Universe* 54) in cisnormative YA texts. At the same time, these authors are documenting and effecting a shift towards the recognition of marginalized people as authoritative voices regarding their own identities, experiences, and stories.

Conclusion

The depictions of relationships between cisgender parent and transgender adolescent characters under consideration in this chapter offer implied transgender readers the opportunity to examine the relationships that exist in their nontextual world. Coats argues that "as readers, we learn about the ways characters, indeed people, are constructed though their actions and the way society views those actions" ("Young Adult Literature" 319). As well as creating tense and dramatic storylines that are perhaps most relevant to transgender teenagers, given the fact that the most immediate conflict for many adolescents is home-centered, the novels I have discussed in this chapter mostly construct a shared reality of misrecognition, misunderstanding, and transphobia that is yoked to the quotidian lives of their transgender teenage characters. In one manner or another, works including the Nemesis series, *Cemetery Boys*, and *Pet* embrace versions of trans adolescence that afford teenagers more power in their relationships with their parents. In doing so, these novels offer new perspectives on how authority might exist in the intersectional relationships shared by cisgender adults and transgender teenagers. Through positioning marginalized teenagers' experiences as an alternative to the "accumulated baggage of experience" (Beauvais, *The Mighty Child* 19) that adults are seen to possess, a number of works I have examined in this chapter are representing and reinforcing the recognition of lived experience as a form of authority. Beauvais's link between authority and authorship—"conveniently, of course, the term [authority] is also a first cousin of authorship" ("The Problem of 'Power'" 81)—can be pushed further to acknowledge that authorship, at least in traditional, mainstream publishing, is associated with an authority to tell stories. Such recognition is tied to the growth and marketability of trans-authored fiction that I have already explored, as well as to trans young adults having space for their own stories in the memoirs I interrogate in the next and final chapter.

Chapter 5

TRANSGENDER MEMOIRS FOR YOUNG ADULT READERS

Literature for young people is mostly "written by adults, illustrated by adults, edited by adults, marketed by adults, purchased by adults, and often read by adults" (Jenkins, "Introduction" 23). As a result, young people's own stories are seldom included in the mainstream book market. Alison Waller suggests that, as adults usually "create and control narrative" in YA literature, texts are "most likely to portray *adult* impressions of adolescence that are shaped by prevailing discourses" (*Constructing Adolescence in Fantastic Realism* 99). To this point, I have dealt with fictional constructions of trans adolescence that have been authored by both transgender and cisgender adults. In this final chapter, I examine six transgender YA memoirs (see table 5.1) that provide opportunities to revisit and update the picture of the market and to consider the role that young transgender people play as creators, as well as readers, of YA texts. As I will show, the authorial, editorial, and marketing decisions relating to these memoirs privilege self-representation and have also increasingly prioritized transgender teenagers as their intended readership.

To my knowledge, these titles are the only full-length transgender YA memoirs published in the US and UK mainstream markets.[1] Trans-authored trans fiction, that which "draws heavily from an author's [. . .] identity and experiential knowledge of belonging to a marginalized group" (Booth and Narayan, "Identifying Inclusion" 3), has become exponentially more prevalent during the course of my research. However, autobiographical work that represents the author's identity, experiential knowledge, and also their own

Table 5.1. Transgender YA memoirs published in the US or UK from 2014 through 2020.

Memoirist	Cowriter*	Title	Publisher	Date
Arin Andrews	Joshua Lyon	Some Assembly Required: The Not-So-Secret Life of a Transgender Teen	Simon & Schuster	2014
Katie Rain Hill	Ariel Schrag	Rethinking Normal: A Memoir in Transition	Simon & Schuster	2014
Jazz Jennings	Joshua Lyon	Being Jazz: My Life as a (Transgender) Teen	Penguin Random House	2016
Skylar Kergil	None	Before I Had the Words: On Being a Transgender Teen	Skyhorse	2017
Alex Bertie	None	Trans Mission: My Quest to a Beard	Hachette	2017
Miles McKenna	None	Out! How to Be Your Authentic Self	AMBRAMS	2020

* I have chosen to use "cowriter" instead of "ghostwriter" as it is not clear how involved the transgender young people were in the writing process. Throughout this chapter, I refer to the memoirs using the surname of the memoirist.

experiences (with or without a cowriter) remains unusual. While not substantial in number, these memoirs are a vital part of the landscape of transgender YA literature: as Kate Douglas and Anna Poletti argue, life writing can offer "a powerful and effective means for young people to engage with and respond to the discourses that construct them" (8). Trans young adults are the implied authors, if not also always the actual authors, of the memoirs, and the plots are retellings of their lived experiences.

All of these memoirs portray a teenager navigating their childhood and adolescence and the additional or alternative challenges that being transgender brings to their life in the twenty-first century. In all of them, a young person rejects the gender they were assigned at birth, identifies their transness, comes out to their family and friends, and begins (or even completes) their social and physical gender transitions. *Some Assembly Required* and *Rethinking Normal* recount the intertangled experiences of Arin Andrews and Katie Rain Hill, respectively, as they both discover their transgender identity, come out, meet in a support group for trans teens, have a romantic relationship with each other that gains media attention, transition, and break up. *Being Jazz* chronicles the childhood and adolescence of Jazz Jennings, a transgender teenager whose unusually early transition has become a topic of fascination in popular culture. Indeed, the American reality TV series about Jennings's life and family, *I Am Jazz*, premiered its sixth season in 2020 (a seventh season was confirmed in June 2021). *Trans Mission, Before I Had the Words*, and *Out!* narrate the experiences of transgender young adults—Alex Bertie, Skylar Kergil, and Miles McKenna, respectively—who have each gained popularity with YouTube channels that document the processes of their gender transitions.[2] As I write, Bertie's channel has 282,000 subscribers, Kergil's channel has 111,000 subscribers, and McKenna's channel has a staggering 1.15 million subscribers. As these brief insights suggest, all three memoirists have a level of cultural prominence that predates the publication of their memoir.

Robert Bittner points out that young people are rarely the producers of life writing, "unless their personal stories are considered exceptional" ("Trans and Nonbinary Teen Voices and Memoir" 44). Trans-ness constitutes "exceptional" content from the perspective of a cisnormative book market, and the preexisting popularity of these transgender teenagers perhaps explains why they were chosen to tell their stories by traditional publishers. Literature by transgender young people does not, therefore, necessarily equate to literature that is representative of trans youth in the twenty-first century. In addition to the online celebrity status of these memoirists, they are also mostly white and have binary gender identities. Andrews notes that he "understood why the cameras like us [Andrews and Hill] so much. We were safe for the masses—white, telegenic, and heteronormative" (213). This evident normativity reflects a broader cultural problem in transgender representation and links to the Western-centric concept of trans-ness that I highlighted in chapter 1. As Chiara Pellegrini has noted of transgender autobiographies for adults, "the narrative production of what counts as an intelligible trans life is intrinsically tied with the whiteness of the canon" ("Posttranssexual Temporalities" 50). As such, while the six full-length memoirs are the focus of this final chapter, I also want to bring attention to two other notable examples of transgender young people being included as active voices in the YA book market. Susan Kuklin's *Beyond Magenta: Transgender Teens Speak Out* (2014) and Juno Roche's *Gender Explorers: Our Stories of Growing Up Trans and Changing the World* (2020) both include myriad voices in the form of short interviews and discussions with transgender young people and do important work to diversify the representation of trans adolescence in the YA book market.

Some Assembly Required, *Rethinking Normal*, *Being Jazz*, *Before I Had the Words*, *Trans Mission*, and *Out!* have intersected with multiple different literary traditions and genres, such as YA literature, transgender autobiography for adults, and the more recent genre of "YouTube memoir" (Rebellino 20), but they also constitute a discrete "genre world" as a "a sector of the publishing industry, a social formation, and a body of texts" (Fletcher et al. 997). Recognizing them as such gives attention to the sociocultural and industry contexts of their production in ways that usefully reveal how the literature has developed in only a few short years. The diachronic approach I have loosely adopted throughout this book now comes to the fore. Inspired by Jodi McAlister's "snapshot approach" (4) to defining and redefining genres, I offer an account of transgender YA memoir at two key periods of the genre's development that draws on the methods of peritextual and textual analysis already established in other chapters' examinations of fictional texts. As McAlister argues, when "the industry and the marketplace develop, so too do the conventions of texts in a given genre" (2). My analysis considers how the conventions of transgender YA memoirs have shifted in response to their changing sociocultural, multimedia contexts, finding an increased emphasis on the needs of transgender teenagers.

In the first section, I give a snapshot that spans 2014 through 2016 and explores the overlaps between Andrews's, Hill's, and Jennings's memoirs and transgender autobiographies for adults, arguing that these young adult memoirists and their cisgender cowriters have narrativized the transgender journey in ways that offer intriguing stories of difference. I suggest that, while they are most clearly pitched to a mainstream audience, these texts' introspective accounts of trans-ness can implicitly function to guide trans teenagers. In the second section, I give a snapshot from 2017 through 2020 that shows how Kergil's, Bertie's, and McKenna's memoirs are more clearly influenced by, built within, and marketed through contemporary digital transgender youth cultures and offer more explicit guidance to an implied transgender readership. In the third section, I use the representative example of "the haircut"[3] to further argue that transgender YA memoirs have increasingly prioritized mentorship, functioning to guide, educate, and mentor transgender teenagers in ways that emulate the memoirists' YouTube content.[4]

Online spaces, such as YouTube, that have gained popularity in recent years have had a significant impact on transgender teenagers' access to information and supportive communities, radically altering "the forms of selfhood and connectedness available to queer adolescents" (McCallum and Tuhkanen 11). As Bittner suggests, YouTube is the space "where many young trans individuals began to document their experiences of transition, since they lacked access to the realm of mainstream publishing" ("Trans and Nonbinary Teen Voices and Memoir" 48). Online spaces have also impacted more traditional modes of publishing. In "Oversharing on and off the Internet: Crossing from Digital to Print (and Back) in Young Adult Works Authored by YouTube Stars," Rachel L. Rickard Rebellino investigates how online conventions have shaped a recent corpus of YA memoirs written or co-written by YouTube celebrities and highlights "converging and diverging roles of connectivity and intimacy across media platforms" (22). My findings confirm Rebellino's argument, and they also tell us something more specific about how transgender YouTube conventions, as well as broader online trends, have shaped the self-authorship of transgender adolescent identities in traditionally published YA transgender memoirs. Transgender YA memoirs have increasingly brought together traditional and nontraditional forms of trans authorship. As I will show, the genre is expanding the boundaries of trans representation in YA literature by creating connections with digital transgender youth culture and appealing to transgender young people who engage with trans stories in online spaces.

Some Assembly Required, Rethinking Normal, Being Jazz, and the Legacy of Transgender Life Writing for Adults

Transgender autobiographical writing for, and by, adults dates back at least as far as Lili Elbe's posthumous 1933 autobiography, *Man into Woman: The First Sex Change,* and continues to be published with regularity. With the exception of the 1940s, transgender autobiographies (or transsexual autobiographies) have been published in every decade since, including Roberta Cowell's *Roberta Cowell's Story by Herself* (1954), Christine Jorgensen's *Christine Jorgensen: A Personal Autobiography* (1967), Jan Morris's *Conundrum* (1974), Renee Richards's (and John Ames's) *Second Serve: The Renee Richards Story* (1983), Leslie Feinberg's *Stone Butch Blues* (1993), Jennifer Finney Boylan's *She's Not There: A Life in Two Genders* (2003), and Juliet Jacques's *Trans: A Memoir* (2015).[5] These are only a sample of a far larger corpus, as autobiography is the genre of adult literature in which transgender representation has been most prominent. As Colby Gordon pithily notes, "trans people have a genre problem: we are trapped in memoir" (195).[6] Transgender adolescents are not "trapped in memoir." To the contrary, fictional depictions of trans young people are far more common that autobiographical depictions, likely due to both the dominance of adult authorship in the YA market and the tendency to represent marginalized identities in problem novels. Transgender YA memoirs emerged as a much later contribution to the market, at a time when demands for transgender representation were growing. These memoirs have a theoretically separate adolescent readership from adult autobiography, but they nevertheless operate within this broader context of transgender life writing.

In *Second Skins: The Body Narratives of Sexuality* (1998), Jay Prosser used a corpus of fifty texts published between 1954 and 1996 to show transgender autobiography as having an "archetypal story structured around shared tropes and fulfilling a particular narrative organization of consecutive stages" (101). Prosser noted tropes including the representation of "strong, early, and persistent transgendered identification" (101), the use of wrong-body discourse (104), and the portrayal of transgender identity as a journey (116). He identified the consecutive stages of this journey as "suffering and confusion; the epiphany of self-discovery; corporeal and social transformation/ conversion; and finally the arrival 'home'—the reassignment" (Prosser 101). Prosser attributed these conventions to the fact that autobiographical accounts have traditionally reproduced or reflected the narrative demanded by medical gatekeepers, who have historically been cisgender men: "[T]he autobiographical act for the transsexual begins even before the published autobiography—namely, in the clinician's office where, in order to be diagnosed as transsexual, s/he must recount a transsexual autobiography" (101). Published autobiographies thus played an important role in enabling transgender people's access to medical treatment: they provided a "narrative map" for "the subject's self-construction as transsexual" (124) that adhered to the medical discourses controlled by cisgender clinicians, and some included "support/group medical help telephone numbers" (125). Prosser's 1998 analysis inevitably does not take into account more recent transgender autobiographies that have disrupted this archetype (see, for example, Evan Vipond's "Becoming Culturally [Un]intelligible: Exploring the Terrain of Trans Life Writing" [2018]), but it nevertheless offers valuable insights into transgender autobiography as a formative genre.

At the same time as providing a "narrative map" for trans readers, these autobiographies have presented intriguing accounts of trans-ness to a mainstream audience. Vipond points out that many popular adult transgender memoirs are "considered mainstream" because they have been "published by well-established publishing houses and are marketed to the general (read: cisgender) public" ("Becoming Culturally [Un]Intelligible" 20). A consequence of such marketing is that "trans life writing continues to be read as an exotic journey of transformation" (Vipond 29). Joanne Meyerowitz makes similar observations in her analysis of Jorgenson's memoir. In addition to opening up identification possibilities for transgender readers, she argues, *Christine Jorgenson* "offered an exoticized travelogue for armchair tourists who had never imagined that one could take a journey across the sex divide" (2). This is, in fact, how transgender life writing was explicitly pitched to readers of the 2005 anthology *Sexual Metamorphosis: An Anthology of Transsexual Memoirs* by editor Jonathan Ames (not to be confused with John Ames, coauthor of *Second Serve*, mentioned above). Ames's introduction suggests that the accounts featured in the anthology "hold the appeal of an adventurer's tale: someone who has gone where you, the reader, will never go—the Amazon, Mount Everest, a change of sex—but you'd like to hear about it" (xiv). The texts that established autobiographical transgender writing as a genre in the adult book market are often marketed to curious, mainstream readers, even as their implied readers include transgender people seeking reflections of their lived experiences.

Some Assembly Required, Rethinking Normal, and Being Jazz occupied a comparable space in the YA book market when they were published in the mid-2010s. In 2014, Andrews's and Hill's memoirs became the first trans memoirs to be published for an explicitly young adult readership, and their joint publication responded to a growing cultural interest in transgender young people. Christian Trimmer, senior editor for both memoirs, describes wanting to capitalize on the "cultural moment" (qtd. in Pavao n.p.) he perceived to be happening as transgender stories were making mainstream news headlines.[7] The memoirs were rushed to print in a matter of months, with professional cowriters drafted to speed the process of their production, in order to take advantage of the media attention that Andrews and Hill were receiving as a young transgender couple in Oklahoma. Articles such as the *Huffington Post*'s "Teenagers Who Swapped Genders End Up Finding Love with Each Other (PICTURES)" were fueling public interest in their stories, the advertisement of "PICTURES" presumably serving to capitalize on cisgender intrigue about transgender bodies. In the same vein, Katy Steinmetz has attributed an unusually high first print run for *Being Jazz* (150,000 copies), published two years later, to "the zeitgeist" and "the publicity machine that comes with a TLC reality show" ("Transgender Teen Star Jazz Jennings to Publish a Memoir" n.p.). The memoirs were overtly distinguished from fictional representations of trans-ness using generic cues in their titles to demonstrate their appeal as intriguing, real-life accounts. As Jonathan Gray suggests, "while genre is not a paratext it can work to paratextually frame a text" (*Show Sold Separately* 6). The subtitle of Hill's memoir ("A Memoir in Transition") and the inclusion of the "Life of" and "On Being" in the subtitles of Andrews's and Jennings's memoirs respectively signaled that they were bringing a new sort of transgender narrative to the YA book market. Though these memoirs intersected a longer history of autobiographical transgender writing for adults, the public interest in trans children and adolescents undoubtedly contributed to the memoirs' commission and publication at that time.

Megan Paslawski suggests that "the mainstream visibility of transgender youth is probably the biggest change that the millennial status quo has to offer" (110), and these YA memoirs are presented as inside stories about growing up transgender in near-contemporary society. The opening to Jennings's memoir declares: "[E]ver since I could form coherent thoughts, I knew I was a girl trapped inside a boy's body" (1). To a similar effect, Hill's memoir suggests: "[F]rom the age of two, I knew that something with my body was off. I couldn't explain why, but I was certain that my penis was not supposed to be there" (36). In a more playful memory of his childhood gender identification, Andrews describes modelling with Play-Doh, and the snake he originally made "started to take on another familiar form. [He] stuck a round ball on the tip and walked up to the mirror, holding it between [his] legs. *That's more like it*, [he] thought" (30). These wrong-body scenes function in *Some Assembly Required*, *Rethinking Normal*, and *Being Jazz* to position the memoirists' gender embodiments as unusual and remarkable, yet comprehensible, to mainstream readers. The representation of early childhood experiences is arguably expected in YA memoirs because the teens have evidently become aware of their trans-ness in time to have (and narrate) the experiences portrayed in their memoirs. While adult memoirists are often "distanced [from childhood] to such an extent that there can be questions about accuracy and the influence of nostalgia in such recollections" (Bittner, "Trans and Nonbinary Teen Voices and Memoir" 44), the close proximity of young adult memoirists to their childhood and adolescent experiences promises to bring a new vantage point to the market.

These memoirs foreground the most sensational and seemingly interesting (i.e. nonnormative) of the popular young people's real-life transgender journeys. This begins from the peritextual materials which, as we saw in chapter 2, are pivotal in creating an identity for the book and the author. Memoir is, after all, "a way to construct, package, and market identity so that others will want to buy it" (Rak, *Boom!* 7). The peritextual materials of the memoirs advertise the texts in ways that capitalize on intrigue and the promise of revelation as a means of enticing readers, a promise that is made by implying a close relationship between the memoir and memoirist. Philippe Lejeune's theorization of an "autobiographical pact" reads autobiographical writing as "a contract of identity [. . .] sealed by a proper name" (6). Lejeune differentiates autobiography (or rather, life writing as opposed to fiction) as a type of literature that promises the author and narrator are one and the same. In doing so, the pact positions life writing as a referential genre, one that claims "to provide information about a 'reality' exterior to the text" (Lejeune 6). Therein lies the danger, for Lejeune, because the reader of life writing can become convinced by the "games of illusion and not see through the transparent veils that cover the production of the text" (194); not notice that the author is "responsible for his writing as he is for his life" (194). Lejeune's pact has been described as "the most often quoted and hotly debated in autobiographical criticism" (Broughton 15), and Lejeune himself eventually came to think of the definition of "autobiography" within his work as "a 'definition' of dogmatic appearance, with a rather uncertain theoretical status" (Lejeune 120). Nevertheless, for my purposes, the pact usefully opens up the question of how the memoirist's name, and identity more broadly, functions among the peritextual elements to construct an identity for the text.

Lejeune pictured the author's (and narrator's) name as a feature of the peritext that connects the text with the world: "[T]he author is not just a person, he is a person who writes and publishes. With one foot in the text, and one outside, he is the point of contact between the two" (200). The author/narrator's name appears then to anchor the text to the author's lived experiences in the "real" (nontextual) world for a potential reader. Each of the memoirs portrays the transgender young adult as the sole author and includes their name prominently on the book cover. In addition, Andrews's and Jennings's include "a transgender teen" within their full titles, and Jennings's title also includes Jennings (Jazz) by name. Though it is in no way unusual for a memoirist to be featured prominently in their memoir's packaging—making a clear and visible connection between the memoir and the memoirist is, in fact, an often-used "promotional lure" (Sutton 3)—the identities of the popular trans young adults, which have already been commodified by the mainstream media, are further commodified to market these stories. The connection between the text and the memoirist's identity functions in such a way that readers might feel they are accessing an intriguing, inside story, in spite of the fact that the texts have been co-written by professional writers, whose names are absent from these memoirs' outer materials.

To the same end, the packaging of all three memoirs employs similar themes of truth, transformation, and sensationalism to appeal to readers. The back cover of Andrews's memoir advertises it as a "first-of-its-kind memoir," in which, "in his captivatingly witty, honest voice, Arin reveals the challenges he faced as a boy in a girl's body. [. . .] *Some Assembly Required* is a true coming-of-age story" (n.p.). The back cover of Hill's memoir describes it as a "first-person account [in which] Katie reflects on her pain-filled childhood and the events leading up to the life-changing decision to undergo gender reassignment surgery as a teenager," all of which is "told in an unwaveringly honest voice" (n.p.). The inside cover of *Being Jazz* labels it a "remarkable memoir" that shows Jennings "navigating the physical, social, and emotional upheavals of adolescence, made even more complicated by the unique challenges of being transgender." The language used across these materials—including "captivatingly," "honest," "reveals," "true," "first-person," "life-changing," "remarkable," "unique"—emphasizes the sensational and exceptional qualities of Andrews's Hill's, and Jennings's memoirs. In this sense, the memoirs are what Julie Rak would call "unusual accounts packaged for mainstream audiences" ("Memoir, Truthiness" 228), signaling the publishers' intentions to attract cisgender readers.

The peritexts emphasize that the three texts offer authentic, real-life accounts to set them apart from fictional representations of trans-ness in the mainstream book market, which were exclusively written by cisgender authors until 2016 (despite the fact that the memoirists' cowriters are also assumed to be cisgender). Though the peritextual materials' emphasis on intrigue speaks most clearly to a mainstream readership, the opportunity to encounter and explore trans-ness through first-hand accounts may be of most interest to transgender readers and their allies, who can approach these YA memoirs as "roadmap[s]" to help them grow (Paslawski 114). For example, these YA memoirs' backmatter includes additional resources that may be helpful to transgender readers (reminiscent of the "support group/medical help telephone numbers" [Prosser 125] included in some adult autobiographies). Bittner suggests that YA memoirs can provide "vital space for young trans people to safely explore their own identity and development" and function as "powerful tool[s]" to build "greater knowledge of gender and sexualities outside of cisnormative curricula and media representations" ("Trans and Nonbinary Teen Voices and Memoir" 56). Later publications make this trend more explicit: the following section indicates that mentorship and guidance have become more established in the peritextual and textual conventions of the most recent trans YA memoirs. Yet, in creating introspective accounts of Andrews's, Hill's, and Jennings's experiences and packaging them for mainstream audiences, these earlier memoirs, like the archetypal adult autobiographies, nevertheless offer practical information to transgender readers.

For example, scenes in *Some Assembly Required* and *Rethinking Normal* that show the memoirists learning about trans-ness convey the important role that online information played in the memoirists' self-discoveries when they were young teenagers and function implicitly to give readers information and/or hints regarding how to conduct additional independent research. Hill recalls her research process during attempts to identify and understand her gender identity, and she and her cowriter construct a sensationalized, triumphant scene in which Hill first learns about trans-ness. After several attempts to "Google for answers" to no avail, "one cold night in January when [she] was fifteen, it happened" (Hill 87). Hill "sat down and typed the usual, 'I feel like I'm a girl trapped in a boy's body,' and this time [she] was greeted with something new" (87). Hill recalls her first encounter with "the magical word: transgender," reading it in an article called "I'm a Girl—Understanding Transgender Children" (87). The article—written about Jazz Jennings—showed Hill that she was not alone and led her to "other transgender stories" from which she "learned that there were actually thousands" (Hill 87) of trans people. As Dawn Latta Kirby and Dan Kirby have observed of other twenty-first-century memoirs, *Rethinking Normal* "resides at the intersection of narration and reflection, of storytelling and exposition [...] employ[ing] the techniques of fiction" (24). Scene-setting details, such as it being a "cold night in January," are interlaced with practical information regarding the search terms Hill used and the resources she discovered. Hill's reference to Jennings reinforces the popularity of the "exceptional" (Bittner, "Trans and Nonbinary Teen Voices and Memoir" 44) teenager, but it also signals the important role that other transgender people have had in the memoirists' lives and preempts a more explicit emphasis on community building that comes to the fore in later memoirs.

Some Assembly Required creates a comparable opportunity for trans readers to infer information and guidance from its introspective account. Andrews recalls "deciding to do some research, hoping to find someone—anyone—who had the same sorts of dreams and feelings" (87). Andrews "knew that 'LGBT' was the phrase to search for to find the smart, personal stories, as opposed to just typing in 'gay' and getting hundreds of videos of pretty boys lip-synching to pop songs in their bedrooms" (87). Though *Some Assembly Required* does not problematize the stereotypical association between "gay" and "pretty boys," it nevertheless offers teenagers tips for their own online searches. In another intertextual reference that operates in the same way as the earlier example from Hill's memoir, Andrews encounters a YouTube video made by Skylar Kergil—"a guy with short, tousled blonde hair" (88). The memoir suggests that Kergil's video stood as a representative of his own identity. For Andrews, Kergil was "what I wanted to be. He was who I *was*. He even had the same haircut I fantasized about" (88). In this scene, Kergil's video not only fuels Andrews's own desire for short hair but is also a catalyst for Andrews's realization that he, too, is transgender. After Andrews's discovery of Kergil's video journal introduced the concept of trans-ness to him, his searches became more focused on transgender identity:

> I blew up Google that night, researching everything I could about being transgender, and with everything I read, I clicked a mental check mark next to every question I'd ever had about myself. [. . .] It's hard to describe what it all actually felt like. I imagine it's sort of similar to having some horrible disease for years, and then one day your doctor calls you and says, "We found the cure!" [. . .] I was bursting with new information, priceless information that finally explained everything that was wrong with me. [. . .] I now had a clear set of steps that could help guide me to becoming the person I knew I was." (89)

Andrews and his cowriter's attempt to capture "what it all actually felt like" for Andrews to make this discovery of trans-ness with the more culturally recognizable metaphor of illness presumes a cisgender reader, creating the sense of an "exoticized travelogue for armchair tourists" in much the same way as earlier adult autobiographical texts. The comparison of trans-ness to a "horrible disease" and research to "the cure" also repeats the problematic trope of presenting trans-ness as a resolvable issue, popularized in YA fiction by cisgender-authored problem novels to explain trans-ness to a mainstream audience. At the same time, transgender readers are able to gather information from Andrews's experiences. The memoir implies that online research will yield "priceless information" to enable readers to identify their own "set of steps" for transition and offers hints regarding what sorts of searches and resources proved most useful to Andrews. The inward-looking account of Andrews's experiences can tacitly serve the educational needs of transgender teenagers.

As I have shown, trans YA memoirs intersect with a longer history of trans autobiographical writing for adults, and the overlaps between the two indicate shared positions and functions within their respective book markets. The peritextual and textual conventions of *Some Assembly Required*, *Rethinking Normal*, and *Being Jazz* suggest they are broadly pitched to mainstream readerships, but they nonetheless invite an implied transgender reader to search for representation and guidance within their introspective narratives. The diachronic approach taken in this chapter is underpinned by the fact that "genres are not stable categories, but are endlessly evolving and shifting signifiers" (McAlister 4), and the memoirs I discuss in the following section reveal significant developments. With the publication of *Before I Had the Words*, *Trans Mission*, and *Out!*, transgender YA memoirs have become increasingly connected to the multimedia landscape of online transgender youth culture and have more explicitly focused on offering community and mentorship to guide transgender teen readers through the obstacles frequently faced during transgender adolescence.

Before I Had the Words, *Trans Mission*, *Out!*, and Digital Transgender Youth Culture

In "Theory Rises, Maginot Line Endures," Caroline Hunt argues for the necessity of taking "a broader view of 'reading'" (210) to reflect how teenagers read. Hunt suggests that "for many educators and cultural critics, 'reading' evidently means 'reading the classics'—in print form," but that digital reading practices are posing a challenge to that view (210). Open access online spaces, such as YouTube, blogs, and social media platforms, have allowed transgender young people to self-publish details regarding their lives and, particularly, their gender transitions while "bypass[ing] traditional modes of publishing" (Douglas and Poletti 24). With the growing popularity of nontraditional modes of online authorship, Rebellino argues that YA literature critics "must also be willing to wade into the constantly shifting digital stream of texts and to explore the fascinating symbiotic relationship between traditional print literature and digital youth culture" (30). Recent trans YA memoirs have developed from earlier texts by bringing together traditional and digital modes of authorship.

Kergil's, Bertie's, and McKenna's memoirs replicate the experience of engaging with their YouTube channels in myriad ways, creating what Henry Jenkins might call "transmedia storytelling" ("Transmedia Storytelling" n.p.). The concept of "transmedia storytelling" describes "a process where integral elements of a fiction get dispersed systematically across multiple delivery channels for the purpose of creating a unified and coordinated entertainment experience" (H. Jenkins, "Transmedia Storytelling" n.p.). Through the creation of multiple points of entry into a narrative world, such as narratives that are spread across comics, TV series, and films, transmedia storytelling practices can expand potential engagement. Jenkins's concept refers to fictional narratives, but similar ideas can be applied to nonfiction. For example, Rebellino suggests that a new genre of YouTube memoir—memoirs written or cowritten by YouTube celebrities—offers readers and viewers multiple means of engaging with the creators' lives and stories. She suggests that "YouTube memoirs seem intentionally created to connect an author's print book to her or his online presence" (Rebellino 23). These recent transgender YA memoirs can also be considered YouTube memoirs, but I want to nuance Rebellino's conclusions by considering how, and to what effect, Kergil's, Bertie's, and McKenna's memoirs emulate the sorts of storytelling devices that specifically typify trans YouTube vlogs.

Although YouTube vlogs are not the only form of autobiographical digital content made by transgender teenagers, they are the form most closely connected with the transgender young adult memoirists. According to Matthew G. O'Neill, "trans youth have a need for artistic expression, and YouTube offers a valuable performance and discursive space" (36). In fact, Laura Horak notes that YouTube has "almost singlehandedly transformed the trans mediascape" (575) in the twenty-first century. Trans content on YouTube, particularly transition vlogs (video diaries that relate to a transgender person's transition), have "strong conventions" (Horak 574) that make their format recognizable, easy to recreate, and quick to circulate. The creators usually sit in front of the camera and deliver a first-person, direct address to their audience and often include retrospective images that are designed to demonstrate progress in their physical gender transitions (Horak 572–72). In these vlogs, teenagers frequently "list their current physical changes and current state of mind" and "track and archive transition as a bodily and psychosocial process" (Raun 368). Though there are inevitable differences between video media and written texts, each of the memoirs includes conventions that provide connections to the memoirist's own YouTube content in an effort to recreate the structure of YouTube storytelling that has already proven its appeal to transgender young adult audiences.

For instance, the chapter structure of Kergil's *Before I Had the Words* signals an effort to replicate the episodic format of Kergil's YouTube channel, Skylarkeleven. *Before I Had the Words* comprises a series of sixty-three short chapters, plus additional materials that include conversations with Kergil's mother, father, and brother. The chapters are a mix of prose, poems, and journal entries, and they share brief insights into Kergil's childhood, adolescence, and feelings at the time of writing, including "Speaking" (1–3), "You Can Call Me Mike!" (4–5), "Not Twins, but Close" (6–8), "Cross Country Doesn't Feel Super Far (When You're Six)" (9–10), and "Cool Bike, Yo" (11–15). Eschewing the more developed, polished narrative structure of Andrews's, Hill's, and Jennings's memoirs in favor of brief and varied chapters, Kergil's memoir mimics the type of engagement that his YouTube channel fosters. On Skylarkeleven, transition vlogs such as "two years on testosterone—changes & reflections," "march seventh—transitional update," "two years post top surgery," and "37 days post hysterectomy update" are included alongside less transition-focused content. Conversations between Kergil and his mother ("Q&A: MOM & TRANSGENDER SON"), music cover videos (e.g. "i'll be yr bird—m. ward cover" and "Say Yes—Elliot Smith [cover]"), and videos relating to Kergil's life ("Tiger's morning attitude," for example, is a thirty-six-second-long video clip of Kergil and his cat) are interspersed among his more transgender-specific content. The structure encourages readers to move quickly from chapter to chapter, mimicking the interaction with multiple short clips on YouTube. *Before I Had the Words* spreads Kergil's storytelling style across platforms and, as such, offers multiple avenues for transgender young people to engage with Kergil's life.

Bertie's memoir also emulates the conventions of YouTube transition vlogs that he and other transgender people have created. A number of YouTube videos from Bertie's channel (TheRealAlexBertie) demonstrate how Bertie's body had changed as a result of hormone treatment: "1 MONTH ON T!," "2 MONTHS ON T," "3 MONTHS ON T," "5 MONTHS ON T," "1 YEAR ON T: FTM TRANSGENDER," "TRANSGENDER: 2 YEARS ON TESTOSTERONE." They do so using a popular temporal framing in transition vlogs that Horak has dubbed "hormone time" (579)—a system of time that is "linear and teleological, directed toward the end of living full time in the desired gender" (580)—as their organizational format. It is unsurprising that "hormone time" has found relevance in YA memoirs considering the parallels between "hormone time" and the construction of adolescence as a period defined by "growth towards the ultimate goal of maturity" (Waller, *Constructing Adolescence in Fantastic Realism* 1). Chapter 1 argued that both trans-ness and adolescence are characterized by liminality, in-between-ness, and a sense of journeying towards a preconceived destination, where "[a]dolescence bears the ideological weight of all transitory and contingent moments of self-making so that adulthood can represent a final arrival at selfhood" (Owen, "Adolescence, Trans Phenomena" 563). In hormone time—as in adolescence—"time begins with a moment of rupture and points in a particular direction," focused as it is on "progressive change" (Horak 580). The passages in *Trans Mission* that give details of how Bertie's body changed as a result of him receiving testosterone treatment similarly employ the number of months since his treatment began as a storytelling framework: "[A]fter two months [menstruation] stopped (174), "within three months my voice had deepened" (174), "between four and six months on testosterone, I noticed [. . .] that I had gained weight" (175). At the same time as being aligned with the developmental trajectory of YA narratives, the structural allusions in *Trans Mission* to the format of Bertie's YouTube videos reveal an effort to tap into the storytelling conventions that engage viewers of his and others' transition vlogs.

The visual formatting of *Trans Mission* is also pivotal in creating cross-media connections. Nonfiction literature for young people often contains illustrated material (Coats, *The Bloomsbury Introduction* 292), but Bertie's memoir contains more visually creative ways of communicating than previous transgender YA memoirs. As a standard feature of the memoir form, the three earlier titles include autobiographical images. Andrews's and Hill's memoirs include small black-and-white photographs of the memoirists through childhood and adolescence on the first page of each chapter, Jennings's memoir includes photo collages of her childhood and adolescence as glossy inserts, and, similarly, *Trans Mission* includes childhood photographs of Bertie. Whereas the narratives of earlier memoirs are formatted in standard prose, *Trans Mission* employs illustrations and creative methods of presenting the text that hint at a desire to recreate Bertie's dynamic personality on the page. With the exception of its cover material, *Trans Mission* is printed in black and white (the costs of color printing perhaps played a part in this decision). The text is frequently enlarged, emboldened, and makes use of different fonts; paragraphs are more dynamically presented on the page when compared with standard prose texts; and black doodled illustrations decorate the pages, thematically designed to complement the narrative. For example, *Trans Mission*'s chapter on Bertie's childhood begins with the emboldened claim that "[a]s kids, nobody cared about who you were or what you wore," followed by paragraphs of text overlayed on a doodle of a dress.

The multimodal formatting weaves together text and illustration to reflect Bertie's dynamic YouTube personality and create a visually engaging reading experience for teenager readers who "live in an image-saturated culture" (Coats, *The Bloomsbury Introduction* 167). As Rebellino suggests, "the frequency with which the format of YouTube memoirs veers towards the non-traditional implies a pervasive belief that print, prose text needs augmentation to connect with readers" (23). *Trans Mission* was published by Wren & Rook, a nonfiction children's and YA literature imprint of Hachette that is dedicated to a visually creative collection of "personality-led" titles.[8] Publishing operations like these are recognizing and responding to young people's growth as "both critical consumers of images as well as prosumers—that is, people who produce and promote, rather than just consume, visual media through social networks" (Coats, *The Bloomsbury Introduction* 167).

The format of McKenna's *Out!* also recreates the experience of engaging with McKenna's online content. *Out!* has also been published by a house that specializes in illustrated books (ABRAMS) and, unlike any other of the trans YA memoirs, McKenna's memoir favors visually creative ways of communicating over elongated prose chapters. Included in McKenna's memoir are full-color photographs, graphics, doodles, replications of personal materials (such as handwritten notes), and a gallery of fan art that create a diverse range of content for readers to access, evoking the "seemingly endless variety" (Rebellino 23) that the internet has to offer.

The visual similarities between McKenna's channel and his printed text—bright colors, quirky graphics—portray *Out!* as an extension of the earlier, popular YouTube content, capitalizing on the recognizable and multimedia branding that has already been proven (by the popularity of McKenna's online content) to attract and engage a teenage audience. For instance, the repeated contrast of colored and emboldened font within black, standard text creates a dynamic voice for McKenna as narrator, playing with the reading experience in ways that, like Bertie's memoir, attempt to capture the exuberant and animated personality that can be seen in his YouTube content. Rebellino suggests that memoirs by popular YouTubers, such as Tyler Oakley, Jenn McAllister, and Shane Dawson, "attempt to capture the 'feel' of their online personalities through formatting reminiscent of digital content and an overarching tone fitting with a YouTuber's particular brand" (23), and the same can be said of the formatting choices made in McKenna's memoir. The influence of YouTube celebrities and their digital content has shaped the trans YA memoir in ways that signal a shift in the genre's function.

The latest texts attempt to connect with, and address, an implied transgender teenage reader by engaging in a process of intentional community making between trans teenagers that builds on the ethos of the memoirists' YouTube channels. For example, Horak points out how "the YouTube talking head"—the digital framing used by Kergil, Bertie, and McKenna in their vlogs—"brings trans individuals close to the viewer, both in seeming physical proximity and feelings of intimacy" (576). As print extensions of the YouTube content created by Kergil, Bertie, and McKenna, the memoirs construct narrative intimacy by creating the perception of a close relationship between memoirist and reader. Aidan Chambers argues that "the child, finding within the book an implied author whom he can befriend because he is of the tribe of childhood as well, is thus wooed into the book" ("The Reader in the Book" 7). While the concept of "befriending" most often lends itself to considerations of how power operates in adult-child relationships between author and reader, it also usefully opens up interesting ways of thinking about the narrative intimacy that is created when the actual author and the implied author are one and the same, and the gaps between reader and author are narrowed. Kergil's, Bertie's, and McKenna's memoirs are self-authored, forming as intimate of a connection between author and reader as is feasible in traditional publishing (owing to the collaboration of editors, publishers, and other industry professionals), and the memoirists are also closer in age to their intended readership than is often the case in YA literature. In this regard, *Before I Had the Words*, *Trans Mission*, and *Out!* are designed to appeal to and "befriend" transgender teenagers seeking community, perhaps especially teenagers who are already familiar with the memoirists' online content. Compared with earlier, cowritten transgender memoirs pitched to a mainstream audience, these recent titles have driven a shift towards an implied transgender readership by blending conventions from digital transgender youth culture into traditionally published texts.

The popularity of Kergil's, Bertie's, and McKenna's YouTube content—like YouTube vlogs more broadly—is dependent upon their ability to engage an audience. According to Liam Berriman and Rachel Thompson, success on YouTube "emerges not at the moment of production but rather accumulates through the attention of their [content creators'] audience" (11). Rachel Berryman and Misha Kavka point out that the "celebrification" of popular YouTubers is "contingent upon viewers' positive responses not only to the video content, but even more so to the YouTubers' ability to combine 'natural' self-promotion with the digital technologies of intimacy" (309). For Berryman and Kavka, "technolog[y] of intimacy" describes the feeling of intimacy created between viewer and creator that is produced by "patterns of direct address and self-revelation," among other spatial, temporal, and editing effects (309–10). Horak has similarly argued that YouTube vlogs are designed to "create a sense of intimacy between vloggers and viewers," as "trans youth creatively exploit the platform's predilections in order to author and affirm their bodies and selves, in the process generating far-flung communities of support" (573). In this regard, YouTube has provided trans teenagers with what Howard Rheingold would call a "virtual community" (4). In the YouTube community, "users seek to form friendship and find a sense of companionship. [. . .] To many of the users, contact with their peers is the most important foundation of the community" (Rotman and Preece 325). While Andrews's, Hill's, and Jennings's memoirs are more clearly pitched to a mainstream audience, Kergil's, Bertie's, and McKenna's narratives signal an intended transgender reader by recreating the communities of support that typify digital transgender youth culture.

These memoirs create communities by reflecting on the memoirists' experiences of online communities and linking those experiences to their motivation for writing. For example, Kergil describes starting his YouTube channel as "speaking into my camera as if there might be someone listening," remarking that "YouTube gave me a community when I needed one" (154–55). Kergil then describes *Before I Had the Words* as "a reflection of my experiences that I wish I could have shown my younger self back then. [. . .] I finished writing this book for the transgender youth who have contacted me over the years" (viii). To a similar effect, Bertie explains: "my [YouTube] channel has gained a bigger following than I ever imagined, and it's become my passion to share my transition story. Nothing will ever beat the feeling I get when I'm approached by someone saying my videos have helped them" (11). Bertie links the desire to help others with his decision to widely share his transition story, naming his memoir as "the first time [he has] ever put out [his] story from start to finish" (11), a feat which differs from the fragmented, rolling nature of digital content including YouTube videos.

McKenna's memoir goes even further in positioning the memoir as a textual community for the benefit of transgender readers. McKenna explains that his YouTube channel became his "safe space" and that it is "because of the Internet" that he could "communicate with hundreds of thousands of other edgy teens" (60). McKenna invites readers of the book to "think of [him] like an older sibling, mentor, fairy godbrother, or, if you're willing, a member of your chosen family" (4). The framing of McKenna's authorial identity in this way acknowledges the complex and, at times, problematic relationship that chapter 4 suggested trans teenagers often have with their biological families by offering trans teenagers alternative forms of connection. The subtitle of *Out!—How to Be Your Authentic Self*—similarly implies that the memoir is particularly attuned to the anticipated needs of transgender readers, which McKenna has explicitly identified to be community and mentorship. These recent memoirs' attention to transgender readers has transformed the genre of transgender YA memoir, moving away from introspective accounts of individual experiences towards community-focused texts that reflect how young people are engaging with transgender stories online.

Transgender Young Adult Memoirs and the Textual Guide to The Haircut

As I suggested in chapter 3's discussion of speculative texts, Coats's concept of the distorted mirror stresses the "important function" that literary texts have in allowing readers to "reflect" on their own lives by "fram[ing] experiences and situations and offer[ing] them back to us for analysis and contemplation": "they reflect in their ways so that we can reflect in ours" (*The Bloomsbury Introduction* 2), she argues. A defining feature of trans YA memoirs, compared to trans YA fiction, is that they seemingly represent the real "experiences and situations" of transgender teenagers for readers to explore (albeit through mediated narratives). The most recent trans memoirs perform this reflective function, but they also surpass it by explicitly directing readers to take action in their own lives. The haircut serves as a useful example to unpack how this new convention of overt literary mentorship operates, and it does so for three reasons. First, the haircut trope lends itself particularly well to YA literature because haircuts are considered both accessible and affordable. Second, hairstyles are deemed an important and immediately obvious signifier when either constructing or interpreting identity. Third, the haircut is prominent within the transgender community as a means of embodying masculinity. Haircutting is among the "technologies" masculine transgender people use to "reflect and solidify their internal senses of self" (Farber 11). As we will see, recollections of the memoirists' own haircuts are used as the basis for overt guidance addressed to an implied transgender readership.

In his memoir, Kergil explains that his desire for short hair had been "brewing" for a long time (49) but that his small-town US environment made short hair feel unachievable for an ostensibly female body. Bertie refers to how "short hair is often seen by society as more masculine" to explain his disassociation with his own long hair: "for 14 years I had long, straight, ash blonde hair down to my butt. My mum loved it and it even made people a little jealous, but fuck, I hated it" (57). McKenna's memoir takes a more nuanced approach, articulating how McKenna's relationship with his hair as a child and adolescent was complex and bewildering at times. He explains, "[T]he reason why I wanted it short wasn't clear to me for the longest time when I was a kid. I just didn't have the language to know I was a boy or that I was trans" (144). McKenna continues:

> It was super confusing navigating my personal style as a teenager while also caring about what people thought (because I was a teenager). I was constantly complimented on how my hair looked "so pretty," which made my desire to cut my hair even more confusing for a teen who really wanted to feel good and fit in. What if I was making a mistake? A part of me acknowledges today that it is just hair and it's ridiculous that so many people have opinions on how someone else looks. If anything, it's the one area that should be easiest for us to play with, but straying from what everyone else in your community is doing or saying can be hard. (144–45)

McKenna's uncertainty, underscored by the rhetorical question signaling his teenage doubt, emphasizes the challenges of navigating being both transgender and adolescent in a cisnormative society. The benefit of hindsight allows McKenna to recognize the influencing power of social norms that, as a teenager, he was only aware of via their impact on his feelings. Hair "occupies an extraordinary position, mediating between the natural and cultural" (Rosenthal 1): it is often (though not always) a natural material, but grooming practices are culturally constructed and are not as bound to biological sex as other markers. Hair theorist Anthony Synnott argues that "[male] gender identity is usually not that tangled up with head hair" (105), but, whether or not this is usually the case, it is clear that the hair and the male gender identities of the transgender memoirists are very much entangled (as we have also seen in Andrews's encounter with Kergil's YouTube vlog that I discussed earlier). The haircut exemplifies a way of navigating the emotional and practical challenges that gender dysphoria can cause for transgender teenagers.

For each of the memoirists, the haircut represents a significant moment in their personal transgender journeys. In *Before I Had the Words*, Kergil recalls being "transformed in a way that [he] can't articulate" as the hairdresser "began to chop away bits and pieces" (50), feeling "a quite literal weight being lifted" (50). Kergil suggests that "the way that hair alludes to gender, the way that hair frames and changes a face, [and] the way that others would comment on [his] hair—all of these things changed in an instant" (50) when he had his first masculine haircut. In *Trans Mission*, Bertie's hair was "separated into ponytails and chopped off one by one" (59), also bringing about a feeling of physical and emotional weightlessness that heightens the intensity of the haircut. Bertie was "amazed at how light it felt" (59), suggesting "it was almost like taking a mask off to reveal what had been underneath the whole time.

You could finally see *me*" (59). In *Out!*, McKenna was "surprisingly emotional" when he "ended up getting 'the big haircut'" because it was "as if I looked in the mirror and actually saw myself for the first time" (145). The importance of the haircut to the memoirists is emphasized by the satisfaction its descriptions are designed to cause for readers. These extracts create a similar effect to that of transition videos, which generate spectacularism with images of drastic aesthetic material change. As Horak observes, "transition videos have become particularly popular because they also exploit the platform's inclination for the spectacular" (576). Videos containing retrospective slideshows and time-lapses create "temporal compression," meaning "trans bodies morph as if by magic, drawn inexorably toward their felt gender" (Horak 578). These haircut scenes similarly work to show the memoirists taking a sudden and tangible step towards embodying their male identities.

Casting themselves as older, wiser mentor figures, Bertie and McKenna then deliver explicit advice to their intended transgender readership regarding their own haircuts. Bertie explains that "other trans guys ask me how to approach their first 'male' haircut all the time" (61), assuring transgender readers of his authority and knowledge of the topic based on his role within his online community. Bertie admits that "talking to the hairdresser can be daunting" (61) and offers readers a "pro tip" (61). While Bertie positions himself as the "pro," the implied reader is represented by this rhetoric as an inexperienced trans teen who has not yet had the haircut. Bertie recommends readers find pictures of the types of haircut they would like and suggests that "getting your haircut is almost like ordering a fancy coffee. You can be as simple or precise as you like, so long as you know what to say" (61–62). The comparison, further stressed by its emboldened repetition in a stylized font occupying the whole of the following page, implies that Bertie *does* know what to say. He tells readers about hair being "measured in 'grades,' with grade one being short and grade eight being slightly longer" (61), likening it to "knowing your shoe size" (61). The relationship with the implied trans reader that Bertie creates is one of polar opposites: experienced/unexperienced, wise/naïve, knowing/unknowing, knowledgeable/unknowledgeable.

To an even greater extent, *Out!* translates the participatory culture of McKenna's YouTube community into print form with instructional elements aimed towards an inexperienced transgender teenager. In a distinct subsection that immediately follows the recollection of McKenna's haircutting experiences, *Out!* includes a glossy, highly illustrated, five-page-long "Guide to a Masculine Haircut" (148–53). The introductory paragraph to the guide functions to overtly position McKenna as a mentor figure and reinforce an intimate bond between him and the implied transgender reader. An excerpt of the paragraph reads:

> No matter what style your first chop is, it'll be epic. [. . .] Worst case scenario: It's a bad haircut. But a bad haircut will always grow out, and you'll know more about what you do and don't want! My advice is to always bring in a picture of the type of cut you want. [. . .] Here's a little guide to some cuts you may want to try to compliment your facial structure/vibe. (McKenna 149)

The passage creates the sense of a one-to-one connection between McKenna and the implied trans adolescent addressee. His authorial voice takes on a familiar and reassuring tone that is designed to build rapport with readers. While Mike Cadden has noted that the first-person narration of YA literature is frequently ironic, given that "novels constructed by adults to simulate an authentic adolescent's voice are inherently ironic because the so-called adolescent voice is never—and can never be—truly authentic" ("The Irony of Narration in the Young Adult Novel" 146), the self-authored memoirs offer as close to "authentic" narration as is feasible in the mainstream book market. The guide goes further than any other text I have considered in this chapter to combine personal anecdote with explicit advice to readers. The pages of the guide include a series of illustrations of different haircuts with captions that give McKenna's experiences, opinions, and/or advice about the haircut. Take, for instance, the "Mohawk" that is described as "the power move I [McKenna] wish I'd chosen for my first short haircut!" or the "Spikey Windswept Fringe" that is described as "my haircut when I add product to tame my curls!" (152). The graphic elements, combined with McKenna's captions, provide a visually creative guide to the haircut that serves to direct and shape readers' own experiences.

The haircut reveals how transgender YA memoirs are increasingly providing a private form of communication from young people who have lived the experiences their memoirs describe to young trans readers who are perhaps navigating, or may soon be navigating, similar issues and situations. Any number of examples would almost certainly yield a similar pattern of literary mentorship: a first dose of hormone therapy, changing names and pronouns, and pursuing surgical transition options are just a few of the moments that occur in the transgender YA memoirs. The most recent transgender memoirs can be read as an attempt to expand the boundaries of traditionally published trans representation with the introduction of conventions that emulate the transgender content that young people have access to online, and that they are choosing to produce themselves.

Conclusion

The genre world of the trans YA memoir has evolved significantly over its short publication history. In only six years, texts have shifted from introspective accounts of trans-ness that were cowritten with professional writers and mostly pitched to a mainstream readership, to texts in which transgender young people draw on the conventions of their own self-authored YouTube content and directly address other transgender young people to offer guidance and mentorship. Transgender representation in the YA book market can never achieve the same level of self-authorship as the YouTube vlogs that have also been produced by the memoirists because traditionally published texts are molded by adults who are inextricably implicated in their production, such as editors and publishers. Yet, this chapter has shown that trans YA memoirs have increasingly pushed the boundaries of trans YA literature by blending the conventions of traditionally and nontraditionally published forms of trans life narrative.

The diachronic picture put together in this chapter indicates that the publishing industry is becoming more receptive and responsive to transgender young people as creators and consumers of texts. As Kim Wilkins suggests, "genres are not static, ahistorical categories. Rather, genres are processes. They are formed, negotiated and reformed, both tacitly and explicitly, by the interactions of authors, readers and (importantly) institutions" ("The Process of Genre" n.p.). Technological trends and advancements continue to reshape transgender digital youth culture, and I suspect future memoirs will make different connections to this culture than those I have been able to discuss in this chapter. It will certainly be necessary to build on this chapter by looking at how the specific conventions, tropes, and community-building capacities of TikTok (and other digital innovations) shape the next snapshot of transgender YA memoirs.

CONCLUSION

A book-length exploration of trans YA literature would not have been possible twenty years ago. However, researching between 2017 and 2021, I had to be selective as to which texts to include in my analysis, due to the considerable increase in the field. Since 2004, there have been at least 140 YA texts published in the United States and the United Kingdom that feature explicit transgender representation. At least 70 YA texts include transgender protagonists, and at least 70 are written or cowritten by openly transgender authors. Trans representation has also featured in a range of genres (including contemporary realism, problem novels, fantasy, science fiction, superhero fiction, mystery, and thriller) and forms (including novel, memoir, short story, and graphic novel). Capitalizing on this growth, this book has traced shifting trends in transgender YA texts and tied them to the sociocultural moment of their publication and the changing shape of YA literature. It has also demonstrated that attention to trans people as creators and readers in the YA literature market has increased over my research period. Indeed, transgender YA literature has participated in a broader cultural recognition of both the authority of marginalized people and the importance of representing marginalized experiences in mainstream texts.

As I suggested in the introduction, the cultural relevance of conversations about inclusive literature has grown in the last few years, though the beginnings of these conversations predate this book by several decades. In 1990, children's literature scholar Rudine Sims Bishop proposed that all children need and deserve representation in literature that functions as mirrors, windows, and sliding glass doors to their own and others' lived experiences. Many subsequent calls for more diversity and inclusivity in children's and

YA literature have taken on Bishop's metaphor, advocating that marginalized young people should be able to see elements of their identities and experiences reflected in the books they read. While there is much still to be done to promote inclusivity and improve transgender visibility in the publishing industry, this book has built on earlier calls to action with a critical stance that interrogates what sorts of trans representation are available to contemporary readers. In "think[ing] more carefully about the qualities of the mirror itself" (Coats, *The Bloomsbury Introduction* 1), this book has asked not only who is represented in YA literature but also how they are represented, and by whom.

Openly cisgender authors introduced trans representation into YA literature via the problem novel. As I argued in chapter 1, acceptance arcs reinscribed trans-ness outside of what the YA texts present as "normal." This occurred in novels such as Ellen Wittlinger's *Parrotfish* (2007), Cris Beam's *I Am J* (2011), Kirstin Cronn-Mills's *Beautiful Music for Ugly Children* (2012), Kristin Elizabeth Clark's *Freakboy* (2013), and Lisa Williamson's *The Art of Being Normal* (2015). Each of these novels stressed transgender identity's divergence from cisnormative structures, even as they brought explicitly transgender characters into mainstream publishing. Catherine Butler suggested as recently as 2020 that transgender representation continues to be hamstrung by a reluctance to "move on" from tropes of "coming out, disclosure to cisgender characters, and so on" and "the educative function of such literature for cisgender readers [which] is in partial tension with its usefulness to trans readers" (7). Though much of the field is still concerned with exploring and affirming trans-ness, recent contributions have also branched out from earlier work.

This book has brought multiple developments to the fore, including shifts in the authorship, character diversity, and generic variety of transgender YA literature. For example, there have been several speculative texts published that have created alternative strategies for exploring trans issues by blending the generic conventions of the transgender problem novel with the possibilities of fantastic literature. Though few speculative texts step away from the realities of being a transgender teenager in a cisnormative society (and some, in fact, exaggerate them), Chapter 3 showed that imaginary worlds have also served to empower transgender teenagers. Imaginary worlds and the fantastic trans characters who inhabit them, such as Bells Broussard and Danielle Tozer from the superhero universes of C. B. Lee's Sidekick Squad series

(2016–2022) and April Daniels's Nemesis series (2017–) respectively, have offered transgender readers opportunities to explore themes such as identity and power through allegory and metaphor. Speculative fiction showcases different types of representation, intervening in the "horizons of expectation" (Todorov 18) that were established by early problem novels and continue to shape some existing critical impressions of trans YA literature.

The expansion of transgender representation beyond contemporary realist problem novels can be linked to broader shifts in the market demands. As I suggested in chapter 2, the We Need Diverse Books movement and the heightened visibility of transgender celebrities in the mainstream media in the mid-2010s also spurred on mainstream YA publishers to introduce and cultivate transgender authorship in their catalogs. Not uncoincidentally, many texts have since offered more intersectionality and variety regarding the transgender identities represented. Several trans-authored YA texts have been published that represent nonbinary experiences, such as Hal Schrieve's *Out of Salem* (2016), Mason Deaver's *I Wish You All the Best* (2019), and Kacen Callender's *Felix Ever After* (2020). These texts partially fill the "empty space within publishing" (949) that Robert Bittner and colleagues' 2016 investigation of transgender representation in children's and YA literature identified. Moreover, intersectional diversity has also somewhat improved since B. J. Epstein observed in 2012 that YA fiction suggests "it may not be possible to be GLBTQ and something else" ("We're Here, We're [Not?] Queer" 296). For example, titles including Anna-Marie McLemore's *When the Moon Was Ours* (2016) and Sonia Patel's *Jaya and Rasa* (2017) include nonwhite transgender teenagers. From 2014, transgender YA memoirs have also introduced additional representation into the book market by sharing transgender young people's experiences of being transgender in near-contemporary US and UK societies. Chapter 5 showed how the publication of the most recent memoirs has further expanded the boundaries of transgender representation in YA literature by blending traditionally and nontraditionally published forms of transgender self-authorship.

This book's analysis of trans YA literature moves across genres and forms, but each strand of the discussion is underpinned by the claim that the literary trends identified cannot be extricated from the wider cultural context of the books' publication. In the introduction, I suggested that Michelle Ann Abate and Kenneth Kidd's question as to whether "queer literature for young readers [can] effect, as much as document, change" (146) inspired my investigation, and these chapters have shown that transgender YA texts reflect and respond to the contemporary world for transgender teenagers and have become increasingly invested in disrupting and challenging the problematic, cisnormative structures that inflect their lived experiences. For example, chapter 4 unpicked how some novels are using conflict to empower transgender teenage characters. I suggested that these texts are offering new perspectives on how authority might exist in these relationships that are almost always considered to be cis- and aetonormative. Daniels's Nemesis series, Akwaeke Emezi's *Pet* (2019), and Aiden Thomas's *Cemetery Boys* (2020), in particular, show marginalized teens with the authority to speak on their identity, with narrative arcs and moments that recognize their knowledge. These examples are reinforcing the recognition of lived experience as a form of authority that is also evident from the growth of, and demand for, transgender authorship.

In spite of the increased emphasis on transgender people as authors and readers, there still remains a neoliberal, capitalist tendency to market and advertise trans-ness to cisgender readers who represent the majority of consumers in the market. This continues to limit transgender teenagers' access to nuanced mirrors and perpetuates the association of trans-ness with a social issue. While the packaging of some trans-authored novels reference the lived experiences of transgender teens, such as the inclusion of the protagonist's top surgery scars in the cover illustration of Callender's *Felix Ever After*, in ways that speak most clearly to transgender teenagers, a number of other texts have used trans-ness as a hook or a lure. Chapters 2 and 5 suggested that several recent texts have marketed transgender subjects to a mainstream, cisgender readership through the use of curiosity and sensationalism. There are also a number of texts written by openly cisgender authors that have continued to treat trans-ness as an intriguing difference to explore, such as John Boyne's *My Brother's Name Is Jessica* (2019), even as demands for more authentic depictions of marginalized identities have proliferated.

The idea of progress—of representation fundamentally *getting better* over time—has preoccupied scholars of LGBTQ+ fiction, and inclusive fiction more generally. In his recent monograph, Derritt Mason attempted to complicate the linear trajectory from "bad" to "good" representation, instead "hop[ing] to move beyond a conception of queer YA as a literary genre grounded in visibility" (18). Transgender representation has not reached a point where conversations can feasibly "move beyond" visibility because trans teenagers still need more, and more varied, literary mirrors, but trans

YA literature has grown into a somewhat diverse body of texts with varied authorship, trends, characters, conventions, genres, forms, implied readers, and ideologies. This book brought together texts through the transgender identity of their characters, but others might go on to produce analyses of transgender characters within broader investigations of YA literature as these characters become increasingly present across different genres in the market. In 2018, Malinda Lo tweeted that "coming out stories are still important, but I do think straight people sometimes forget that the LGBTQ experience can also involve happiness, adventure, saving the world/slaying dragons/solving mysteries. You know, LIFE" (@malindalo). To that I add: with the growth of trans representation, trans YA books will hopefully go on to feature in a far broader range of scholarly investigations within and beyond studies of transgender and LGBTQ+ literature.

APPENDIX

A selection of YA literature that includes transgender characters in major or minor roles.

Title	Author	Year	Country of publication	Format	Publisher
Luna	Julie Anne Peters	2004	US	Novel	Hachette
Jongensdroom	Lorna Minkman	2007	Netherlands	Novel	Lannoo
Parrotfish	Ellen Wittlinger	2007	US	Novel	Simon & Schuster
"The Missing Person" (in How Beautiful the Ordinary)	Jennifer Finney Boylan	2009	US	Short Story	Harper Collins
Almost Perfect	Brian Katcher	2009	US	Novel	Penguin Random House
f2m: The Boy Within	Haxel Edwards and Ryan Kennedy	2010	Australia	Novel	Ford Street Publishing
Jumpstart the World	Catherine Ryan Hyde	2010	US	Novel	Penguin Random House
Beauty Queens	Libba Bray	2011	US	Novel	Scholastic
I Am J	Cris Beam	2011	US	Novel	Hachette
Meisje van Mars	Anna Woltz and Vicky Janssen	2011	Netherlands	Novel	Em. Querido's Uitgeverij BV
Beautiful Music for Ugly Children	Kirstin Cronn-Mills	2012	US	Novel	North Star Editions
Being Emily	Rachel Gold	2012	US	Novel	Bella Books

Title	Author	Year	Country of publication	Format	Publisher
Everyday	David Levithan	2012	US	Novel	Penguin Random House
Happy Families	Tanita S. Davis	2012	US	Novel	Penguin Random House
One in Every Crowd	Ivan Coyote	2012	Canada	Short Story Collection	Arsenal Pulp
Roving Pack	Sassafras Lowrey	2012	US	Novel	PoMo Freakshow
Freakboy	Kristin Elizabeth Clark	2013	US	Verse Novel	Macmillan
Love in the Time of Global Warming	Francesca Lia Block	2013	US	Novel	Macmillan
The Coldest Girl in Coldtown	Holly Black	2013	US	Novel	Hachette
The Other Me	Suzanne van Rooyen	2013	US	Novel	Dreamspinner Press
Two Boys Kissing	David Levithan	2013	US	Novel	Penguin Random House
A Boy Like Me	Jennie Wood	2014	US	Novel	215 Ink
Beloved Pilgrim	Christopher Hawthorne Moss	2014	US	Novel	Dreamspinner Press
Beyond Magenta	Susan Kuklin (editor)	2014	US	Interview Collection	Candlewick Press
Breaking Free	Winter Page	2014	US	Novel	Dreamspinner Press
Changers	T. Cooper and Allison Glock-Cooper	2014	US	Novel	Akashic Books
Freeing Stella	Zoe Lynne	2014	US	Novel	Dreamspinner Press
If We Shadows	D. E. Atwood	2014	US	Novel	Dreamspinner Press
Just Girls	Rachel Gold	2014	US	Novel	Bella Books
Lessons on Destroying the World	Gene Gant	2014	US	Novel	Dreamspinner Press

Appendix

Title	Author	Year	Country of publication	Format	Publisher
Maxine Wore Black	Nora Olsen	2014	US	Novel	Bold Strokes Books
Rethinking Normal	Katie Rain Hill (and Ariel Schrag)	2014	US	Memoir	Simon & Schuster
Some Assembly Required	Arin Andrews (and Joshua Lyon)	2014	US	Memoir	Simon & Schuster
"The Most Handsome" (in *Summer Love: An LGBTQ Collection*)	S.J. Martin	2015	US	Short Story	Interlude Press
About a Girl (*Metamorphoses #3*)	Sarah McCarry	2015	US	Novel	Macmillan
Alex	Sylvia Aguilar-Zeleny	2015	US	Novel	ABDO Press
Fairy Tales for Modern Queers	Emily Reed	2015	US	Short Story Collection	Dreamspinner Press
Fathersonfather	Evan Jacobs	2015	US	Novel	Saddleback Educational Publishing
Lizard Radio	Pat Schmatz	2015	US	Novel	Candlewick Press
Only We Know	Simon Packham	2015	UK	Novel	Piccadilly Press
The Art of Being Normal	Lisa Williamson	2015	UK	Novel	David Fickling Books
Traffick	Ellen Hopkins	2015	US	Novel	Simon & Schuster
What We Left Behind	Robin Talley	2015	US	Novel	HarperCollins
A Fine Bromance	Christopher Hawthorne Moss	2016	US	Novel	Dreamspinner Press
Beast	Brie Spangler	2016	US	Novel	Penguin Random House
Being Jazz	Jazz Jennings (and Joshua Lyon)	2016	US	Memoir	Penguin Random House
If I Was Your Girl	Meredith Russo	2016	US	Novel	Macmillan

Title	Author	Year	Country of publication	Format	Publisher
Jess, Chunk, and the Road Trip to Infinity	Kristin Elizabeth Clark	2016	US	Novel	Macmillan
Look Past	Eric Devine	2016	US	Novel	Running Press
Magic Fell (Mages' Guild #1)	Andi Van	2016	US	Novel	Dreamspinner Press
Not Your Sidekick (Sidekick Squad #1)	C.B. Lee	2016	US	Novel	Interlude Press
Spirit Level	Sarah N. Harvey	2016	Canada	Novel	Orca Book Publishers
Symptoms of Being Human	Jeff Garvin	2016	US	Novel	HarperCollins
The Hammer of Thor (Magnus Chase and the Gods of Asgard #2)	Rick Riordan	2016	US	Novel	Disney-Hyperion Books
The Santa Hoax	Francis Gideon	2016	US	Novel	Dreamspinner Press
The Unintentional Time Traveler	Everett Maroon	2016	US	Novel	Lethe Press
When the Moon Was Ours	Anna-Marie McLemore	2016	US	Novel	Macmillan
Where No One Knows	Jo Ramsey	2016	US	Novel	Dreamspinner Press
As the Crow Flies	Melanie Gillman	2017	US	Graphic Novel	Iron Circus Comics
At the Edge of the Universe	Shaun David Hutchinson	2017	US	Novel	Simon & Schuster
Before I Had the Words	Skylar Kergil	2017	US	Novel	Skyhorse
Dreadnought (Nemesis #1)	April Daniels	2017	US	Novel	Diversion Books
Jaya and Rasa	Sonia Patel	2017	US	Novel	Cinco Puntos Press
Like Water	Rebecca Podos	2017	US	Novel	HarperCollins
Looking for Group	Rory Harrison	2017	US	Novel	HarperCollins
Mask of Shadows	Linsey Miller	2017	US	Novel	Sourcebooks

Appendix

Title	Author	Year	Country of publication	Format	Publisher
Mick & Michelle	Nina Rossing	2017	US	Novel	Dreamspinner Press
Not Your Villain (*Sidekick Squad #2*)	C.B. Lee	2017	US	Novel	Interlude Press
Rainbow Islands	Devin Harnois	2017	US	Novel	October Night Publishing
Sharing Secrets	Matthew J. Metzger	2017	UK	Novel	Bonnier Books
Sovereign (*Nemesis #2*)	April Daniels	2017	US	Novel	Diversion Books
The 57 Bus: A True Story of Two Teenagers and the Crime That Changed Their Lives	Dashka Slater	2017	US	Non-fiction	Macmillan
The Missing	J.R. Lenk	2017	US	Novel	Month9Books
Trans Mission	Alex Bertie	2017	UK	Memoir	Hachette
"A Play in Many Parts" (in *Unbroken: 13 Stories Starring Disabled Teens*)	Fox Benwell	2018	US	Short Story	Macmillan
"Every Shade of Red" (in *All Out The No-Longer-Secret Stories of Queer Teens throughout the Ages*)	Elliot Wake	2018	US	Short Story	Harlequin Trade Publishing
"Roja" (in *All Out: The No-Longer-Secret Stories of Queer Teens throughout the Ages*)	Anna-Marie McLemore	2018	US	Short Story	Harlequin Trade Publishing
"Somewhere That's Green" (in *Meet Cute*)	Meredith Russo	2018	US	Short Story	Houghton Mifflin Harcourt

Title	Author	Year	Country of publication	Format	Publisher
"The Day The Dragon Came" (in *Unbroken: 13 Stories Starring Disabled Teens*)	Marieke Nijkamp	2018	US	Short Story	Macmillan
Anger Is A Gift	Mark Oshiro	2018	US	Novel	Macmillan
Avi Cantor Has Six Months to Live	Sacha Lamb	2018	US	Novella	Book Smugglers Publishing
Big Man	Matthew J. Metzger	2018	US	Novel	NineStar Press
Blanca & Roja	Anna-Marie McLemore	2018	US	Novel	Macmillan
Clean	Juno Dawson	2018	UK	Novel	Hachette
Girl Made of Stars	Ashley Herring Blake	2018	US	Novel	HMH Books
I Was Born For This	Alice Oseman	2018	US	Novel	HarperCollins
Jonny Appleseed	Joshua Whitehead	2018	Canada	Novel	Arsenal Pulp Press
Luminosity (*The Sun Dragon #5*)	Annabelle Jay	2018	US	Novel	Dreamspinner Press
Magic Wept (*Mages' Guild #2*)	Andi Van	2018	US	Novel	Dreamspinner Press
My Crunchy Life	Mia Kerick	2018	US	Novel	Dreamspinner Press
On a Summer Night	Gabriel D. Vidrine	2018	US	Novel	NineStar Press
Power Surge	Sara Codair	2018	US	Novel	NineStar Press
The Brightsiders	Jen Wilde	2018	US	Novel	Feiwel & Friends
The Brilliant Death	Amy Rose Capetta	2018	US	Novel	Penguin Random House
The Disasters	M.K. England	2018	US	Novel	HarperCollins
Trans Teen Survival Guide	Fox Fisher and Owl Fisher	2018	UK	Non-fiction	Hachette
"Murders at the Rue Apartelle, Boracay" (in *His Hideous Heart*)	Rin Chupeco	2019	US	Short Story	Macmillan

Appendix

Title	Author	Year	Country of publication	Format	Publisher
"Parker Outside the Box" (in *Take the Mic: Fictional Stories of Everyday Resistance*)	Ray Stoeve	2019	US	Short Story	Scholastic
"The Other Team" (in *Proud*)	Michael Lee Richardson	2019	UK	Short Story	Little Tiger Group
Birthday	Meredith Russo	2019	US	Novel	Macmillan
Demon in the Whitelands	Nikki Z. Richard	2019	US	Novel	Month9Books
I Wish You All the Best	Mason Deaver	2019	US	Novel	Hachette
Magic Triumphed (*Mages' Guild* #3)	Andi Van	2019	US	Novel	Dreamspinner Press
Mooncakes	Suzanne Walker and Wendy Xu (artist)	2019	US	Graphic Novel	Oni Press
My Brother's Name Is Jessica	John Boyne	2019	US	Novel	Penguin Random House
Not Your Backup (*Sidekick Squad* #3)	C.B. Lee	2019	US	Novel	Interlude Press
Out of Salem	Hal Schrieve	2019	US	Novel	Seven Stories
Pet	Akwaeke Emezi	2019	US	Novel	Penguin Random House
Something Like Gravity	Amber Smith	2019	US	Novel	Simon & Schuster
Squad	Mariah MacCarthy	2019	US	Novel	Macmillan
The Other F Word	Angie Manfredi (editor)	2019	US	Anthology	Abrams
The Lost Coast	Amy Rose Capetta	2019	US	Novel	Candlewick Press
The Music of What Happens	Bill Konigsberg	2019	US	Novel	Arthur A. Levine Books
The Past and Other Things That Should Stay Buried	Shaun David Hutchinson	2019	US	Novel	Simon & Schuster

Title	Author	Year	Country of publication	Format	Publisher
The Princess of Baker Street	Mia Kerick	2019	US	Novel	Dreamspinner Press
The Wise and the Wicked	Rebecca Podos	2019	US	Novel	HarperCollins
They Are The Tide (The Psionics #3)	Tash McAdam	2019	US	Novel	NineStar Press
This Is The Circle (The Psionics #4)	Tash McAdam	2019	US	Novel	NineStar Press
We Are The Catalyst (The Psionics #2)	Tash McAdam	2019	US	Novel	NineStar Press
What Makes You Beautiful	Bridget Liang	2019	Canada	Novel	James Lorimer & Company
Blood Sport	Tash McAdam	2020	Canada	Novel	Orca Books
Cemetery Boys	Aiden Thomas	2020	US	Novel	Macmillan
Dark and Deepest Red	Anna-Marie McLemore	2020	US	Novel	Macmillan
Euphoria Kids	Alison Evans	2020	Australia	Novel	Bonnier Books UK
Even If We Break	Marieke Nijkamp	2020	US	Novel	SourceBooks
Felix Ever After	Kacen Callender	2020	US	Novel	HarperCollins
Gender Explorers	Juno Roche (editor)	2020	UK	Interview Collection	Jessica Kingsley Publishers
Harmonious Hearts - Stories from the 2019 LGBTQ+ Challenge	Various	2020	US	Short Story Collection	Dreamspinner Press
Kids From G.H.O.S.T.	Kaye Vassey	2020	US	Graphic Novel	Month9Books
Out!	Miles McKenna	2020	US	Memoir	ABRAMS
Somebody Told Me	Mia Siegert	2020	US	Novel	Lerner Publishing Group
Spellhacker	M.K. England	2020	US	Novel	HarperCollins
Stay Gold	Tobly McSmith	2020	US	Novel	HarperCollins

Title	Author	Year	Country of publication	Format	Publisher
The Mermaid, the Witch, and the Sea	Maggie Tokuda-Hall	2020	US	Novel	Walker Books Group
The Ninth Life	Taylor Barton	2020	US	Novel	HarlequinTeen
The Storm of Life (The Brilliant Death #2)	Amy Rose Capetta	2020	US	Novel	Penguin Random House
Under Shifting Stars	Alexandra Latos	2020	US	Novel	Houghton Mifflin Harcourt
What's The T?	Juno Dawson	2020	UK	Non-fiction	Hachette
Wonderland	Juno Dawson	2020	UK	Novel	Hachette
A Dark and Hollow Star	Ashley Shuttleworth	2021	US	Novel	Simon & Schuster
Act Cool	Tobly McSmith	2021	US	Novel	HarperCollins
Between Perfect and Real	Ray Stoeve	2021	US	Novel	Abrams
Can't Take That Away	Steven Salvatore	2021	US	Novel	Bloomsbury
Earth Reclaimed	Sara Codair	2021	US	Novel	Aurelia Leo
If You Should Ever Leave Me	Phoebe North	2021	US	Novel	HarperCollins
May the Best Man Win	Z.R. Ellor	2021	US	Novel	Macmillan
Meet Cute Diary	Emery Lee	2021	US	Novel	HarperCollins
Out Loud	Taylor Barton	2021	US	Novel	HarperCollins
The (Un)popular Vote	Jasper Sanchez	2021	US	Novel	HarperCollins
The Ghosts We Keep	Mason Deaver	2021	US	Novel	Scholastic
The Heartbreak Bakery	Amy Rose Capetta	2021	US	Novel	Candlewick
The Many Half-Lived Lives of Sam Sylvester	Maya MacGregor	2021	US	Novel	Boyds Mills Press
The Passing Playbook	Isaac Fitzsimons	2021	US	Novel	Penguin Random House
The Sisters of Reckoning	Charlotte Nicole Davis	2021	US	Novel	Macmillan

Title	Author	Year	Country of publication	Format	Publisher
The Unpopular Vote	Jasper Sanchez	2021	US	Novel	Katherine Tegen Books
The Witch King	H.E. Edgmon	2021	US	Novel	Inkyard Press
Victories Greater than Death	Charlie Jane Anders	2021	US	Novel	Macmillan
A Million Quiet Revolutions	Robin Gow	2022	US	Novel	Macmillan
Acting the Part	ZR Ellor	2022	US	Novel	HarperCollins
Alice Austen Lived Here	Alex Gino	2022	US	Novel	Scholastic
And They Lived...	Steven Salvatore	2022	US	Novel	Bloomsbury
Arden Grey	Ray Stoeve	2022	US	Novel	Abrams
At the End of Everything	Marieke Nijkamp	2022	US	Novel	SourceBooks
Beating Heart Baby	Lio Min	2022	US	Novel	Macmillan
Blackwater	Jeannette Arroyo and Ren Graham	2022	US	Graphic Novel	Macmillan
Dreams Bigger Than Heartbreak (Unstoppable Series #2)	Charlie Jane Anders	2022	US	Novel	Macmillan
Hell Followed With Us	Andrew Joseph White	2022	US	Novel	Peach Tree Publishing Company
Lakelore	Anna-Marie McLemore	2022	US	Novel	Macmillan
Lark and Kasim Start a Revolution	Kacen Callender	2022	US	Novel	Abrams
Magical Boy Vol #1	The Kao	2022	US	Graphic Novel	Scholastic
Magical Boy Vol #2	The Kao	2022	US	Graphic Novel	Scholastic
Man O'War	Cory McCarthy	2022	US	Novel	Penguin Random House
My Name is Magic	Xan van Rooyen	2022	UK	Novel	Tiny Ghost Press

Title	Author	Year	Country of publication	Format	Publisher
Not Your Hero (Sidekick Squad #4)	C.B. Lee	2022	US	Novel	Interlude Press
Self-Made Boys	Anna-Marie McLemore	2022	US	Novel	Macmillan
The Fae Keeper (The Witch King #2)	H.E. Edgmon	2022	US	Novel	Inkyard Press
The Feeling of Falling in Love	Mason Deaver	2022	US	Novel	Scholastic
The Honeys	Ryan La Sala	2022	US	Novel	Scholastic
The Many Half-Lived Lives of Sam Sylvester	Maya MacGregor	2022	US	Novel	Boyds Mills Press
The One True Me and You	Remi K. England	2022	US	Novel	Macmillan
The Sunbearer Trials (The Sunbearer Trials Duology #1)	Aiden Thomas	2022	US	Novel	Macmillan
The Wicked Bargain	Gabe Cole Novoa	2022	US	Novel	Random House
This Rebel Heart	Katherine Locke	2022	US	Novel	Penguin Random House
Welcome to St Hell: My trans teen misadventure	Lewis Hancox	2022	UK	Graphic Memoir	Scholastic
When The Angels Left The Old Country	Sacha Lamb	2022	US	Novel	Levine Querido

NOTES

Introduction

1. Histories of young adult fiction frequently cite one of three texts as the defining moment for the field: Maureen Daly's *Seventeenth Summer* (1942), J. D. Salinger's *The Catcher in the Rye* (1951), or S. E. Hinton's *The Outsiders* (1967). See, for example, the various editions of Michael Cart's history of young adult literature (such as *From Romance to Realism: 50 Years of Growth and Change in Young Adult Literature* [1996] and *Young Adult Literature: From Romance to Realism* [2016]), Kimberley Reynolds's *Radical Children's Literature: Future Visions and Aesthetic* (2007), and Crag Hill's (editor) *The Critical Merits of Young Adult Literature: Coming of Age* (2014).

2. Due to practical constraints and the rapid increase of transgender characters in young adult literature (as I will shortly discuss), this list cannot provide a comprehensive account of the field.

3. Though outside the scope of this book's investigation for various reasons, other notable contributions to the YA book market have emerged in these years. Catherine Ryan Hyde's *Jumpstart the World* (2010) and Tanita S. Davis's *Happy Families* (2012) both feature transgender characters whose status as adults precludes the titles from my study, while self-published titles during these years include Rachel Eliason's *Run, Clarissa, Run* (2012) and *The Best Boy Ever Made* (2014). I have also observed a number of titles from publishing houses that fall outside of my geographical remit: Haxel Edwards and Ryan Kennedy's *f2m: The Boy Within* was published in Australia in 2010, Ivan Coyote's *One in Every Crowd* was published in Canada in 2012, and Lorna Minkman's *Jongensdroom* (2007) and Anna Woltz and Vicky Janssen's *Meisje van Mars* (2011) were published in the Netherlands (in Dutch).

4. Author Corinne Duyvis introduced #OwnVoices in September 2015 as a way to label book recommendations on Twitter. The purpose was to allow readers to suggest books written by authors who shared the diverse identities of their main characters. Initially, it was a specific tool and not intended for broader use. However, over time, the publishing industry embraced the hashtag and transformed it into a catch-all marketing term, encompassing a wide range of representation. See chapter 2 for further discussion of Own Voices in the context of trans authorship.

5. See Megan L. Musgrave's *Digital Citizenship in Twenty-First-Century Young Adult Literature: Imaginary Activism* for further discussion of the real-world impacts of literature. Musgrave makes the case that "imaginary forms of activism depicted in literature can prompt young people to contemplate their real-world choices and take action" (xi).

6. Caroline E. Jones's "From Homoplot to Progressive Novel: Lesbian Experience and Identity in Contemporary Young Adult Novels" (2013) offers an example of subsequent scholarship that has revised Jenkins and Cart's model.

7. It is important to recognize the historical context of the terminology adopted in this book as that with its "origins as a specifically white, Western concept" (Pearce et al. 7). See chapter 1 for further discussion.

8. A Twitter thread by Laura M. Jiménez was, to my knowledge, the first to criticize Aronson's article (@booktoss).

Chapter 1: The Transgender Problem: A New Subcategory of Young Adult Fiction

1. Julie Anne Peters's *Luna* (2004) and Brian Katcher's *Almost Perfect* (2009) are two notable exceptions with teenage transgender representation. *Luna* includes major secondary (and titular) character, Luna, the sister of the cisgender protagonist (as discussed in the introduction), and *Almost Perfect* includes Sage, the transgender love interest of its cisgender, straight, male, teenage protagonist. In addition, a small number of contemporary novels published by conglomerates included adult transgender characters in secondary roles: for example, Catherine Ryan Hyde's *Jumpstart the World* (2010) and Tanita S. Davis's *Happy Families* (2012).

2. The claims this chapter makes could, in many ways, also apply to Robin Talley's *What We Left Behind* (2015), but I have chosen not to focus on Talley's novel as its university-aged protagonists align more closely with new adult publishing (see Amy Pattee and Jodi McAlister for further discussion of the new adult category). I have also chosen not to examine Simon Packman's *Only We Know* (2015) in this chapter, though I do consider it in the following chapter, as the protagonist's trans-ness is concealed until late in the narrative.

3. My analysis focuses on US and UK representations, but my reading of transgender YA fiction as problem narratives tracks with international analyses such as Åsa Warnqvist's reading of transgender fiction in Sweden, where "many of the children's and young adult books depicting transgender experiences focus on the hardships of trans lives and mirror the difficulties pointed out by real-life transgender people" (286).

4. "Stealth" refers to the practice of a transgender person publicly identifying as their true gender, without it being known that they are transgender.

5. See Sandercock's *Youth Fiction and Trans Representation* for a discussion of young adult body-swap films that argues "implied adolescent audiences are being positioned, in both explicit and subtle ways, to think about bodies and identities as wrong or right, valuable or worthless, and how these understandings are imbricated with race, gender, class, sexuality, disability, and other factors" (154). See Jennifer Gouck's *"If People Were Rain, I Was Drizzle and She Was a Hurricane": An Exploration of the Manic Pixie Dream Girl in Contemporary American Young Adult Literature* for a discussion of whiteness in Katcher's *Almost Perfect*.

Chapter 2: The Peritextual Materials of Transgender Young Adult Fiction

1. The arguments I make regarding the constructions of authenticity in this chapter can also be applied to some of the openly cisgender authors discussed in the previous chapter, who also have experiences with trans-ness. Cris Beam published a nonfiction title, *Transparent: Love, Family, and Living the T with Transgender Teenagers* (2007) following her time volunteering at a high school for transgender and queer teenagers (M. Phillips n.p.); Lisa Williamson's novel was inspired by her time working at the Gender Identity Development Service, a national medical service for transgender children and young people in the United Kingdom; and Kristin Elizabeth Clark, whose work I also discuss in this chapter, has a transgender daughter.

2. While this concept has the potential to disrupt chapter 1's assertion that transgender representation was introduced into the market by cisgender authors, these authors are "openly cisgender" in the sense that they have explicitly identified themselves as such in various peritextual and epitextual materials.

3. "Catfish" refers to the act of creating and using one or more false online identities, particularly with the purpose of pursuing deceptive online romances.

4. "Top surgery" refers to the medical procedure performed to remove breast tissue.

5. A term used to refer to "how transgender and other nonbinary individuals are scrutinized for pleasure and consumption by cisgender individuals" (V. E. Thomas 5).

6. It is important to note that many of *Pet*'s epitextual materials—such as interviews, reviews, marketing, and publicity announcements—do signal the protagonist's transgender identity, so a potential reader who first encounters the book through these materials will likely do so with a preunderstanding of its trans-ness. While outside the scope of this chapter, the epitextual materials of transgender YA fiction certainly provide interesting possibilities for future investigations.

7. I also recognize my limitations as a cisgender scholar who has not had the transgender lived experiences depicted in these narratives.

8. J. K. Rowling's recent online essay, "J. K. Rowling Writes about Her Reasons for Speaking Out on Sex and Gender Issues" (10 June 2020), has catalyzed online discussion and debate about transphobia, particularly in the publishing industry.

9. Bacha posh is a Pakistani-Afghanistan cultural practice in which families without sons select a daughter to live and behave as male.

Chapter 3: Can Transgender Representation Get More Fantastic? Speculative Young Adult Fiction

1. Throughout this chapter, I borrow Hunt's concept of the "known world" in place of phrases such as the "real world" or "reality" to acknowledge that our sense of the world is mediated by our own experiences. For Hunt, "fantasy cannot be 'free-floating' or entirely original [. . .]. It must be understandable in terms of its relationship to, or deviance from, our known world" (7).

2. Thirty texts were published by mainstream publishers in 2013, compared with 108 in 2018 (Lo, "A Decade of LGBTQ YA Since Ash" n.p.).

3. While Black's inclusion of a transgender character is significant in that it predates Schmatz's *Lizard Radio*, the character has a very minor role in the narrative, and I do not, therefore, consider the book to be a work of speculative transgender YA fiction.

4. The first of McAdam's series, *I Am the Storm* (2014), was originally self-published under the title *SLAM*. McAdam is a Welsh Canadian author with books, such as *Blood Sport*, published by Canadian publishers. NineStar Press is based in the United States.

5. Alex Fierro, the gender fluid character of Riordan's Magnus Chase series, was not introduced until the second novel (*The Hammer of Thor*), published in 2016.

6. As I mentioned in the introduction, Pierce has since revealed that "Alanna has always defied labels. She took the best bits of being a woman and a man, and created her own unique identity. I think the term is 'gender-fluid,' though there wasn't a word for this (to my knowledge) when I was writing her" (@TamoraPierce), but Alanna can be (and has been) read as an example of female cross-dressing based on primary textual evidence.

7. I return to this scene in the next chapter to further unpack the relationship between Jam and her parents and to consider why *Pet* is unusual in its portrayal of the coming-out process as a preteen moment.

8. The novels in Lee's series each take the point of view of a different character from the group of adolescent heroes as their focalizing perspective. The first, *Not Your Sidekick*, is a novel from the perspective of an Asian American, bisexual protagonist. *Not Your Villain* positions the series' major transgender character, Bells Broussard, as its protagonist.

9. A brief survey of the titles of children's and YA literature criticism can demonstrate how far power is central in their discussions: Pat Pinsent's *The Power of the Page: Children's Books and Their Readers* (1993), Trites's *Disturbing the Universe: Power and Repression in Adolescent Literature* (2000), Joanne Brown and Nancy St. Clair's *Declarations of Independence: Empowered Girls in Young Adult Literature* (2002), Maria Tatar's *Enchanted Hunters: The Power of Stories in Childhood* (2009), Maria Nikolajeva's *Power, Voice, and Subjectivity in Literature for Young Readers* (2010), June Pulliam's *Monstrous Bodies: Feminine Power in Young Adult Horror Fiction* (2014), and Clémentine Beauvais's *The Mighty Child: Time and Power in Children's Literature* (2015) offer a few notable examples.

Chapter 4: There's No Place Like Home: Parent-Adolescent Relationships in Transgender Young Adult Fiction

1. The much larger market of cisgender YA has already started to feature stories shaped by Covid-19, such as a YA anthology, *Together, Apart* (2020), featuring nine short stories from popular YA authors about finding love in lockdown; *hello (from here)* (2021), a novel on the same theme by Chandler Baker and Wesley King; and Lilliam Rivera's *We Light Up the Sky* (2021), in which teenage Luna is grieving the loss of her cousin to the pandemic.

2. Adolescent transgender characters are exclusively depicted in otherwise cisgender families. Transgender parents of cisgender children are included in a small number of titles that fall beyond my scope in this book, and future research might consider the additional insights offered by this adult/child, transgender/cisgender configuration of characters. Notably, Tanita S. Davis's young adult novel, *Happy Families* (2012), depicts teenage twins Ysabel and Justin coming to accept their parent's identity as a transgender woman; Sarah Hagger-Holt's middle-grade novel, *Nothing Ever Happens Here* (2020), includes a family from Littlehaven with a transgender parent; and Kit Rosewater and Sophie Escabasse's

illustrated middle-grade novel, *Kenzie Kickstarts a Team* (2020), includes a transgender parent in a small, supporting role.

3. A 2015 investigation by the Pew Research Center into the contemporary American family revealed that less than half (46 percent) of children are living with two parents who are both in their first marriage (n.p.). The Office for National Statistics reported that in the United Kingdom in 2020, there were 2,030,000 lone mother families and 348,000 lone father families with dependent children, as well as 255,000 multifamily households (n.p.).

4. As I explained in chapter 3, the Brujx binary community is divided into brujos (males) and brujas (females) who have different powers within the imaginary world of *Cemetery Boys*.

5. To my knowledge, there are no other YA fiction books that depict a preteen child coming out as transgender to their parents published up to 2021. Jazz Jennings's memoir *Being Jazz* (2016) includes Jennings coming out at six years old, and indeed Jennings is notable precisely for being one of the youngest publicly documented people to be identified as transgender. It should be noted that this claim is made in reference only to the YA book market. Though outside of the scope of this investigation, scholars have noted a recent trend in picture books and books for younger readers that depict transgender children (Crawley 35).

Chapter 5: Transgender Memoirs for Young Adult Readers

1. Lewis Hancox's YA graphic memoir, *Welcome to St. Hell: My Trans Teen Misadventure*, was also published in 2022.

2. It is worth noting that Andrews, Hill, and Jennings also have YouTube channels, but their cultural popularity can be attributed to the mainstream media in a way that the latter three cannot.

3. As a term borrowed from Bertie's *Trans Mission*, "the haircut" denotes the first masculine, short haircut that many masculine transgender people have as a form of gender-affirming transition. The haircut is a real-world occurrence, but it also constitutes a shared narrative moment.

4. In this regard, the most recent memoirs also share connections with self-help guides published for transgender teens, or LGBTQ+ teens more broadly, that are becoming increasingly prevalent in the YA book market, such as Owl Fisher and Fox Fisher's *Trans Teen Survival Guide* from Jessica Kingsley Publishers (UK) in 2018 and Juno Dawson's *What's the T? The No-nonsense Guide to All Things Trans and/or Non-binary for Teens* from Wren & Rook imprint of Hachette (UK) in 2021.

5. This list has been collated, in part, from the GLBTQ Archives Encyclopaedia Project.

6. There is no definitive reason why transgender representation has not developed in the young adult book market in the same way, though I suspect it is due both to young people's lack of cultural capital as writers and a belief among publishing houses that young people are more vulnerable to the harms associated with sharing intimate personal details in public spaces.

7. Though it is evident that Trimmer was keen to publish the teens' stories, I have not encountered any suggestion that the teenagers were in any way exploited.

8. Other titles include Dawson's *What's the T?* and Milli Hill's *My Period: Find Your Flow and Feel Period Positive!* (2021).

REFERENCES

Abate, Michelle Ann, and Kenneth Kidd. "Introduction." *Over the Rainbow: Queer Children's and Young Adult Literature*, edited by Michelle Ann Abate and Kenneth Kidd, University of Michigan Press, 2011, pp. 1–14.
"About Us." *BellaBooks*, https://www.bellabooks.com/about-us/. Accessed 17 Aug. 2021.
Albertalli, Becky. "I Know I'm Late." *Medium*, 31 Aug. 2020, https://medium.com/@rebecca.albertalli/i-know-im-late-9b31de339c62. Accessed 13 Jul. 2021.
Alston, Ann. *The Family in English Children's Literature*. Routledge, 2008.
Ames, Jonathan, editor. *Sexual Metamorphosis: An Anthology of Transsexual Memoirs*. Vintage, 2005.
Anders, Charlie Jane. *Victories Greater Than Death*. Macmillan, 2021.
Andrews, Arin, and Joshua Lyon. *Some Assembly Required: The Not-So-Secret Life of a Transgender Teen*. Simon & Schuster, 2014.
Appel, Markus, and Barbara Malečkar. "The Influence of Paratext on Narrative Persuasion: Fact, Fiction, or Fake?" *Human Communication Research*, vol. 38, no. 4, 2012, pp. 459–84. https://doi.org/10.1111/j.1468-2958.2012.01432.x.
Appleyard, J. A. *Becoming a Reader: The Experience of Fiction from Childhood to Adulthood*. Cambridge University Press, 1991.
Aronson, Marc. "Nonfiction Windows So White." *The Horn Book*, Mar. 2021, https://www.hbook.com?detailStory=nonfiction-windows-so-white. Accessed 11 May. 2021.
Bachmann, Chaka L., and Becca Gooch. *LGBT in Britain: Trans Report*. 2018.
Banks, William P. "Literacy, Sexuality, and the Value(s) of Queer Young Adult Literatures." *The English Journal*, vol. 98, no. 4, 2009, pp. 33–36.
Bardugo, Leigh. *Wonder Woman: Warbringer*. Penguin Random House, 2017.
Barthes, Roland. *Image, Music, Text*. Fontana, 1977.
Barthes, Roland. "The Reality Effect." 1969. *The Rustle of Language*, edited by François Walch, translated by Richard Howard, 1989, pp. 141–48.
Barthes, Roland. "The Structuralist Activity." 1963. *European Literary Theory and Practice: From Existential Phenomenology to Structuralism*, Delta Books, 1973, pp. 157–63.
Batchelor, Katherine E., et al. "Opening Doors: Teaching LGBTQ-Themed Young Adult Literature for an Inclusive Curriculum." *The Clearing House: A Journal of Educational Strategies, Issues and Ideas*, vol. 91, no. 1, 2018, pp. 29–36. https://doi.org/10.1080/00098655.2017.1366183.

Battis, Jes. "Introduction: Supernatural Youth." *Supernatural Youth: The Rise of the Teen Hero in Literature and Popular Culture*, edited by Jes Battis, Lexington Books, 2011, pp. 1–14.

Beam, Cris. *I Am J*. Hachette, 2011.

Beam, Cris. *Transparent: Love, Family, and Living the T with Transgender Teenagers*. Harcourt, 2007.

Beauvais, Clémentine. *The Mighty Child: Time and Power in Children's Literature*. John Benjamins, 2015.

Beauvais, Clémentine. "The Problem of 'Power': Metacritical Implications of Aetonormativity for Children's Literature Research." *Children's Literature in Education*, vol. 44, no. 1, 2013, pp. 74–86. https://doi.org/10.1007/s10583-012-9182-3.

Bernstein, Robin. "The Queerness of Harriet the Spy." *Over the Rainbow: Queer Children's and Young Adult Literature*, edited by Michelle Ann Abate and Kenneth Kidd, University of Michigan Press, 2011, pp. 111–20.

Berriman, Liam, and Rachel Thomson. "Spectacles of Intimacy? Mapping the Moral Landscape of Teenage Social Media." *Journal of Youth Studies*, vol. 18, no. 5, 2015, pp. 583–97. https://doi.org/10.1080/13676261.2014.992323.

Berryman, Rachel, and Misha Kavka. "'I Guess a Lot of People See Me as a Big Sister or a Friend': The Role of Intimacy in the Celebrification of Beauty Vloggers." *Journal of Gender Studies*, vol. 26, no. 3, 2017, pp. 307–20. https://doi.org/10.1080/09589236.2017.1288611.

Bertie, Alex. *Trans Mission: My Quest to a Beard*. Hachette, 2017.

Best, Amy L. *Prom Night: Youth, Schools, and Popular Culture*. Routledge, 2000.

Bettcher, Talia Mae. "Trapped in the Wrong Theory: Rethinking Trans Oppression and Resistance." *Signs: Journal of Women in Culture and Society*, vol. 39, no. 2, Jan. 2014, pp. 383–406. https://doi.org/10.1086/673088.

Birdsall, Bridget. *Double Exposure*. Simon and Schuster, 2014.

Bishop, Rudine Sims. "Evaluating Books by and about African-Americans." *The Multicolored Mirror: Cultural Substance in Literature for Children and Young Adults*, edited by Merri V. Lindgren, Highsmith Press, 1991, pp. 31–44.

Bishop, Rudine Sims. "Mirrors, Windows, and Sliding Glass Doors." *Perspectives*, vol. 6, no. 3, 1990, pp. ix–xi.

Bishop, Rudine Sims. "Reframing the Debate about Cultural Authenticity." *Stories Matter: The Complexity of Cultural Authenticity in Children's Literature*, edited by Dana L. Fox and Kathy G. Short, 2003, pp. 25–40. https://eric.ed.gov/?id=ED480339.

Bishop, Rudine Sims. "Windows and Mirrors: Children's Books and Parallel Cultures." *California State University Reading Conference: 14th Annual Conference Proceedings*, 1990, pp. 3–12.

Bittner, Robert. "(Im)Possibility and (in)visibility: Arguing against 'Just Happens to Be' in Young Adult Literature." *Queer Studies in Media & Popular Culture*, vol. 1, no. 2, 2016, pp. 199–214. https://doi.org/10.1386/qsmpc.1.2.199_1.

Bittner, Robert. "Trans and Nonbinary Teen Voices and Memoir: (Non-)Traditional Mirrors of (Non-) Traditional Lives." *Sexuality in Literature for Children and Young Adults*, edited by Paul Venzo and Kristine Moruzi, Routledge, 2021, pp. 44–58.

Bittner, Robert, et al. "Queer and Trans-Themed Books for Young Readers: A Critical Review." *Discourse: Studies in the Cultural Politics of Education*, vol. 37, no. 6, 2016, pp. 948–64. https://doi.org/10.1080/01596306.2016.1195106.

Black, Holly. *The Coldest Girl in Coldtown*. Hachette, 2013.
Boffone, Trevor. "Call for Chapters: 'TikTok Cultures.'" April 2021.
@booktoss (Laura M. Jimenez). "Because . . . When You're Accustomed to Privilege, Equality Feels like Oppression. @HornBook this article should have been shelved for the self serving whinging it is." *Twitter*, 20 March 2021, https://twitter.com/booktoss/status/1373271184368922625.
Booth, Emily, and Bhuva Narayan. "'The Expectations That We Be Educators': The View of Australian Authors Young Adult Fiction on Their OwnVoices Novels as 'Windows' for Learning about Marginalized Experiences." *Young Adult Library Services Association*, 2020. https://opus.lib.uts.edu.au/handle/10453/137198.
Booth, Emily, and Bhuva Narayan. "Identifying Inclusion: Publishing Industry Trends and the Lack of #OwnVoices Australian Young Adult Fiction." *Research on Diversity in Youth Literature*, vol. 3, no. 1, 2021, pp. 1–38.
Boylan, Jennifer Finney. *She's Not There: A Life in Two Genders*. Broadway Books, 2003.
Boyne, John. *My Brother's Name Is Jessica*. Penguin Books, 2019.
Boyne, John. *My Brother's Name Is Jessica*. Penguin Books, 2020.
Bradlow, Josh, et al. *Shut Out: The Experiences of LGBTQ Young People Not in Education, Training or Work*. 2020, pp. 1–52.
Bray, Libba. *Beauty Queens*. Scholastic, 2011.
Brocklebank, Lisa. "Rebellious Voices: The Unofficial Discourse of Cross-Dressing in d'Aulnoy, de Murat, and Perrault." *Children's Literature Association Quarterly*, vol. 25, no. 3, 2000, pp. 127–36. https://doi.org/10.1353/chq.0.1336.
Broughton, Trev Lynn. *Autobiography: Critical Concepts in Literary and Cultural Studies*. Routledge, 2007.
Brown, Joanne, and Nancy St. Clair. *Declarations of Independence: Empowered Girls in Young Adult Literature, 1990–2001*. Scarecrow, 2002.
Brown, Megan. "'Tell Me Who I Am': An Investigation of Cultural Authenticity in YA Disability Peritexts." *Beyond the Blockbusters: Themes and Trends in Contemporary Young Adult Fiction*, edited by Rebekah Fitzsimmons and Casey Alane Wilson, University Press of Mississippi, 2020, pp. 140–55.
Browne, Katelyn R. "Reimagining Queer Death in Young Adult Fiction." *Research on Diversity in Youth Literature*, vol. 2, no. 2, 2020, pp. 1–25.
Brownie, Barbara, and Danny Graydon. *The Superhero Costume: Identity and Disguise in Fact and Fiction*. Bloomsbury Academic, 2016.
Brugman, Alyssa. *Alex as Well*. Text, 2013.
Bunker, Lisa. *Felix Yz*. Penguin Random House, 2018.
Butler, Catherine. "Experimental Girls: Feminist and Transgender Discourses in Bill's New Frock and Marvin Redpost: Is He a Girl?" *Children's Literature Association Quarterly*, vol. 34, no. 1, 2009, pp. 3–20. https://doi.org/10.1353/chq.0.1889.
Butler, Catherine. "Portraying Trans People in Children's and Young Adult Literature: Problems and Challenges." *Journal of Literary Education*, vol. 3, 2020, pp. 1–24. https://doi.org/10.7203/JLE.3.15992.
Butler, Judith. *Undoing Gender*. Taylor & Francis, 2004.
Cadden, Mike. "Introduction." *Telling Children's Stories: Narrative Theory and Children's Literature*, University of Nebraska Press, 2010, pp. i–xxv.
Cadden, Mike. "The Irony of Narration in the Young Adult Novel." *Children's Literature Association Quarterly*, vol. 25, no. 3, 2000, pp. 146–54. https://doi.org/10.1353/chq.0.1467.

Callender, Kacen. *Felix Ever After*. HarperCollins, 2020.
Capetta, Amy Rose. *The Brilliant Death*. Penguin Random House, 2018.
Capetta, Amy Rose. *The Lost Coast*. Candlewick Press, 2019.
Capetta, Amy Rose. *The Storm of Life*. Penguin Random House, 2020.
Capuzza, Jamie C., and Leland G. Spencer. "Regressing, Progressing, or Transgressing on the Small Screen? Transgender Characters on U. S. Scripted Television Series." *Communication Quarterly*, vol. 65, no. 2, 2017, pp. 214–30. https://doi.org/10.1080/01463373.2016.1221438.
Carroll, Lewis. *Alice's Adventures in Wonderland*. 1865. Princeton University Press, 2015.
Cart, Michael. *From Romance to Realism: 50 Years of Growth and Change in Young Adult Literature*. HarperCollins, 1996.
Cart, Michael. *Young Adult Literature: From Romance to Realism*. American Library Association, 2016.
Chambers, Aidan. "Finding the Form: Toward a Poetics of Youth Literature." *The Lion and the Unicorn*, vol. 34, no. 3, 2010, pp. 267–83.
Chambers, Aidan. "The Reader in the Book: Notes from Work in Progress." *Children's Literature Association Quarterly*, vol. 1978, no. 1, 1978, pp. 1–19. https://doi.org/10.1353/chq.1978.0000.
Chappell, Shelley. *Werewolves, Wings, and Other Weird Transformations: Fantastic Metamorphosis in Children's and Young Adult Fantasy Literature*. PhD Thesis, 2007.
Clark, Christina, and Irene Picton. *Children and Young People's Reading in 2020 before and during the COVID-19 Lockdown*. 2020, pp. 1–18.
Clark, Kristin Elizabeth. *Freakboy*. Macmillan, 2013.
Clark, Kristin Elizabeth. *Jess, Chunk, and the Road Trip to Infinity*. Macmillan, 2016.
Coats, Karen. *The Bloomsbury Introduction to Children's and Young Adult Literature*. Bloomsbury Academic, 2017.
Coats, Karen. "From 'Death Be Not Proud' to Death Be Not Permanent: Shifting Attitudes towards Death in Contemporary Young Adult Literature." *The International Journal of Young Adult Literature*, vol. 1, no. 1, 2020, pp. 1–17. https://doi.org/10.24877/ijyal.31.
Coats, Karen. "Young Adult Literature: Growing Up, in Theory." *Handbook of Research on Children's and Young Adult Literature*, edited by Shelby Wolf et al., Routledge, 2011, pp. 315–29.
Codair, Sara. *Power Surge*. Ninestar, 2018.
Cooper, T. *Real Man Adventures*. McSweeney's, 2012.
Corbett, Emily, and Leah Phillips. "Ploughing the Field: A Discussion about YA Studies." *The International Journal of Young Adult Literature*, vol. 1, no. 1, 2020, pp. 1–22. https://doi.org/10.24877/ijyal.28.
"Corporate Information." Simon & Schuster UK. https://www.simonandschuster.co.uk/c/ss-uk-corporate-information. Accessed 17 Aug. 2021.
Cowell, Roberta. *Roberta Cowell's Story by Herself*. Hamilton and Company, 1954.
Coyote, Ivan E. *One In Every Crowd*. Arsenal Pulp, 2012.
Cramer, Katherine Mason, and Jill Adams. "The T* in LGBT*: Disrupting Gender Normative School Culture Through Young Adult Literature." *Teaching, Affirming, and Recognizing Trans and Gender Creative Youth: A Queer Literacy Framework*, edited by sj Miller, Palgrave Macmillan US, 2016, pp. 121–41. https://doi.org/10.1057/978-1-137-56766-6_7.

Crawley, Stephen Adam. "Be Who You Are: Exploring Representations of Transgender Children in Picturebooks." *Journal of Children's Literature*, vol. 43, no. 2, 2017, pp. 28–41.

Crisp, Thomas. "From Romance to Magical Realism: Limits and Possibilities in Gay Adolescent Fiction." *Children's Literature in Education*, vol. 40, no. 4, 2009, pp. 333–48. https://doi.org/10.1007/s10583-009-9089-9.

Cronn-Mills, Kirstin. *Beautiful Music for Ugly Children*. North Star Editions, 2012.

Cronn-Mills, Kirstin. *Beautiful Music for Ugly Children*. North Star Editions, 2014.

Cronn-Mills, Kirstin. *Transgender Lives: Complex Stories, Complex Voices*. Lerner, 2014.

Daly, Maureen. *Seventeenth Summer*. 1942.

Daniels, April. *Dreadnought*. Diversion Books, 2017.

Daniels, April. "An Interview with Author April Daniels." *Intellectual Freedom Blog*, 30 Apr. 2018, https://www.oif.ala.org/oif/?p=14028. Accessed 19 June 2020.

Daniels, April. *Sovereign*. Diversion Books, 2017.

Dashtipour, Parisa. *Social Identity in Question: Construction, Subjectivity and Critique*. Routledge, 2012. https://doi.org/10.4324/9780203103586.

David, Emmanuel. "Capital T: Trans Visibility, Corporate Capitalism, and Commodity Culture." *Transgender Studies Quarterly*, no. 4, vol. 1, 2017, pp. 28–44.

Davis, Charlotte Nicole. *The Sisters of Reckoning*. Macmillan, 2021.

Davis, Mark. "Theorizing the Blurb: The Strange Case at the End of the Book." *Meanjin*, vol. 53, no. 2, pp. 245–57. https://doi.org/10.3316/informit.884277270529025.

Davis, Tanita S. *Happy Families*. Penguin Random House, 2012.

Dawson, Juno. *Clean*. Hachette, 2018.

Dawson, Juno. *What's the T?: The Guide to All Things Trans And/or Nonbinary for Teens*. Hachette, 2021.

Dawson, Juno. *Wonderland*. Hachette, 2020.

de la Peña, Matt. *Superman: Dawnbreaker*. Penguin Random House, 2020.

Deaver, Mason. *I Wish You All the Best*. Hachette, 2019.

Deaver, Mason. "Interview with Mason Deaver, Author of *I Wish You All the Best*." *YA SHELF*, 23 Nov. 2018, https://www.yash3lf.com/interview-with-mason-deaver-author-of-i-wish-you-all-the-best/. Accessed 30 Jan. 2021.

Derrida, Jacques. "The Law of Genre." 1979. *Acts of Literature*, edited by Derek Attridge, Routledge, 1992, pp. 221–52.

Devine, Eric. *Look Past*. Running Press, 2016.

"Do You Use the Phrase: 'Born in the Wrong Body'?" *Mermaids*, Sept. 2020, https://mermaidsuk.org.uk/news/do-you-still-use-the-phrase-born-in-the-wrong-body/. Accessed 24 Nov. 2020.

Donnelly, Colleen Elaine. "Re-Visioning Negative Archetypes of Disability and Deformity in Fantasy: Wicked, Maleficent, and Game of Thrones." *Disability Studies Quarterly*, vol. 36, no. 4, 2016. https://doi.org/10.18061/dsq.v36i4.5313.

Donovan, John. *I'll Get There. It Better Be Worth the Trip*. Harper & Row, 1969.

Douglas, Kate, and Anna Poletti. *Life Narratives and Youth Culture: Representation, Agency and Participation*. Palgrave Macmillan, 2016. https://doi.org/10.1057/978-1-137-55117-7.

Eagleton, Terry. "Enjoy!" *Paragraph*, vol. 24, no. 2, 2001, pp. 40–52. https://doi.org/10.3366/jsp.2001.24.2.40.

Edgmon, H. E. *The Witch King*. Inkyard, 2021.

Edwards, Hazel, and Ryan Kennedy. *F2m: The Boy Within*. Ford Street, 2010.

Elbe, Lili. *Man into Woman: A Comparative Scholarly Edition*. 1933. Bloomsbury, 2020.
Eliason, Rachel. *The Best Boy Ever Made*. Self-published, 2014.
Eliason, Rachel. *Run, Clarissa, Run*. Self-published, 2012.
Emezi, Akwaeke. "Akwaeke Emezi on '*Pet*' and on Making a Better World for Their Protagonist, a Black Trans Girl Named Jam." *Teen Vogue*, 13 Sept. 2019, https://www.teenvogue.com/story/akwaeke-emezi-pet. Accessed 21 Nov. 2020.
Emezi, Akwaeke. *Pet*. Penguin Random House, 2019.
Engdahl, Ulrica. "Wrong Body." *TSQ: Transgender Studies Quarterly*, vol. 1, no. 1–2, 2014, pp. 267–69. https://doi.org/10.1215/23289252-400226.
England, M. K. *The Disasters*. HarperCollins, 2018.
England, M. K. *Spellhacker*. HarperCollins, 2020.
Epstein, B. J. *Are the Kids All Right?: The Representation of LGBTQ Characters in Children's and Young Adult Lit*. Intellect, 2013.
Epstein, B. J. "'The Case of the Missing Bisexuals': Bisexuality in Books for Young Readers." *Journal of Bisexuality*, vol. 14, no. 1, 2014, pp. 110–25. https://doi.org/10.1080/15299716.2014.872483.
Epstein, B. J. "We're Here, We're (: GLBTQ Characters in Children's Books." *Journal of GLBT Family Studies*, vol. 8, no. 3, 2012, pp. 287–300. https://doi.org/10.1080/1550428X.2012.677241.
Farber, Rebecca. "'Transing' Fitness and Remapping Transgender Male Masculinity in Online Message Boards." *Journal of Gender Studies*, vol. 26, no. 3, 2017, pp. 254–68. https://doi.org/10.1080/09589236.2016.1250618.
Feinberg, Leslie. *Stone Butch Blues*. Firebrand Books, 1993.
Fisher, Fox, and Owl Fisher. *Trans Teen Survival Guide*. Jessica Kingsley, 2018.
Fitzsimmons, Rebekah. "Exploring the Genre Conventions of the YA Dystopian Trilogy as Twenty-First-Century Utopian Dreaming." *Beyond the Blockbusters: Themes and Trends in Contemporary Young Adult Fiction*, edited by Rebekah Fitzsimmons and Casey Alane Wilson, University Press of Mississippi, 2020, pp. 3–19.
Fitzsimmons, Rebekah, and Casey Alane Wilson. "Introduction. Boom! Goes the Hypercanon: On the Importance of the Overlooked and Understudied in Young Adult Literature." *Beyond the Blockbusters: Themes and Trends in Contemporary Young Adult Fiction*, edited by Rebekah Fitzsimmons and Casey Alane Wilson, University Press of Mississippi, 2020, pp. ix–xxiv.
Fitzsimons, Isaac. *The Passing Playbook*. Penguin Random House, 2021.
Flanagan, Victoria. "Girl Parts: The Female Body, Subjectivity and Technology in Posthuman Young Adult Fiction." *Feminist Theory*, vol. 12, no. 1, 2011, pp. 39–53. https://doi.org/10.1177/1464700110390596.
Flanagan, Victoria. *Into the Closet: Cross-Dressing and the Gendered Body in Children's Literature and Film*. Routledge, 2008.
Flanagan, Victoria. "'Kindness in a Cruel World': The Formation of Agentic Non-Heteronormative Identity in Contemporary YA Fictions." *Cruel Children in Popular Texts and Cultures*, edited by Monica Flegel and Christopher Parkes, 2018, pp. 257–75. https://doi.org/10.1007/978-3-319-72275-7_13.
Fletcher, Lisa, et al. "Genre Worlds and Popular Fiction: The Case of Twenty-First-Century Australian Romance." *The Journal of Popular Culture*, vol. 51, no. 4, 2018, pp. 997–1015. https://doi.org/10.1111/jpcu.12706.

Forest Park Public Library. "The Need for Diverse Books and De-Centering Whiteness in the Conversation." https://www.fppl.org/2021/02/19/sljfebissue/. Accessed 16 Aug. 2021.

Fowers, Alyssa, and William Wan. "'The Volume Has Been Turned Up on Everything': Pandemic Places Alarming Pressure on Transgender Mental Health." *Washington Post*, 18 Aug. 2020. www.washingtonpost.com, https://www.washingtonpost.com/health/2020/08/18/coronavirus-transgender/.

Fox, Dana L., and Kathy G. Short. "The Complexity of Cultural Authenticity in Children's Literature: Why the Debates Really Matter." *Stories Matter: The Complexity of Cultural Authenticity in Children's Literature*, edited by Dana L. Fox and Kathy G. Short, National Council of Teachers of English, 2003, pp. 3–24. https://eric.ed.gov/?id=ED480339.

Friddle, Megan E. "Who Is a 'Girl'? The Tomboy, the Lesbian, and the Transgender Child." *Gender(Ed) Identities: Critical Rereadings of Gender in Children's and Young Adult Literature*, edited by Tricia Clasen and Holly Hassel, Routledge, 2016, pp. 117–33. https://doi.org/10.4324/9781315691633.

Frisby, Naomi. "The Hidden Sex: Representations of Intersex People in Circus and Sideshow Novels." *Networking Knowledge: Journal of the MeCCSA Postgraduate Network*, vol. 10, no. 3, 2017, pp. 44–56.

Gamble, Sarah, editor. *The Routledge Companion to Feminism and Postfeminism*. Routledge, 2001.

Genette, Gérard. "Introduction to the Paratext." *New Literary History*, translated by Marie Maclean, vol. 22, no. 2, 1991, pp. 261–72. https://doi.org/10.2307/469037.

Gillingham, Erica. *Lesbian Love Stories in Young Adult Literature and Graphic Memoirs: Narrative Constructions of Same-Sex Relationships between Female Characters across Genre and Form*. PhD Thesis, 2018.

Gill-Peterson, Jules. *Histories of the Transgender Child*. University of Minnesota Press, 2018.

Gold, Rachel. *Being Emily*. Bella Books, 2012.

Gold, Rachel. *Just Girls*. Bella Books, 2014.

Gordon, Colby. "The Sign You Must Not Touch: Lyric Obscurity and Trans Confession." *Postmedieval*, vol. 11, no. 2, 2020, pp. 195–203. https://doi.org/10.1057/s41280-020-00172-x.

Gouck, Jennifer. *If people were rain, I was drizzle and she was a hurricane": An Exploration of the Manic Pixie Dream Girl in Contemporary American Young Adult Literature*. PhD Thesis, 2023.

Graham, Ruth. "Against YA." *Slate Magazine*, 5 June 2014, https://slate.com/culture/2014/06/against-ya-adults-should-be-embarrassed-to-read-childrens-books.html. Accessed 17 Mar. 2019.

Gray, Jonathan. *Show Sold Separately: Promos, Spoilers, and Other Media Paratexts*. NYU Press, 2010.

Gray, Jonathan. "When Is the Author?" *A Companion to Media Authorship*, edited by Jonathan Gray and Derek Johnson, John Wiley & Sons, Ltd, 2013, pp. 88–111. https://doi.org/10.1002/9781118505526.ch5.

Gregorio, I. W. *None of the Above*. HarperCollins, 2015.

Guin, Ursula K. Le. *The Language of the Night: Essays on Fantasy and Science Fiction*. Ultramarine, 1979.

Guin, Ursula K. Le. *The Left Hand of Darkness*. 1969. Hachette UK, 2012.

Hagger-Holt, Sarah. *Nothing Ever Happens Here*. Usborne, 2020.

Halberstam, Jack. *Trans*: A Quick and Quirky Account of Gender Variability*. University of California Press, 2018.
Hall, Granville Stanley. *Adolescence: Its Psychology and Its Relations to Physiology, Anthropology, Sociology, Sex, Crime, Religion and Education*. Appleton, 1904.
Hancox, Lewis. *Welcome to St. Hell: My Trans Teen Misadventure*. Scholastic, 2022.
Harnois, Devin. *Rainbow Islands*. October Night, 2018.
Hawke, Lisa D., et al. "Mental Health among Transgender and Gender Diverse Youth: An Exploration of Effects during the COVID-19 Pandemic." *Psychology of Sexual Orientation and Gender Diversity*, vol. 8, no. 2, 2021, pp. 180–87. https://doi.org/10.1037/sgd0000467.
Henderson, Alex. "*Let's Talk about Love*, *Tash Hearts Tolstoy*, and the Asexual Coming-of-Age Story." *RoundTable*, vol. 2, no. 2, 2019, pp. 1–19. https://doi.org/10.5334/rt.52.
Henderson, Alex. "Playing with Genre and Queer Narrative in the Novels of Malinda Lo." *The International Journal of Young Adult Literature*, vol. 2, no. 1, 2021, pp. 1–17.
Hill, Crag. *The Critical Merits of Young Adult Literature: Coming of Age*. Routledge, 2014.
Hill, Katie Rain, and Ariel Schrag. *Rethinking Normal: A Memoir in Transition*. Simon & Schuster, 2014.
Hill, Milli. *My Period: Find Your Flow and Feel Period Positive!* Hachette, 2021.
Hinton, S. E. *The Outsiders*. Puffin Books, 1967.
Hollindale, Peter. "The Adolescent Novel of Ideas." *Children's Literature in Education*, vol. 26, no. 1, 1995, pp. 83–95. https://doi.org/10.1007/BF02360343.
Horak, Laura. "Trans on YouTube: Intimacy, Visibility, Temporality." *TSQ: Transgender Studies Quarterly*, vol. 1, no. 4, 2014, pp. 572–85. https://doi.org/10.1215/23289252-815255.
Hughes-Hassell, Sandra, et al. "Lesbian, Gay, Bisexual, Transgender, and Questioning (LGBTQ)-Themed Literature for Teens: Are School Libraries Providing Adequate Collections?" *School Library Research*, vol. 16, 2013, pp. 1–18. https://eric.ed.gov/?id=EJ1012828.
Hume, Kathryn. *Fantasy and Mimesis: Responses to Reality in Western Literature*. Methuen, 1984.
Hunt, Caroline. "Theory Rises, Maginot Line Endures." *Children's Literature Association Quarterly*, vol. 42, no. 2, 2017, pp. 205–17. https://doi.org/10.1353/chq.2017.0017.
Hunt, Caroline. "Young Adult Literature Evades the Theorists." *Children's Literature Association Quarterly*, vol. 21, no. 1, 1996, pp. 4–11. https://doi.org/10.1353/chq.0.1129.
Hunt, Peter. "Introduction." *Alternative Worlds in Fantasy Fiction*, edited by Peter Hunt and Millicent Lenz, Continuum, 2001, pp. 1–41.
Hutchinson, Shaun David. *The Past and Other Things That Should Stay Buried*. Simon & Schuster, 2019.
Hyde, Catherine Ryan. *Jumpstart the World*. Penguin Random House, 2010.
Iser, Wolfgang. "Interview: Wolfgang Iser." *Diacritics*, vol. 10, no. 2, 1980, pp. 57–74. https://doi.org/10.2307/465093.
Jackson, Rosemary. *Fantasy: The Literature of Subversion*. Routledge, 2002.
Jacques, Juliet. *Trans: A Memoir*. Verso, 2015.
Jenkins, Christine A. "Young Adult Novels with Gay/Lesbian Characters and Themes 1969–92: A Historical Reading of Content, Gender, and Narrative Distance." *Journal of Youth Services in Libraries*, vol. 7, no. 1, 1993, pp. 43–55.
Jenkins, Christine A., and Michael Cart. *The Heart Has Its Reasons: Young Adult Literature with Gay/Lesbian/Queer Content, 1969–2004*. Scarecrow Press, 2006.

Jenkins, Christine A., and Michael Cart. *Representing the Rainbow in Young Adult Literature: LGBTQ+ Content since 1969*. Rowman & Littlefield, 2018.
Jenkins, Elwyn. "Reading Outside the Lines: Peritext and Authenticity in South African Children's Books." *The Lion and the Unicorn*, vol. 25, no. 1, 2001, pp. 115–27. https://doi.org/10.1353/uni.2001.0007.
Jenkins, Henry. "Introduction: Childhood Innocence and Other Modern Myths." *The Children's Culture Reader*, edited by Henry Jenkins, New York University Press, 1998, pp. 1–38.
Jenkins, Henry. "Transmedia Storytelling 101." *Henry Jenkins*, 21 Mar. 2007, http://henryjenkins.org/blog/2007/03/transmedia_storytelling_101.html. Accessed 31 Nov. 2018.
Jennings, Jazz, and Joshua Lyon. *Being Jazz: My Life as a (Transgender) Teen*. Crown, 2016.
Jiménez, Laura M. "Representations in Award-Winning LGBTQ Young Adult Literature from 2000–2013." *Journal of Lesbian Studies*, vol. 19, no. 4, 2015, pp. 406–22. https://doi.org/10.1080/10894160.2015.1057795.
Jones, Caroline E. "From Homoplot to Progressive Novel: Lesbian Experience and Identity in Contemporary Young Adult Novels." *The Lion and the Unicorn*, vol. 37, no. 1, 2013, pp. 74–93. https://doi.org/10.1353/uni.2013.0003.
Joosen, Vanessa. *Adulthood in Children's Literature*. Bloomsbury Academic, 2018.
Jorgensen, Christine. *Christine Jorgensen: A Personal Autobiography*. 1967. Cleis, 2000.
Kamblé, Jayashree. *Making Meaning in Popular Romance Fiction: An Epistemology*. Springer, 2014.
Katcher, Brian. *Almost Perfect*. Penguin Random House, 2009.
Keegan, Cael M. "Moving Bodies: Sympathetic Migrations in Transgender Narrativity." *Genders*, no. 57, 2013. https://go.gale.com/ps/i.do?p=AONE&sw=w&issn=08949832&v=2.1&it=r&id=GALE%7CA324981029&sid=googleScholar&linkaccess=abs. Accessed 18 Sep. 2020.
Kemp, Gene. *The Turbulent Term of Tyke Tiler*. Faber, 1977.
Kennon, Patricia. "Asexuality and the Potential of Young Adult Literature for Disrupting Allonormativity." *The International Journal of Young Adult Literature*, vol. 2, no. 1, 2021, pp. 1–24.
Kergil, Skylar. *Before I Had the Words: On Being a Transgender Young Adult*. Skyhorse, 2017.
Khuman, Bhagirath Jetubhai, and Madhumita Ghosal. "Ungendered Narrative: A New Genre in the Making." *Concentric: Literary and Cultural Studies*, vol. 44, no. 2, 2018, pp. 271–93.
Kidd, Kenneth. "Introduction: Lesbian/Gay Literature for Children and Young Adults." *Children's Literature Association Quarterly*, vol. 23, no. 3, 1998, pp. 114–19. https://doi.org/10.1353/chq.0.1284.
Kidd, Kenneth, and Derritt Mason. *Queer as Camp: Essays on Summer, Style, and Sexuality*. Fordham University Press, 2019.
Killeen, Erlene Bishop. "#WeNeedDiverseBooks!" *Teacher Librarian*, vol. 42, no. 5, 2015, p. 52.
Kirby, Dawn Latta, and Dan Kirby. "Contemporary Memoir: A 21st-Century Genre Ideal for Teens." *The English Journal*, vol. 99, no. 4, 2010, pp. 22–29.
Kittredge, Katharine. "The Girl-Hero for the New Millennia." *The Wiley Blackwell Companion to Contemporary British and Irish Literature*, edited by Richard Bradford et al., John Wiley & Sons, Ltd, 2020, pp. 671–81. https://doi.org/10.1002/9781118902264.ch62.

Kokkola, Lydia. *Fictions of Adolescent Carnality: Sexy Sinners and Delinquent Deviants.* John Benjamins, 2013.
Kokorski, Karin. "I Want More! The Insatiable Villain in Children's Literature and Young Adults' Fiction." *Global Perspectives on Villains and Villainy Today*, edited by Burcu Genc and Corinna Lenhardt, BRILL, 2011, pp. 147–54. https://doi.org/10.1163/9781848880528.
Kuklin, Susan. *Beyond Magenta: Transgender Teens Speak Out.* Candlewick, 2014.
Kwaymullina, Ambelin. "Privilege and Literature: Three Myths Created by Misdiagnosing a Lack of Indigenous Voices (and Other Diverse Voices) as a 'Diversity Problem.'" *ALPHA Reader*, 10 Mar. 2016, http://alphareader.blogspot.com/2016/03/privilege-and-literature-three-myths.html. Accessed 2 Oct. 2020.
Lam, Laura. *Masquerade.* Macmillan, 2017.
Lam, Laura. *Pantomime.* Macmillan, 2013.
Lam, Laura. *Shadowplay.* Macmillan, 2014.
Landgraff, Molly. *Fatebane Series.* Self-published, 2017.
Lapinski, L. D. *The Strangeworlds Travel Agency.* Hachette, 2020.
Latos, Alexandra. *Under Shifting Stars.* Houghton Mifflin Harcourt, 2020.
Lavoie, Alaina. "Why We Need Diverse Books Is No Longer Using the Term #OwnVoices." *WNDB*, 6 June 2021, https://diversebooks.org/why-we-need-diverse-books-is-no-longer-using-the-term-ownvoices/. Accessed 12 Apr. 2022.
Lee, C. B. *Not Your Backup.* Duet Books, 2019.
Lee, C. B. *Not Your Hero.* Duet Books, 2022.
Lee, C. B. *Not Your Sidekick.* Duet Books, 2016.
Lee, C. B. *Not Your Villain.* Duet Books, 2017.
Lefebvre, Benjamin. "From Bad Boy to Dead Boy: Homophobia, Adolescent Problem Fiction, and Male Bodies That Matter." *Children's Literature Association Quarterly*, vol. 30, no. 3, 2005, pp. 288–313. https://doi.org/10.1353/chq.2006.0008.
Lejeune, Philippe. *On Autobiography.* Edited by Paul John Eakin, translated by Katherine Leary, University of Minnesota Press, 1989.
Lenk, J. R. *The Missing: The Curious Cases of Will Winchester and the Black Cross.* Month9Books, 2017.
Letcher, Mark. "Off the Shelves: Celebrating Love in All Shades: YA Books with LGBTQ Themes." *The English Journal*, vol. 98, no. 4, 2009, pp. 123–26.
Levithan, David. "Boy Meets Boy, Ten Years Later." *Out*, 9 Apr. 2013, https://www.out.com/entertainment/art-books/2013/04/09/david-levithan-boy-meets-boy-10th-anniversary-ya. Accessed 27 Apr. 2020.
Levithan, David. *Everyday.* Penguin Random House, 2012.
Levithan, David. "Supporting Gay Teen Literature." *School Library Journal*, vol. 50, no. 10, 2004, pp. 44–45.
Lewis, Cady. "How Far Have We Come? A Critical Look at LGBTQ Identity in Young Adult Literature." *Language Arts Journal of Michigan*, vol. 30, no. 2, 2015, pp. 53–57. https://doi.org/10.9707/2168-49X.2072.
Liang, Bridget. *What Makes You Beautiful.* James Lorimer, 2019.
Lo, Malinda. "A Decade of LGBTQ YA Since Ash." *Malinda Lo*, 14 May 2019, https://www.malindalo.com/blog/2019/3/18/a-decade-of-lgbtq-ya-since-ash. Accessed 17 Oct. 2020.
Lo, Malinda. "LGBTQ YA by the Numbers: 2015–16." *Malinda Lo*, 12 Oct. 2017, https://www.malindalo.com/blog/2017/10/12/lgbtq-ya-by-the-numbers-2015-16. Accessed 17 Oct. 2020.

Loeb, Jeph, and Tom Morris. "Heroes and Superheroes." *Superheroes and Philosophy: Truth, Justice, and the Socratic Way*, edited by Tom Morris and Matt Morris, Open Court, 2001, pp. 11–20.
Louie, Belinda Y., and Douglas H. Louie. "Empowerment through Young-Adult Literature." *The English Journal*, vol. 81, no. 4, 1992, pp. 53–56. https://doi.org/10.2307/819931.
Love, Heather. "Transgender Fiction and Politics." *The Cambridge Companion to Gay and Lesbian Writing*, edited by Hugh Stevens, Cambridge University Press, 2011, pp. 148–66.
Lovelock, Michael. "Call Me Caitlyn: Making and Making over the 'Authentic' Transgender Body in Anglo-American Popular Culture." *Journal of Gender Studies*, vol. 26, no. 6, Routledge, 2017, pp. 675–87. https://doi.org/10.1080/09589236.2016.1155978.
Maas, Sarah J. *Catwoman: Soulstealer*. Penguin Random House, 2019.
MacFarlane, Elizabeth, et al. "Introducing the Superhero Body." *Superhero Bodies: Identity, Materiality, Transformation*, edited by Elizabeth MacFarlane et al, Routledge, 2019, pp. 1–13.
@malindalo (Malinda Lo). "Coming out stories are still important, but I do think straight people sometimes forget that the LGBTQ experience can also involve happiness, adventure, saving the world/slaying dragons/solving mysteries. You know, LIFE." *Twitter*, 13 April 2018, https://twitter.com/malindalo/status/984507355076456448.
Mallan, Kerry. "(M)Other Love: Constructing Queer Families in Girl Walking Backwards and Obsession." *Children's Literature Association Quarterly*, vol. 29, no. 4, 2004, pp. 345–57. https://doi.org/10.1353/chq.0.1473.
Malo-Juvera, Victor, and Crag Hill. *Critical Explorations of Young Adult Literature: Identifying and Critiquing the Canon*. Routledge, Taylor & Francis Group, 2019.
Martin, George R. R. *A Song of Ice and Fire Series*. Bantam Books, 1996.
Mason, Derritt. *Queer Anxieties of Young Adult Literature and Culture*. University Press of Mississippi, 2020.
Matos, Angel Daniel. "Adolescence." *The Routledge History of American Sexuality*, edited by Kevin P. Murphy et al., Routledge, 2020, pp. 10–20.
Matos, Angel Daniel. "The Undercover Life of Young Adult Novels." *ALAN Review*, vol. 44, no. 2, 2017, pp. 85–91.
Matthews, Nicole. "Introduction." *Judging a Book by Its Cover: Fans, Publishers, Designers, and the Marketing of Fiction*, edited by Nicole Matthews and Nickianne Moody, Routledge, 2016, pp. xi–xxi.
McAdam, Tash. *Blood Sport*. Orca Books, 2020.
McAdam, Tash. *The Psionics Series*. NineStar, 2016.
McAlister, Jodi. "Defining and Redefining Popular Genres: The Evolution of 'New Adult' Fiction." *Australian Literary Studies*, 2018, pp. 1–19. https://doi.org/10.20314/als.0fd566d109.
McCallum, E. L., and Mikko Tuhkanen. "Introduction." *The Cambridge History of Gay and Lesbian Literature*, edited by E. L. McCallum and Mikko Tuhkanen, Cambridge University Press, 2014, pp. 1–12. https://doi.org/10.1017/CHO9781139547376.001.
McCallum, Robyn. *Ideologies of Identity in Adolescent Fiction: The Dialogic Construction of Subjectivity*. Routledge, 1999.
McKenna, Miles. *Out!: How to Be Your Authentic Self*. ABRAMS, 2020.
McLemore, Anna-Marie. *Blanca & Roja*. Macmillan, 2018.
McLemore, Anna-Marie. *Dark and Deepest Red*. Macmillan, 2020.
McLemore, Anna-Marie. *Lakelore*. Macmillan, 2022.

McLemore, Anna-Marie. *When the Moon Was Ours*. Macmillan, 2016.
Mendlesohn, Farah. *Rhetorics of Fantasy*. Wesleyan University Press, 2008.
Mesch, Rachel. *Before Trans: Three Gender Stories from Nineteenth-Century France*. Stanford University Press, 2020.
Meyer, Anneke. "The Moral Rhetoric of Childhood." *Childhood*, vol. 14, no. 1, 2007, pp. 85–104. https://doi.org/10.1177/0907568207072532.
Meyerowitz, Joanne. *How Sex Changed: A History of Transsexuality in the United States*. Harvard University Press, 1980.
Miller, Linsey. *Mask of Shadows*. Sourcebooks, 2017.
Miller, Linsey. *Ruin of Stars*. Sourcebooks, 2018.
Miller, Mary Catherine. "Identifying Effective Trans* Novels for Adolescent Readers." *Bookbird: A Journal of International Children's Literature*, vol. 52, no. 1, 2014, pp. 83–86. https://doi.org/10.1353/bkb.2014.0042.
Miller, sj. "Introduction: The Role of Recognition." *Teaching, Affirming, and Recognizing Trans and Gender Creative Youth: A Queer Literacy Framework*, edited by sj Miller, Palgrave Macmillan US, 2016, pp. 1–24.
Minkman, Lorna. *Jongensdroom*. Lannoo, 2007.
Mock, Janet. *Redefining Realness: My Path to Womanhood, Identity, Love and So Much More*. Atria Books, 2014.
Moore, Perry. *Hero*. Hyperion Books for Children, 2007.
Morgan, Cheryl. "Tipping the Fantastic: How the Transgender Tipping Point Has Influenced Speculative Fiction." *Gender Identity and Sexuality in Current Fantasy and Science Fiction*, edited by edited by F. T. Barbini, Luna Press Publishing, 2017, pp. 83–103.
Morris, Jan. *Conundrum*. Harcourt Brace Jovanovich, 1974.
Moss, Christopher Hawthorne. *Beloved Pilgrim*. Dreamspinner, 2014.
Mukherjee, Utsa. "Rainbows, Teddy Bears and 'Others': The Cultural Politics of Children's Leisure Amidst the COVID-19 Pandemic." *Leisure Sciences*, vol. 43, no. 1–2, 2021, pp. 24–30. https://doi.org/10.1080/01490400.2020.1773978.
Musgrave, Megan L. *Digital Citizenship in Twenty-First-Century Young Adult Literature: Imaginary Activism*. Palgrave Macmillan, 2016.
Myers, Christopher. "The Apartheid of Children's Literature." *The New York Times*, Mar. 2014, https://www.nytimes.com/2014/03/16/opinion/sunday/the-apartheid-of-childrens-literature.html. Accessed 19 Jul. 2019.
Nash, Jackson Jesse. *The Transgender Tipping Point and Trans Representation in Contemporary Young Adult YA Fiction*. PhD Thesis, 2019.
Nijkamp, Marieke. *Even If We Break*. Sourcebooks Fire, 2020.
Nikolajeva, Maria. *Power, Voice and Subjectivity in Literature for Young Readers*. Routledge, 2010.
Nikolajeva, Maria. *The Rhetoric of Character in Children's Literature*. Scarecrow, 2002.
Nodelman, Perry. *The Hidden Adult: Defining Children's Literature*. Johns Hopkins University Press, 2008.
Nodelman, Perry. *The Pleasures of Children's Literature*. Longman, 1996.
Norton, Jody. "Transchildren and the Discipline of Children's Literature." *The Lion and the Unicorn*, vol. 23, no. 3, 1999, pp. 415–36. https://doi.org/10.1353/uni.1999.0034.
Nova, Cole. *The Wicked Bargain*. Penguin Random House, 2022.
O'Connor, Amy. "John Boyne Deletes Twitter Account after Trans Article Backlash." *The Irish Times*, 16 Apr. 2019, https://www.irishtimes.com/culture/books/john-boyne-deletes-twitter-account-after-trans-article-backlash-1.3862249. Accessed 16 Apr. 2019.

Office for National Statistics. *Families and Households in the UK: 2020*. Mar. 2021.

O'Keefe, Deborah. *Readers in Wonderland: The Liberating Worlds of Fantasy Fiction: From Dorothy to Harry Potter*. Continuum, 2003.

Olsen, Nora. *Maxine Wore Black*. Bold Stroke Books, 2014.

O'Neill, Matthew G. "Transgender Youth and YouTube Videos: Self-Representation and Five Identifiable Trans Youth Narratives." *Queer Youth and Media Cultures*, edited by Christopher Pullen, Springer, 2014, pp. 34–45.

Oseman, Alice. *I Was Born for This*. HarperCollins, 2018.

Owen, Gabrielle. *A Queer History of Adolescence: Developmental Pasts, Relational Futures*. University of Georgia Press, 2020.

Owen, Gabrielle. "Adolescence, Trans Phenomena, and the Politics of Sexuality Education." *The Palgrave Handbook of Sexuality Education*, Palgrave Macmillan, 2017, pp. 555–70.

Packham, Simon. *Only We Know*. Piccadilly, 2015.

Page, Winter. *Breaking Free*. Dreamspinner, 2014.

Pallotta-Chiarolli, Maria. "Only Your Labels Split Me: Interweaving Ethnicity and Sexuality in English Studies." *English in Australia*, vol. 112, 1995, pp. 33–44.

Paslawski, Megan. *The Way We Dream Now: History, Theory, and LGBTQ Memoir in America*. PhD Thesis, 2018.

Patel, Sonia. *Jaya and Rasa: A Love Story*. Cinco Puntos, 2017.

Pattee, Amy. "Between Youth and Adulthood: Young Adult and New Adult Literature." *Children's Literature Association Quarterly*, vol. 42, no. 2, 2017, pp. 218–30. https://doi.org/10.1353/chq.2017.0018.

Pavao, Kate. "Both Sides of the Story: Transgender Teens Release Memoirs." *Publishers Weekly.Com*, 7 Aug. 2014, https://www.publishersweekly.com/pw/by-topic/childrens/childrens-book-news/article/63590-both-sides-of-the-story-transgender-teens-release-memoirs.html. Accessed 18 May 2020.

Pearce, Ruth, Deborah Lynn Steinberg, and Igi Moon. "Introduction: The Emergence Of 'Trans.'" *Sexualities*, vol. 22, nos. 1–2, 2019), pp. 3–12.

Pellegrini, Chiara. "Posttranssexual Temporalities: Negotiating Canonical Memoir Narratives in Kate Bornstein's *Gender Outlaw* and Juliet Jacques's *Trans*." *Auto/Biography Studies*, vol. 34, no. 1, 2019, pp. 45–65. https://doi.org/10.1080/08989575.2019.1542820.

Pendragon, J. K. *Junior Hero Blues*. Riptide, 2016.

Peters, Julie Anne. *Luna*. Hachette, 2004.

Pew Research Centre. *Parenting in America*. Dec. 2015.

Phillips, Leah. *Female Heroes in Young Adult Fantasy Fiction*. Bloomsbury, 2023.

Phillips, Leah. *Myth (Un)Making: The Adolescent Female Body in Mythopoeic YA Fantasy*. PhD Thesis, 2016.

Phillips, Leah. "Mythopoeic YA: Worlds of Possibility." *Beyond the Blockbusters: Themes and Trends in Contemporary Young Adult Fiction*, edited by Rebekah Fitzsimmons and Casey Alane Wilson, University Press of Mississippi, 2020, pp. 123–39.

Phillips, Maureen. "Book Review: Cris Beam's *Transparent*." *Xtra Magazine*. Jan. 2007, https://xtramagazine.com/culture/book-review-cris-beams-transparent-19688. Accessed 29 Jan. 2021.

Pierce, Tamora. The Song of the Lioness series. Atheneum Books, 1983.

Pini, Barbara, et al. "Transphobic Tropes and Young Adult Fiction: An Analysis of Brian Katcher's Almost Perfect." *The Lion and the Unicorn*, vol. 42, no. 1, 2018, pp. 57–72. https://doi.org/10.1353/uni.2018.0004.

Pinsent, Pat. *The Power of the Page: Children's Books and Their Readers*. D. Fulton, 1993.
Plum-Ucci, Carol. *What Happened to Lani Garver*. Houghton Mifflin, 2002.
Prosser, Jay. *Second Skins: The Body Narratives of Transsexuality*. Columbia University Press, 1998.
Pulliam, June. *Monstrous Bodies: Feminine Power in Young Adult Horror Fiction*. McFarland, 2014.
Putzi, Jennifer. "'None of This 'Trapped-in-a-Man's-Body' Bullshit': Transgender Girls and Wrong-Body Discourse in Young Adult Fiction." *Tulsa Studies in Women's Literature*, vol. 36, no. 2, 2017, pp. 423–48. https://doi.org/10.1353/tsw.2017.0029.
Rak, Julie. *Boom!: Manufacturing Memoir for the Popular Market*. Wilfrid Laurier University Press, 2013.
Rak, Julie. "Memoir, Truthiness, and the Power of Oprah." *Prose Studies*, vol. 34, no. 3, 2012, pp. 224–42. https://doi.org/10.1080/01440357.2012.751260.
Ramdarshan Bold, Melanie. "The Eight Percent Problem: Authors of Colour in the British Young Adult Market (2006–2016)." *Publishing Research Quarterly*, vol. 34, no. 3, 2018, pp. 385–406. https://doi.org/10.1007/s12109-018-9600-5.
Ramdarshan Bold, Melanie. *Inclusive Young Adult Fiction: Authors of Colour in the United Kingdom*. Springer International, 2019.
Ramdarshan Bold, Melanie. "The Thirteen Percent Problem: Authors of Colour in the UKYA Market, 2017–2019 Edition." *The International Journal of Young Adult Literature*, vol. 2, no. 1, 2021, pp. 1–35.
Ramdarshan Bold, Melanie, and Leah Phillips. "Adolescent Identities: The Untapped Power Of YA." *Research on Diversity in Youth Literature*, vol. 1, no. 2, 2019, pp. 1–9.
Raun, Tobias. "Video Blogging as a Vehicle of Transformation: Exploring the Intersection between Trans Identity and Information Technology." *International Journal of Cultural Studies*, vol. 18, no. 3, 2015, pp. 365–78. https://doi.org/10.1177/1367877913513696.
Rawson, K. J., and Cristan Williams. "Transgender*: The Rhetorical Landscape of a Term." *Present Tense*, vol. 3, no. 2, 2014, pp. 1–9.
Reay, Barry. "Transgender Orgasms." *Feminist Formations*, vol. 28, no. 2, 2016, pp. 152–61. https://doi.org/10.1353/ff.2016.0034.
Rebellino, Rachel L. Rickard. "Oversharing on and off the Internet: Crossing from Digital to Print (and Back) in Young Adult Works Authored by YouTube Stars." *Beyond the Blockbusters: Themes and Trends in Contemporary Young Adult Fiction*, edited by Rebekah Fitzsimmons and Casey Alane Wilson, University Press of Mississippi, 2020, pp. 20–32.
Reimer, Mavis. "Homing and Unhoming: The Ideological Work of Canadian Children's Literature." *Discourses of Children's Literature in Canada*, edited by Mavis Reimer, Wilfrid Laurier University Press, 2008, pp. 1–26.
Reynolds, Kimberley. *Radical Children's Literature: Future Visions and Aesthetic Transformations in Juvenile Fiction*. Springer, 2007.
Rheingold, Howard. *The Virtual Community: Homesteading on the Electronic Frontier*. MIT Press, 2000.
Richard, Nikki. *Demon in the Whitelands*. Month9Books, 2019.
Richards, Renée, and John Ames. *Second Serve: The Renée Richards Story*. Stein and Day, 1983.
Riordan, Rick. Magnus Chase and the Gods of Asgard series. Disney Hyperion, 2015.
Roche, Juno. *Gender Explorers: Our Stories of Growing Up Trans and Changing the World*. Jessica Kingsley, 2020.

Rose, Jacqueline. *The Case of Peter Pan, Or, The Impossibility of Children's Fiction*. Macmillan, 1984.
Rosenberg, Robin S., and Peter MacFarland Coogan. *What Is a Superhero?* Oxford University Press, 2013.
Rosenthal, Angela. "Raising Hair." *Eighteenth-Century Studies*, vol. 38, no. 1, 2004, pp. 1–16.
Rosewater, Kit, and Sophie Escabasse. *Kenzie Kickstarts a Team*. Amulet Books, 2020.
Rotman, Dana, and Jennifer Preece. "The 'WeTube' in YouTube—Creating an Online Community through Video Sharing." *International Journal of Web Based Communities*, vol. 6, no. 3, 2010, pp. 317–33. https://doi.org/10.1504/IJWBC.2010.033755.
Rowling, J. K. "J. K. Rowling Writes about Her Reasons for Speaking Out on Sex and Gender Issues." *J. K. Rowling*, 10 June 2020, https://www.jkrowling.com/opinions/j-k-rowling-writes-about-her-reasons-for-speaking-out-on-sex-and-gender-issues/. Accessed 10 June 2020.
Rubenstein, Roberta. *Home Matters: Longing and Belonging, Nostalgia and Mourning in Women's Fiction*. Springer, 2001.
Russo, Meredith. *Birthday*. Macmillan, 2019.
Russo, Meredith. *If I Was Your Girl*. Macmillan, 2016.
Salinger, J. D. *The Catcher in the Rye*. Little, Brown, 1951.
Sandercock, Tom. *Youth Fiction and Trans Representation*. Routledge, 2023.
Sandercock, Tom. "Transing the Small Screen: Loving and Hating Transgender Youth in Glee and Degrassi." *Journal of Gender Studies*, vol. 24, no. 4, 2015, pp. 436–52. https://doi.org/10.1080/09589236.2015.1021307.
Santana, Sol. *Just Ash*. Carolrhoda Lab, 2021.
Saunders, Ben. *Do The Gods Wear Capes?: Spirituality, Fantasy, and Superheroes*. A&C Black, 2011.
Saxey, Esther. *Homoplot: The Coming-out Story and Gay, Lesbian and Bisexual Identity*. Peter Lang, 2008.
Schiffer, Davida Jae. "Researching While Trans: Being Clocked and Cooling Cistress." *Journal of Contemporary Ethnography*, vol. 51, no. 5, 2022, pp. 700–725.
Schmatz, Pat. *Lizard Radio*. Candlewick, 2015.
Schrieve, Hal. *Out of Salem*. Seven Stories, 2019.
Serano, Julia. *Whipping Girl: A Transsexual Woman on Sexism and the Scapegoating of Femininity*. Basic Books, 2016.
Shrier, Abigail. *Irreversible Damage: The Transgender Craze Seducing Our Daughters*. Simon and Schuster, 2020.
Shuttleworth, Ashley. *A Dark and Hollow Star*. Simon and Schuster, 2021.
Siegert, Mia. *Somebody Told Me*. Lerner, 2020.
Sivashankar, Nithya, et al. "Centering the Margins: Investigating Relationships, Power, and Culture through Critical Peritextual Analysis." *Children's Literature in Education*, vol. 51, no. 4, 2020, pp. 480–501. https://doi.org/10.1007/s10583-019-09395-4.
Skylarkeleven (Skylar Kergil). "37 days post hysterectomy update." YouTube, 15 February 2012, https://www.youtube.com/watch?v=HHOeF79eXoE. Accessed 21 Sept. 2021.
Skylarkeleven (Skylar Kergil). "i'll be yr bird—m. ward cover." YouTube, 14 February 2013, https://www.youtube.com/watch?v=Ev5zyD_aWLg. Accessed 21 Sept. 2021.
Skylarkeleven (Skylar Kergil). "march seventh—transitional update." YouTube, 7 March 2011, https://www.youtube.com/watch?v=JDXNfhqDosQ. Accessed 21 Sept. 2021.

Skylarkeleven (Skylar Kergil). "Q&A: MOM & TRANSGENDER SON." YouTube, 29 August 2014, https://www.youtube.com/watch?v=ID2ZmEsgqIU. Accessed 21 Sept. 2021.

Skylarkeleven (Skylar Kergil). "Say Yes—Elliot Smith (cover)." YouTube, 3 November 2014, https://www.youtube.com/watch?v=RGFCVpt_wEM. Accessed 21 Sept. 2021.

Skylarkeleven (Skylar Kergil). "Tiger's morning attitude." YouTube, 25 February 2015, https://www.youtube.com/watch?v=rceUbH87WD8. Accessed 21 Sept. 2021.

Skylarkeleven (Skylar Kergil). "two years on testosterone—changes & reflections." YouTube, 21 January 2011, https://www.youtube.com/watch?v=ixfra-v4q34. Accessed 21 Sept. 2021.

Skylarkeleven (Skylar Kergil). "two years post top surgery." YouTube, 30 December 2011, https://www.youtube.com/watch?v=5A3lC890nvQ. Accessed 21 Sept. 2021.

Slagle, R. Anthony. "Queer Criticism and Sexual Normativity." *Journal of Homosexuality*, vol. 45, no. 2–4, 2003, pp. 129–46. https://doi.org/10.1300/J082v45n02_06.

Smith, Amber. *Something like Gravity*. Simon & Schuster, 2019.

Smolkin, Laura B., and Craig A. Young. "Missing Mirrors, Missing Windows: Children's Literature Textbooks and LGBT Topics." *Language Arts*, vol. 88, no. 3, pp. 217–25.

Smolkin, Laura B., and Joseph H. Suina. "Artistic Triumph or Multicultural Failure? Multiple Perspectives on a 'Multicultural' Award-Winning Book." *Stories Matter: The Complexity of Cultural Authenticity in Children's Literature*, edited by Dana L. Fox and Kathy G. Short, National Council of Teachers of English, 2003, pp. 213–30. https://eric.ed.gov/?id=ED480339.

Sokoll, Talya. "Representations of Trans Youth in Young Adult Literature: A Report and a Suggestion." *Young Adult Library Services*, vol. 11, no. 4, 2013, pp. 23–26.

Spangler, Brie. *Beast*. Penguin Random House, 2016.

Spencer, Leland G. "Performing Transgender Identity in *The Little Mermaid*: From Andersen to Disney." *Communication Studies*, vol. 65, no. 1, 2014, pp. 112–27. https://doi.org/10.1080/10510974.2013.832691.

Steinmetz, Katy. "Transgender Teen Star Jazz Jennings to Publish a Memoir." *EW.Com*, 26 Jan. 2016, https://ew.com/article/2016/01/26/jazz-jennings-memoir/. Accessed 21 Sept. 2021.

Steinmetz, Katy. "The Transgender Tipping Point." *Time*, 2014, https://time.com/135480/transgender-tipping-point/. Accessed 21 Sept. 2021.

Stoeve, Ray. *Between Perfect and Real*. Amulet Books, 2021.

Stoeve, Ray. "Trans Representation in YA Fiction Is Changing, But How Much?" *Autostraddle*, https://www.autostraddle.com/trans-representation-in-ya-fiction-is-changing-but-how-much/. Accessed 17 Aug. 2021.

Stone, Sandy. "The Empire Strikes Back: A Posttranssexual Manifesto." *The Transgender Studies Reader*, edited by Susan Stryker and Stephen Whittle, Routledge, 2006, pp. 221–35.

Stryker, Susan. "My Words to Victor Frankenstein above the Village of Chamounix: Performing Transgender Rage." 1993. *The Transgender Studies Reader*, edited by Susan Stryker and Stephen Whittle, Routledge, 2006, pp. 244–56.

Stryker, Susan. *Transgender History: The Roots of Today's Revolution*. 2nd ed., Basic Books, 2017.

Stryker, Susan, and Paisley Currah. "Introduction." *Transgender Studies Quarterly*, vol. 1, nos. 1–2, 2014, pp. 1–18.

Suico, Terri. "History Repeating Itself: The Portrayal of Female Characters in Young Adult Literature at the Beginning of the Millennium." *Gender(Ed) Identities: Critical Rereadings of Gender in Children's and Young Adult Literature*, edited by Tricia Clasen and Holly Hassel, Routledge, 2016, pp. 11–27. https://doi.org/10.4324/9781315691633.

Sullivan, C. W. "Fantasy." *Stories and Society: Children's Literature in Its Social Context*, edited by Dennis Butts, Palgrave Macmillan UK, 1992, pp. 97–111. https://doi.org/10.1007/978-1-349-22111-0_7.

Sun, Simón(e) D. "Stop Using Phony Science to Justify Transphobia." *Scientific American Blog Network*, https://blogs.scientificamerican.com/voices/stop-using-phony-science-to-justify-transphobia/. Accessed 16 Aug. 2021.

Sutton, Matthew. "Amplifying the Text: Paratext in Popular Musicians' Autobiographies." *Popular Music and Society*, vol. 38, no. 2, 2015, pp. 208–23. https://doi.org/10.1080/03007766.2014.994325.

Synnott, Anthony. *The Body Social: Symbolism, Self, and Society*. Routledge, 1993.

Talley, Robin. *What We Left Behind*. HarperCollins, 2015.

@TamoraPierce (Tamora Pierce). "Alanna has always defied labels. She took the best bits of being a woman and a man, and created her own unique identity. I think the term is 'gender-fluid,' though there wasn't a word for this (to my knowledge) when I was writing her." *Twitter*, 4 December 2019, https://twitter.com/TamoraPierce/status/1202294877213450240.

Tarttelin, Abigail. *Golden Boy*. Simon and Schuster, 2013.

Tatar, Maria. *Enchanted Hunters: The Power of Stories in Childhood*. W. W. Norton, 2009.

"Teenagers Who Swapped Genders End Up Finding Love with Each Other (PICTURES)." *The Huffington Post*, 23 July 2013, https://www.huffingtonpost.co.uk/2013/07/23/teenagers-gender-swap_n_3639594.html. Accessed 21 Sept. 2021.

TheRealAlexBertie (Alex Bertie). "1 MONTH ON T!" YouTube, 18 May 2016, https://www.youtube.com/watch?v=B1Z6npi2_lA. Accessed 21 Sept. 2021.

TheRealAlexBertie (Alex Bertie). "2 MONTHS ON T." YouTube, 18 June 2016, https://www.youtube.com/watch?v=WY-Ghaem7no. Accessed 21 Sept. 2021.

TheRealAlexBertie (Alex Bertie). "3 MONTHS ON T." YouTube, 18 July 2016, https://www.youtube.com/watch?v=ppSFeZ3eozk. Accessed 21 Sept. 2021.

TheRealAlexBertie (Alex Bertie). "5 MONTHS ON T." YouTube, 15 Sep 2016, https://www.youtube.com/watch?v=kZdpM417SNg. Accessed 21 Sept. 2021.

TheRealAlexBertie (Alex Bertie). "1 YEAR ON T: FTM TRANSGENDER." YouTube, 19 April 2017, https://www.youtube.com/watch?v=ayWoASQHjZQ. Accessed 21 Sept. 2021.

TheRealAlexBertie (Alex Bertie). "TRANSGENDER: 2 YEARS ON TESTOSTERONE." YouTube, 22 April 2018, https://www.youtube.com/watch?v=tb3b-mKxZm8. Accessed 21 Sept. 2021.

Thiel, Elizabeth. *The Fantasy of Family: Nineteenth-Century Children's Literature and the Myth of the Domestic Ideal*. Routledge, 2008.

Thomas, Aiden. *Cemetery Boys*. Macmillan, 2020.

Thomas, Aiden. "Our Friend Is Here! Pride Month Edition—An Interview with Aiden Thomas, Author of Cemetery Boys; On Writing a Love Letter to Their Community and Writing an Unapologetic Latinx, Gay, and Trans Story." *The Quiet Pond*, 11 June 2020, https://thequietpond.com/2020/06/12/our-friend-is-here-pride-month-edition-an-interview-with-aiden-thomas-on-writing-a-love-letter-to-their-community-and-writing-an-unapologetic-latinx-gay-and-trans-story/. Accessed 20 June 2021.

Thomas, Ebony Elizabeth. *The Dark Fantastic: Race and the Imagination from Harry Potter to the Hunger Games*. NYU Press, 2019.

Thomas, Ebony Elizabeth. "Young Adult Literature for Black Lives: Critical and Storytelling Traditions from the African Diaspora." *The International Journal of Young Adult Literature*, vol. 1, no. 1, Nov. 2020, pp 1–15. https://doi.org/10.24877/ijyal.27.

Thomas, P. L., et al. "'I Just Don't See Myself Here': Challenging Conversations about LGBTQ Adolescent Literature." *The English Journal*, vol. 99, no. 3, 2010, pp. 76–79.

Thomas, Victoria E. "Gazing at 'It': An Intersectional Analysis of Transnormativity and Black Womanhood in Orange Is the New Black." *Communication, Culture and Critique*, vol. 13, no. 4, 2020, pp. 519–35. https://doi.org/10.1093/ccc/tcz030.

Thompson, John B. *Merchants of Culture: The Publishing Business in the Twenty-First Century*. 2nd ed., Polity, 2012.

Thorne, Hayden. *Masks: Rise of Heroes*. Prizm, 2008.

Todorov, Tzvetan. *Genres in Discourse*. Cambridge University Press, 1990.

Todres, Jonathan, and Sarah Higinbotham. *Human Rights in Children's Literature: Imagination and the Narrative of Law*. Oxford University Press, 2016.

Tolkein, J. R. R. *The Lord of the Rings*. George Allen & Unwin, 1954.

Town, Caren J. *LGBTQ Young Adult Fiction: A Critical Survey, 1970s-2010s*. McFarland, 2017.

Tribunella, Eric L. *Melancholia and Maturation: The Use of Trauma in American Children's Literature*. University of Tennessee Press, 2009.

Trites, Roberta Seelinger. *Disturbing the Universe: Power and Repression in Adolescent Literature*. University of Iowa Press, 2000.

Trites, Roberta Seelinger. "Queer Performances: Lesbian Politics in Little Women." *Over the Rainbow: Queer Children's and Young Adult Literature*, edited by Michelle Ann Abate and Kenneth Kidd, University of Michigan Press, 2011, pp. 33–58.

Trites, Roberta Seelinger. *Twenty-First-Century Feminisms in Children's and Adolescent Literature*. University Press of Mississippi, 2018.

Vaccaro, Annemarie, et al. *Safe Spaces: Making Schools and Communities Welcoming to LGBT Youth*. ABC-CLIO, 2012.

Venzo, Paul, and Kristine Moruzi, editors. *Sexuality in Literature for Children and Young Adults*. Routledge, 2021.

Vidal-Ortiz, Salvador. "Whiteness." *Transgender Studies Quarterly*, vol. 1, nos. 1–2 (2014): 264–66.

Vincent, Ben, et al. *TERF Wars: Feminism and the Fight for Transgender Futures*. Sage, 2020.

Vipond, Evan. "Becoming Culturally (Un)Intelligible: Exploring the Terrain of Trans Life Writing." *Auto/Biography Studies*, vol. 34, no. 1, 2019, pp. 19–43. https://doi.org/10.1080/08989575.2019.1542813.

Wakarindi, Jane Wangari. "Paratext and the Making of YA Fiction Genre: The Repoussoir." *Eastern African Literary and Cultural Studies*, vol. 5, no. 2, 2019, pp. 94–108. https://doi.org/10.1080/23277408.2019.1635858.

Waller, Alison. "The Art of Being Ordinary: Cups of Tea and Catching the Bus in Contemporary British YA." *The International Journal of Young Adult Literature*, vol. 1, no. 1, 2020, pp.1–25. https://doi.org/10.24877/ijyal.34.

Waller, Alison. *Constructing Adolescence in Fantastic Realism*. Routledge, 2009.

Warnqvist, Åsa. "'I'm Sure This Whole Boy Thing Is Just a Phase': Transgender Narratives in Contemporary Swedish Children's and Young Adult Literature." *International LGBTQ+ Literature for Children and Young Adults*, edited by B. J. Epstein and Elizabeth L. Chapman, Anthem, 2021, pp. 275–302.

Whitby, S. J. *Cute Mutants Series*. Self-published, 2020.

Whitehead, Joshua. *Jonny Appleseed*. Arsenal Pulp, 2018.

Whittle, Stephen. *The Transgender Debate: The Crisis Surrounding Gender Identity*. South Street, 2000.

Wickens, Corrine M. "Codes, Silences, and Homophobia: Challenging Normative Assumptions about Gender and Sexuality in Contemporary LGBTQ Young Adult Literature." *Children's Literature in Education*, vol. 2, no. 42, 2011, pp. 148–64. https://doi.org/10.1007/s10583-011-9129-0.

Wilkins, Kim. "The Process of Genre: Authors, Readers, Institutions." *Text*, vol. 9, no. 2, 2005.

Wilkins, Kim. *Young Adult Fantasy Fiction: Conventions, Originality, Reproducibility*. Cambridge University Press, 2019.

Williamson, Lisa. *The Art of Being Normal*. David Fickling Books, 2015.

Wilson, Mandy. "'I Am the Prince of Pain, for I Am a Princess in the Brain': Liminal Transgender Identities, Narratives and the Elimination of Ambiguities." *Sexualities*, vol. 5, no. 4, 2002, pp. 425–48. https://doi.org/10.1177/1363460702005004003.

Wilson, Melissa B., and Kathy G. Short. "Goodbye Yellow Brick Road: Challenging the Mythology of Home in Children's Literature." *Children's Literature in Education*, vol. 43, no. 2, 2012, pp. 129–44. https://doi.org/10.1007/s10583-011-9138-z.

Wittlinger, Ellen. *Parrotfish*. Simon & Schuster, 2007.

Wittlinger, Ellen. *Parrotfish*. Simon & Schuster, 2015.

Wittlinger, Ellen. "Parrotfish Needed an Update: The Rapidly Changing Language of Transgender Awareness." *The Horn Book*, Nov. 2015, https://www.hbook.com?detailStory=parrotfish-needed-an-update-the-rapidly-changing-language-of-transgender-awareness. Accessed 20 Jan. 2019.

Wolf, Mark J. P. *Building Imaginary Worlds: The Theory and History of Subcreation*. Routledge, 2012.

Wolf, Shelby, et al. *Handbook of Research on Children's and Young Adult Literature*. Routledge, 2011.

Wolf, Virginia L. "From the Myth to the Wake of Home: Literary Houses." *Children's Literature*, vol. 18, no. 1, 1990, pp. 53–67. https://doi.org/10.1353/chl.0.0305.

Woltz, Anna, and Vicky Janssen. *Meisje van Mars*. Em. Querido's Uitgeverij BV, 2011.

Wood, Jennie. *A Boy like Me*. 215 Ink, 2014.

Yampbell, Cat. "Judging a Book by Its Cover: Publishing Trends in Young Adult Literature." *The Lion and the Unicorn*, vol. 29, no. 3, 2005, pp. 348–72. https://doi.org/10.1353/uni.2005.0049.

Zimman, Lal. "'The Other Kind of Coming Out': Transgender People and the Coming Out Narrative Genre." *Gender and Language*, vol. 3, no. 1, 2009, pp. 53–80. https://doi.org/10.1558/genl.v3i1.53.

Zimmerly, Stephen M. *The Sidekick Comes of Age: How Young Adult Literature Is Shifting the Sidekick Paradigm*. Lexington Books, 2019.

INDEX

abuse, 5, 39, 123, 125–29, 135
acceptance, 6, 34–35, 49–54, 86, 92, 96–98, 133–36
adolescence, 37–38, 40, 47–49, 100–103, 109, 117–18, 138–39, 141–43, 156–57
aetonormativity, 85, 110, 115–17, 131–37
Alston, Ann, 122, 124
Andrews, Arin, 142–43, 147–48, 152–53
Art of Being Normal, The, 9, 33, 39, 41, 43, 52, 125, 168
authenticity, 23, 74–79, 132

Barthes, Roland, 24, 116, 118, 124–28
Beam, Cris, 9, 20, 33, 39, 42, 50–51, 60, 122–23, 128, 168
Beautiful Music for Ugly Children, 9, 33, 39, 42, 51, 56–57, 168
Beauvais, Clémentine, 25, 110, 115–16, 131–32, 139
Before I Had the Words, 142–44, 153–56, 159–62
Being Jazz, 48, 142, 144–53
Bertie, Alex, 142–43, 157–63
Birthday, 66, 86, 122, 136
Bittner, Robert, 85, 97, 111, 143–45, 149–52; and colleagues, 13, 49, 51, 55–57, 62, 68, 96, 169
Bold, Melanie Ramdarshan, 4, 8, 23–24, 63–64, 81; and Leah Phillips, 73, 82
Boyne, John, 23–24, 71, 74, 80–81, 114, 122–23, 170
Butler, Catherine, 5, 44, 52–54, 60, 86, 130, 168

Callender, Kacen, 66–68, 70, 78, 122, 169
Cart, Michael, 35–36, 83, 87, 92; and Christine A. Jenkins, 8, 13–16, 20, 37, 70, 81, 87–88, 115, 120, 123
Cemetery Boys, 10, 64, 66, 89, 92, 96, 101, 120, 122, 134, 136, 139, 170
Chambers, Aidan, 26, 258
cisgender: authorship, 26–28, 33–34, 67, 71, 74, 79–80, 86, 89, 110, 122, 150, 153; gaze, 34, 81; readership, 26, 28, 35, 46–50, 58, 62, 72–74, 77–81, 150–53, 168, 170
cisnormativity, 4, 9, 26, 34, 37, 42–47, 51–53, 56–58, 85, 90–100, 118, 120–21, 129–32, 138, 143, 151, 162, 168
Clark, Kristin Elizabeth, 9, 33, 39, 41, 46–47, 50, 53, 68, 77, 121, 133–34, 168
Coats, Karen, 11, 31–34, 47, 57, 92–93, 115–16, 139, 157, 161, 168
coming of age, 47, 52, 104, 150
conversion therapy, 96, 114, 123
Covid, 4, 22, 29, 66, 113–14
Cronn-Mills, Kirstin, 9, 33, 39, 41–43, 50–52, 56–57, 168

Daniels, April, 66–67, 86, 89, 92–95, 100–109, 114, 119, 126–28, 130, 134–35, 138, 169–70
Dawson, Juno, 66, 72, 89, 124, 158
Deaver, Mason, 65, 67–68, 78, 86, 119, 129, 169
disabilities, 67, 76, 101–2

emancipation, 114, 135
Emezi, Akwaeke, 66–67, 73, 89, 94, 97–98, 136–38, 170

211

empowerment, 29, 85–86, 100–105, 110, 115–17, 131–38
Epstein, B. J., 5–6, 13, 16–17, 22, 31, 37, 50–53, 59–60, 67–68, 81, 90, 126, 169

fathers, 39, 41, 50–52, 97, 117, 120–23, 126–30, 133–38, 155
Felix Ever After, 66–68, 70, 78, 122, 169–70
Flanagan, Victoria, 91, 108, 125
Freakboy, 9, 33, 39, 41, 46–47, 53, 68, 168

gender dysphoria, 27, 39, 105, 123, 162
Gender Identity Clinic, 39
Genette, Gérard, 69
genre world, 7–8, 12, 24, 33, 74, 84, 114, 144, 165
Gold, Rachel, 9, 32, 48, 65

haircuts, 144, 152, 161–64
Harnois, Devin, 96
hidden adult, 25
Hill, Katie Rain, 9, 48, 66, 142–44, 147–48, 150–52, 155, 157, 159
hormones, 45, 50, 121, 132, 137–38, 156, 164
Hunt, Caroline, 11, 153–54

I Am J, 9, 20, 33, 39, 41–42, 48–51, 60, 122–23, 132–33, 137, 168
I Wish You All the Best, 65, 67–68, 78, 86, 119, 129–30, 169
If I Was Your Girl, 10, 17, 26, 32, 60–61, 66, 70–73, 78–79, 122, 133–36
implied readers, 3, 14, 26–27, 61, 102, 147, 163, 171
incidental representation, 15, 71, 73, 85, 93
intersectionality, 17, 28, 41, 58, 61, 67–69, 82, 86, 116, 132–34, 139, 169
Iser, Wolfgang, 26

Jennings, Jazz, 48, 142–44, 148–52, 155, 157, 159
Jess, Chunk, and the Road Trip to Infinity, 77, 121, 133

Kergil, Skylar, 142–44, 152–56, 158–62
Kokkola, Lydia, 35–37, 45, 49, 115, 123–24, 130

Lee, C. B., 10, 54, 67, 70, 86, 89, 94, 98–100, 102, 104–5, 109–10, 168
Levithan, David, 9, 14, 136
liminality, 28, 40, 83, 103, 105, 109, 156
Lizard Radio, 10, 84, 87, 90
Lo, Malinda, 69, 87–88, 92, 171
lockdown. *See* Covid
Love, Heather, 5, 32, 40
Luna, 3, 5–6, 8–9, 14, 40, 114, 128–30

Mask of Shadows duology, 54, 68, 71, 89, 93, 122
McKenna, Miles, 20, 142–43, 158, 160–64
McLemore, Anna-Marie, 54, 65–68, 72, 77, 89, 93, 169
mentorship, 39, 45, 51, 144, 151, 153, 160–61, 163–65
Miller, Linsey, 54, 68, 71, 89, 93, 120, 122
mirrors: metaphor for representation, 19, 21–23, 31–32, 34, 47, 49, 57, 69, 74, 77–78, 86, 92–93, 100, 115–16, 124, 161, 167–70; trope or object, 43–44, 46–47, 148, 63
mothers, 41, 46, 48, 50–52, 97, 117–20, 122–24, 132–38, 155
My Brother's Name Is Jessica, 23–25, 71–72, 74, 80–81, 114, 122–23, 170

Nemesis series, 66–67, 86, 89, 92–96, 100–104, 109, 114, 119, 126, 134–35, 139, 169–70
nonbinary, 45–46, 53, 65–68, 73, 77, 129, 169

Out of Salem, 66, 68, 94, 99, 122, 169
Owen, Gabrielle, 20, 27, 40–41, 47, 130, 138, 156
own voices, 10, 65, 75

paratexts: epitext, 19; peritext, 26, 28, 59–82, 88, 144, 149–53
Parrotfish, 9, 20, 33–34, 39, 42, 50, 55–56, 99, 119, 122, 168
Pet, 10, 66–67, 73, 89, 94, 97–98, 136–39, 170
Peters, Julie Anne, 3, 5, 9, 40–41, 114, 128, 130
problem novels, 14, 28, 31–42, 45, 47–50, 57–58, 86, 90, 92, 99, 104, 107, 110, 119, 122, 146, 153, 167–69

Putzi, Jennifer, 34, 38, 42–43, 47–48, 60, 80, 84, 103, 123

race, 5, 8, 10, 21–25, 41, 67, 86, 97–98, 100, 103–4, 132, 143, 169
Rainbow Islands, 96
Rebellino, Rachel L. Rickard, 144–45, 154, 157–58
Rethinking Normal, 9, 48, 66, 142, 144–45, 147–48, 151–53
Russo, Meredith, 10, 17, 26, 32, 60–61, 66, 70–72, 78–80, 86, 122, 133–34, 136

Sandercock, Tom, 16, 19–20, 25, 74
Schmatz, Pat, 10, 84, 87, 90
Schrieve, Hal, 66, 68, 94, 99, 122, 169
Sidekick Squad series, 54, 67, 86, 89, 94, 98, 100, 102–5, 109, 168
sexuality: ambisexuality, 90; asexuality, 17; bisexuality, 17, 67; gay, 13–18, 37–38, 40, 42, 65, 85, 96, 101, 102, 152; heterosexuality, 8, 13, 15–16, 22, 24, 37–38, 41, 56, 79, 85, 98, 100, 102, 119, 171; homosexuality, 6, 15–16, 37, 41, 63, 67; lesbianism, 13–19, 40, 91, 132
Some Assembly Required, 9, 66, 142, 144–45, 147–48, 150–53
stereotypes, 13, 15, 17, 23, 37, 49, 52, 60, 79, 91, 122–23, 152
Stonewall, 87, 113, 118
Stryker, Susan, 8–9, 62, 101, 122; and Paisley Currah, 41

Thomas, Aiden, 10, 64, 66, 89, 92, 96, 101, 120, 122, 134, 136, 138, 170
tipping points, 10, 28, 61–62, 81, 87
Trans Mission, 142–44, 153, 156–57, 159, 162
transgender: definition, 17–18
transphobia, 39, 53, 95–97, 100, 124, 126–30, 138–39
Trites, Roberta Seelinger, 19, 29, 48–49, 104, 109, 116–18, 132, 135, 137–38

Waller, Alison, 21, 40, 100, 104, 109, 125, 133–34, 141, 156
We Need Diverse Books, 10, 28, 61, 63, 65, 76, 169

Williamson, Lisa, 9, 33, 39, 41, 43–45, 50, 52, 125–26, 168
Wittlinger, Ellen, 9, 20, 33–34, 41–42, 50, 55–56, 99, 119, 168
Wonderland, 66, 89, 124
wrong body discourse, 28, 34–35, 41–49, 58, 60, 92, 107, 146, 148

YouTube, 45, 143–45, 152, 154–65

ABOUT THE AUTHOR

Dr. Emily Corbett is a Lecturer at Goldsmiths, University of London, specializing in children's and young adult literature. She also serves as general editor for the *International Journal of Young Adult Literature*.

www.ingramcontent.com/pod-product-compliance
Lightning Source LLC
Chambersburg PA
CBHW022018220426
43663CB00007B/1131